M000211158

THE XX CLUB

a memoir

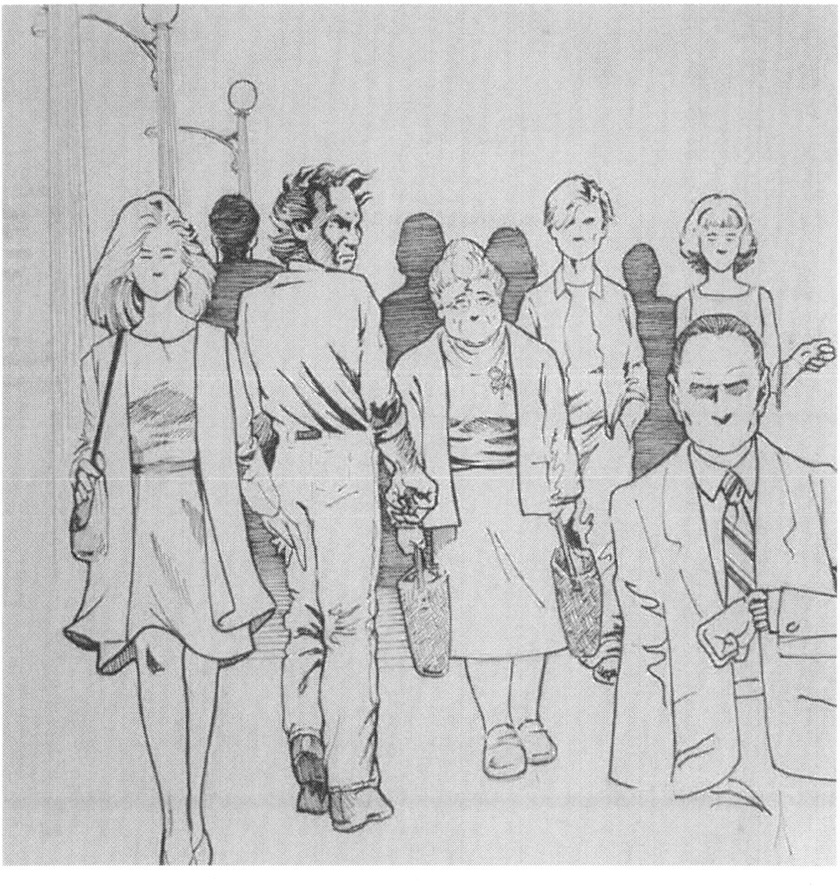

Michelle Berthiaume

In Memoriam

I am the wisp of light at dawn—Gone!
But not forgotten ...

Michael Edmond Barcomb (1954-1994)

What's Your Name?

She stood back on the curb
In the shadow of the building
Where Rodin is entombed
And watched paper faces
With iron stares float by,
No one saw her,
or so she thought—
she melted there on the sidewalk
stabbed through the heart
by one carnivore looking back.

Evelyn Stone (1992 – 1994)

This is a memoir - it is a work of non-fiction laid out in a format designed to be engaging for the reader. Persons, places, organizations and events are real and were laid out as they happened during the 1990s subject only to the frailties of human memory. Names have been altered to protect the privacy of the individuals. The chronology of events has been rearranged or consolidated to provide an ease of flow for the reader, and certain characters are composite--contain more than one person's history, actions or characteristics--to facilitate economy and better enhance an understanding of the transsexual experience.

Text Copyright 2019

Published by: Fyrecurl Publishing Group - Estes Park, Colorado
www.Fyrecurl.pub.com
www.Fyrecurl.Wordpress.com

ISBN: 978-1-7341197-0-1

Cover Design by: Emily McNamee

Illustrations: Kathy McKay [copyright-1994]

Printed in the United States of America

DEDICATION

To my best friend and mother of my children: Deborah Marie (Sprague) who taught me that angels do exist; and to my children: Jennifer Rose, Jacquelyn Marie, and April Michelle, who taught me more about being a woman than I could have ever learned on my own, and without whose love and support, I would not have survived to tell my story.

ACKNOWLEDGMENTS

A big thanks to those who started me on the path to publication of my story, Diane LesBesquets, Roger Wiley Cash, Mitch Wieland, Jo Knowles, Richard Adams Carey, Mark Sundeen and Amy Irvine McHarg, and all of my peers in the 2012-14 SNHU Low-residency Masters in Writing program, for their inspiration, sharing, caring, mentoring, and in some cases cajoling, to get me to focus on writing down my memories truth to preserve an important part of LGBT history. And to my family, for standing by me through the difficult times, particularly my sisters, Kim Barcomb and Kathy Jean Bass, Karyn Barnett and Valerie Barcomb; and to my brother John "Randy" Barcomb, who set his own standard of masculinity that included an equal measure of integrity, courage and compassion. To my mother, Patricia Marilyn Howe Barcomb, whose faith and unconditional love prompted me to believe in myself and led me to accomplish the impossible, and more importantly, to get up on my feet each time I got knocked down and not give up.

A special thanks to Kelly Stone Gamble (editor), and Diane Walters (proofreader)whose patience and contribution in editing and raking through each word of my manuscript, turned it into a readable novel. And to my Beta readers and those friends who volunteered their time, skills and effort, to read and provide input, from its inception to the end, C.G. Fuston, Darren Leo, Tyler Fish, Tina Sears, Randi Sachs, and Ashley (the girl who hates to read), I thank you, your support and friendship.

And to my old friend Traci (wherever you may be) and all the femmes of the XX Club and others who silently passed through the annals of our history seemingly unnoticed. I hope you realized your dream, walked away from yourselves, and blended in to become that woman you were meant to be.

And to all who are still searching: May your journey out of the shadows be as remarkable as mine. May you leave all of the pain behind, and soar with the eagles into those light infused blue skies and beyond—-

Excelsior!

Author's Note:

Memories are like stones, time and distance erode them like acid.
- Ugo Betti

This is a memoir. It is my story. A snippet of life told from my limited perspective. Admittedly, it may leave much to be debated among those fortunate others who have survived similar turbulent times. The reader should not use this as a gauge to measure every person who claims to be transsexual. It is not meant to be an expose nor treatise on any subject but merely a vivisection of one small part of the life of someone who survived transition from male to female during the 1990s; a dangerous time for someone to go against his or her Maker's design.

Essentially, it is memory's truth, subject to all the maladies of the fragile human mind. One does not live with a pen in hand writing down her life as she goes because she may want to recall every detail later. What matters is how she felt at the time she lived the events and how she perceived her actions affected others. When one is on the run from one life to another, there is not much time to unpack your bag and take notes.

I have persevered to accurately recreate the events and emotions I felt, or failed to feel, at the time of my transition during the 1990s. It was a time I was suffering from major depression and searching for my identity. A confusing time when the Gay movement had branched out into particularized groups divided by sex and sexual preference and the concept of Transgender was beginning to emerge from the phenomenon of Transsexualism, that was still a mystery to social scientists and the medical profession. I have consolidated several characters into one for economy and to elucidate salient experiences. Joe is a composite character that contained the experience of several aging transvestites I have met in my journey. Traci represents another group: the passable transsexual who went stealth and walked away from her former life. She was one of the lucky ones who, as Dr. Higgins described in our first and only meeting, blended into society so well she became someone else. Someone she was meant to be.

The XX Club was one of the last institutions, originally funded by a grant from the Ericson Foundation. It was set up by an heiress to assist the most vulnerable part of the gay community, the transsexual, a person who felt trapped in the wrong body and completely and utterly alone, and without its help, I too, would have succumbed to non-existence.

Names of individuals have been altered to protect privacy. Any resemblance to persons should be considered coincidental. Although there are an equal number of female-to-male transsexuals (f-t-m) in the world, this is the story of a male-to-female (m-t-f) transsexual and as such, its perspective is heavily slanted in that direction. References to transsexual or gender without further elaboration should be considered m-t-f. If the transgendered character has a male ego, or identity, he will be referred to in this memoir by male pronouns regardless of how he is dressed. This is to further define some of the larger transgender community from the transsexual, who is *always* gendered opposite his or her birth sex.

In the 1990s, most of the world referred to men who dressed in women's clothing as transvestites. Today, that term has negative connotations as do queer, fagot, dyke, and tranny, to name a few. My point is, in this memoir I will use many of these terms. If you are sensitive, be forewarned.

———

Preface:

The Shadow People - Circa 1990

We are transsexual. Forget what you think you know about our kind. We are not some new category of human called "transgendered." Our gender is as fluid as the rest of humanity. Yes, we are deviant. Women who are born male into a binary society that does not accept nor recognize us. We are an anomaly but we are no more or less perverse than anyone else. We resent that we are treated as though we were born with a mental illness. We are not men who want to become women but simply women who are broken and in need of repair.

We are so few in number for anyone to care how we come into being. In a population of 600,000 it is estimated one may be transsexual. We live on the fringe of society but sometimes a rare few find a way out of the shadows, to infiltrate society and blend in. This is our story of survival.

We are the XX Club.

# # #

Chapter 1

Trinity College (Circa 1992)

"I had known since as far back as my memory began that I was different. My own body felt foreign to me and I feared telling anyone how I felt, particularly my mother and father. Inherently, I knew it would hurt them to learn their son really wasn't a boy."

-- Michael Edmond Barcomb (1954-1994)

Dr. Higgins -

"Most die prior to their 35th birthday by their own hand."

Dr. Higgins leaned back in his big leather chair and put an unlit pipe into his furry mouth. Then, as if reminiscing to himself, he added,

"Or by someone else's."

He stopped talking and shook his pipe out into the waste basket beside his desk before he continued.

"Only a third of the candidates ever complete the requirement of living one year in their chosen gender role, and if you succeed there is a good chance you might die on the operating table or of complications thereafter. Modern science is good but it's not perfect. Sexual re-assignment surgery is still in its infancy. It's experimental."

He grew silent again and stared at his reflection in the frosted window before looking back at me. Usually, when someone showed up in his office asking for help, they were wearing heels and a dress and were sobbing. Rarely, were they poker-faced in jeans and work boots.

"So, do you still want to enter the program? God knows why you'd want to put up with all our rules and hoops to jump through. You certainly have the resources to fly to Thailand and have every known procedure done at a fraction of the cost. Few of our candidates could afford to do that. But there are benefits in following the Harry S. Benjamin standards of care. The risks, although still many, are minimized, and it's not as far to travel if you need follow-up care."

All my life I've prayed for a miracle. After nearly forty years of hiding and living someone else's life, I finally found a way out. I wasn't going to give up now.

I nodded.

He smiled and stretched his hand over his desk toward me. I took it firmly in mine and shook. He wrote down the number for his partner and co-founder of the Gender Identity Clinic of New England, Canon Clinton Jones, an Episcopal priest and the social worker who ran the clinic's support group they pronounced: "The Twenty Club." Someone's clever idea to name a support group for male-to-female transsexuals written out using the Roman numerals XX that resembled the genetic marker of females.

"What are the chances for success for people like me?"

He pulled his unlit pipe from his mouth and studied it for a moment.

"I wish I had an answer, but not many ever come back to tell us about their experience. I'd like to think that they blended into society so well that the person that came in here no longer existed. They got absorbed into their new life."

The XX Club met in Hartford, more than a two-hour drive from the home I shared with my wife, Debbie, in Vermont. Initially, I could commute, but I knew living in my "chosen gender role" for a year would require me to eventually move away from my family.

I smiled. The ultimate goal for a true transsexual is to walk away from his life and become someone else. Someone they were meant to be. If it didn't work. There was always the alternative.

Chapter 2

The XX Club

One is not born a woman, but rather she becomes one. – Simone Lucie Ernestine Marie Bertrand de Beauvoir, "The Second Sex"

The XX Club met in the basement of Christ's Church in downtown Hartford every second and fourth Saturday of the month from 10:00 a.m. until noon. It was a safe place where you shared your deepest, darkest secret with others you just met, learned all you could about becoming a woman, and left. If lucky, your membership would expire in a year. If not, you could be waiting for salvation a long time, sitting around an imperfect circle of folding metal chairs, staring up at four rectangular windows that lined the ceiling along the back wall, and watching the boots of the world march by and throw mud up against the sordid panes.

A parade-of-horribles had passed through my mind on the way down to Hartford from Central Vermont. In the thirty plus years I had been living in a body I hated, responsibility, acne, and a sea of male hormones attached themselves to me and hardened my appearance. A war zone in the battle between the sexes showed most prominently on my face. I wasn't sure what I would find at the XX Club. Tim Curry in makeup and a dress maybe?

Cindy was the speaker that first day I walked into the basement of Christ's church. She sat cross-legged in the overstuffed chair at the corner of our circle looking like she got into a bout with a pit bull. Her lip was split, and her eyes blackened and purple, separated by a narrow white bandage across the bridge of her nose. Everyone was listening intently to what appeared to be a young woman in the "hot seat", a box of tissue in her lap, sputtering in a little-girl voice about her boyfriend.

"After I informed him about my upcoming operation in Montreal, he made it abundantly clear he did not want to ever see me again. He broke my nose. It wasn't pretty," she said and dabbed a dry eye with a tissue.

"He knocked out two of my front teeth. I had to scramble around on the floor after he had gone, looking for them so the dentist could put them back in."

I had pictured a bunch of middle-aged men trying to dress like the woman of their dreams. Lost souls trying to reinvent themselves into some idyllic embodiment of femininity that they imagined when they were teenagers, before puberty rubbed them the wrong way. Instead, there was Cindy with her long brown hair tucked behind each ear, in her too-long sweater and a pair of thread-bare stirrups looking like a rebellious adolescent. When I found out she was a mechanic for a Sears Auto Center, there was a connection. I was not just surprised but ecstatic. I felt there may be hope for me yet.

Caught up in the euphoria, I asked her to lunch. I wanted to know more. We went to a small deli on the outskirts of town. No one gave us a second look. Two girlfriends out to lunch.

Afterward, I let her drive my sporty 5-speed Honda Civic at top speed through the rolling hills of West Hartford to an apartment she shared with Laura. The two of them plied me with whiskey and wine, dressed me up like a prostitute and took me out to a gay bar near Amherst.

I woke up naked between them in an unfamiliar bed that smelled like sweat and vomit. I dressed quickly and drove back to Vermont. I barely glanced in her direction since that first meeting. It wasn't long into my transition that I realized not every member of my support group was the same kind of crazy as me.

Traci was one of the first like me that I had met. At five feet four inches tall with diminutive features and a lovely face, she was that hot new model everyone at the XX Club aspired to be—no matter what variety of fruit they were. Traci was the CFO for a small medical supply company, Boston Precision. She made out well when she took stock options instead of increases in pay during those early start-up years. She amassed almost a half-million before coming into the XX Club. She and I were more financially stable than most of the others. It gave us some perks. Joe, the person I would eventually move in with, was more scrutinized by the gatekeepers. The clinic made him get his wife to sign off on his hormone shots, but he was undaunted.

"They pay more attention to me than you guys," he laughed.

Canon Clinton Jones, the club's co-founder and social worker, often occupied one of the chairs facing the door. He'd nod and smile up at me and the others as we came in. Traci compared him to Saint Peter thinning out the flock of lost souls as they came up to the pearly gates. He seldom spoke unless someone had a question for him. He sat quietly, small white hands folded neatly on his lap, legs crossed at the knee and observed while Jennifer, our club president, ran the meeting. Canon Jones was there, he reminded us, to help us help ourselves. Our job was not so much to learn how to become women, but to unlearn all the years of living behind a mask of masculinity.

Jennifer described it as peeling an onion, one layer at a time. It would bring tears, but it was necessary before you could find that tender heart. Jennifer loved metaphors. She usually misquoted or mixed them up in an endearing sort of way. She was soft-spoken and plain and didn't wear much makeup. Her graying blond hair was tied up in a bun or stuck under some frumpy hat, and she always showed up in a long skirt and loose knit sweater like some old hippie chick. She looked like the grown-up version of Annie Hall.

She was one of the oldest members of the club and the main topic of conversation during our breaks. No one was certain whether she had had SRS or not, but everyone held her in high esteem. We all knew her intentions were good. Besides, Canon Jones, and one of the former members who presided over my first meeting before leaving to parts unknown, she was one of the few people that appeared to care about our progress and tried to be comforting.

She used to be an engineer at a big firm in Manhattan until she walked into the office one day with her thinning blond hair tied back in a bun behind her head and in a long, knit skirt and cowl-neck sweater. Her partners called her into the boardroom and offered her an early retirement package she could not refuse.

When Jennifer was not running our meetings or arguing with her live-in girlfriend Julie, she stayed home by a phone in her anteroom waiting for a call from her son. Gossip had it, when Jennifer's ex-wife informed the boy what was going on with his father, he never returned home from Penn State.

The greatest part of the gossip however was Julie, an ex-priest. She was a bit disconcerting to be around. It was bad enough for most to descend into the bowels of a church dressed in ways that could get you arrested in the 1990's and share intimate secrets with complete strangers but she made it even more uncomfortable.

Julie was that nun from Hell. The one who dragged you out of your seat by the ear and stood you in front of the entire class and told you that your zipper was open then forbade you to look down to see if it really was. Not only did her outfit resemble the Carmelite nuns who taught me for the first eight years of my academic life, her mannerisms were exactly like my Seventh-grade teacher, Sister Aloysius. Right down to the nervous tic of her mouth when she scolded you for slouching in your chair.

With the exception of Julie's starched blouse, that was usually petrified-white, she wore black like a second skin. Black dress, black sweater, black-framed glasses, and her black hair was tied back with a black ribbon. She wore black nun-shoes— the kind with a thick heel and blunt toe. Julie and Jennifer lived together in Jennifer's large stately home off King's Highway in an old established neighborhood in Bridgeport.

Julie was still on the books as the club vice president but

seldom showed for meetings. When someone inquired, Jennifer would say, "Busy bees must make honey while they can," or "busy is, busy does."

It didn't really answer the question but stifled any further inquiry.

Most were thankful she didn't come. No one wanted to be reminded to keep their legs closed or crossed at the knee if you were wearing a dress or skirt, or stopped at some penultimate moment at the climax of a personal story shared with the group for the first time. She would tell someone if she thought the subject matter was inappropriate. On breaks, no one wanted to be reminded again and again that this was not a place to make "new best friends" simply when you stopped to talk to someone after a meeting.

Traci's boots were on the floor under her chair. Her feet securely tucked up under her while she huddled under her parka with the collar pulled up to her chin. Her breath floated aimlessly up through the loose fabric. She caught me staring and gave me the thumbs up. She approved of my casual look—a pair of my daughter Jackie's old jeans hugged my thighs and a long red sweater clung to my budding round bosom. If you could pass in androgynous clothing, you had made it.

Traci said no matter how good we look someone always sees who we once were. Our past creeps through. My eyes narrowed on her pretty face when she said it. I found it hard to tell the difference between her and any of my biological sisters. She was, without question, as cute as any teenage prom queen.

"Don't worry, you'll get there. Give them moaning whores time to do their magic."

That's what she called hormones. I was never quite sure whether she laughed at my insecurity or her little pundit.

It was Traci who convinced me to move in with Joe for my year of living in my chosen gender, as required by the program.

"You can cart each other around from place to place until all your surgeries are complete. No one can go through this alone."

When I asked who assisted her, she just smiled.

Traci planned on going deep stealth. She stayed to herself at meetings and avoided interaction with anyone who might give her away. She barely talked to the others except cordially. Although not formally appointed, she was my mentor. By the time I moved from Vermont to Hartford, she was halfway through with her 'year of living dangerously' as she called that time when we strapped our sex up between our legs and put on a dress, usually for the first time.

I was fortunate she took me under her wing. I came dressed that first day in blue jeans and work boots looking more like gay Bruce Springsteen than a Lola. I had no experience dressing up as a girl except a few times on Halloween but that ended in the sixth grade, after my father told my mother I looked like a squirrel. All I dared wear was a dab of mascara for fear of getting seen by someone I knew.

I had a key to my friend, Frank's, dental office in Brattleboro. He was never there on weekends and I would stop by to use the bathroom and lightly line my eyes with a black pencil and fluff out my curly hair with a pick, making my androgynous appearance a little more feminine. But it wasn't long after the hormones kicked in that my friends and people that I have known for years began talking about me in those hushed whispers reserved for folks who claimed to be abducted by aliens.

"Look at those two idiots."

Traci jerked her head in the direction of two newbies sitting across from us. She kept her voice low.

"The tall blonde calls herself Proud Mary. She showed up at the last meeting in a long red dress and a white sweater. A bloody mess."

Traci had a euphemism for every regular in the club and labeled the newbies if they came back a second time. Whenever she called me Saint Evelyn my stomach knotted but when she used the epithets that she gave the regulars, I got more nervous.

Besides Joe, Jennifer and Scary Julie, the ex-priest, there was Sarah the eunuch and Laura the admirer. Cindy was the whiner of the group and Hawk-nose Kaitlyn was the youngest member to regularly attend our meetings. Both she and Cindy were in their late twenties and were rail thin. Traci called them Zeros. I didn't know it referenced a dress size. I thought she was being derogatory, like all her other labels.

"Joe calls her Big Kathy," I said referring to the tall blonde. "I like her. Her face is pretty and she has a great attitude. She draws like an artist."

Traci was unconcerned with what other people thought. I never realized how prejudiced she was towards our own kind.

"Like most of these freaks she's too tall, works in IT, and is married. Isn't that Barbie?"

Traci nodded in the direction of a newbie in a white dress.

"No, I don't think so. She's Hispanic. Her eyes are slanted. Barbie had big eyes like the doll, remember. That's why we called her that."

"Cripes! That's right. It's hard to keep track of all the freaks. Where do they all come from?"

Jennifer brought her finger up to her thin colorless lips. Petite Cindy was in the 'hot seat' blubbering something about stenosis and an opening the size of a pencil nub. She was always crying or feigning emotional trauma to draw sympathy. Her large dark eyes looked down into her empty lap. Cindy spoke in a monotone-droll-little-girl voice. Her eyes were wide-open and dry. There were no tears, but people around her, especially the newbies, feigned empathy as though it was expected of them.

People didn't normally cry at meetings. Most of our tears were used up long ago as children. Self-pity is unusual for a tranny who survived past puberty. It succumbed to an emotional cancer that spread quietly into the trauma of our teen years when we noticed the developing bodies of the girls born in the right body. Pity was replaced by an emptiness and self-loathing before we became adults.

Some had a chip on their shoulder, but when most first came to the club and realized they were not alone they were elated or relieved. No one cried in a meeting unless it was a story about them. How she was molested by a family member or sitting in a warm bath at the age of six contemplating how to cut off the male genitals that did not belong on her body without bleeding to death.

Jennifer liked Cindy for some reason. She often sat in the hot seat. Cindy retold her story about her botched operation by an incompetent Montreal surgeon at almost every meeting. We were the experimental people. Dr. Menard had tried a new spiral grafting procedure to improve on the healing process of the neo-vagina. However, something went horribly wrong, if you believed Cindy.

"Cindy is a drama queen," Traci said.

She thought Cindy failed to follow directions and insert the prosthetic device into the raw wound twice a day to keep it open until it healed. I pictured the little girl in *The Exorcist* stabbing her crotch when she said it and winced. Physical pain to pacify our emotional trauma.

I turned in time to catch dark eyes peering in my direction. Sarah's hair was cut short like a boy's but he looked and sounded like a woman because he never went through puberty. He contracted syphilis when he was 9. That's when his mother's boyfriend moved into their trailer. Sarah told me he used to sneak into her room at night when her mother passed out from the drugs that he gave her.

"He was a sick man."

She sounded sorry for him.

I felt sorry for Sarah. She didn't talk much. When she did, it was usually to either me, or Laura, who she moved in with when she moved up from the New York City.

Laura and Sarah were not real members of the XX Club. Neither were candidates for sexual reassignment, but Canon Jones let them join the support group whenever they felt like killing themselves.

Sarah didn't make eye contact. She usually looked down at her feet when she spoke or at her lap if she was sitting. Her voice was low, and you'd have to strain to hear it. She didn't talk much to the others even when they tried to engage her, but for some reason, she did talk to me.

Everyone seemed to confide in me and tell me things I did not want to hear, especially Joe. Sometimes people told me too much—those dirty little secrets that should be locked in a box in the back of a closet or swept under a bed. I kept a smile pressed to my lips and listened and tried not to think about how it would affect me.

From meeting to meeting, I barely remembered the ones I saw from the previous month. A handful of newbies came and went. No one noticed when they didn't show up again. We were keenly aware that only a handful would make it out alive and were relieved when we were still sitting in that imperfect circle of chairs.

One week, several newbies appeared at once. A Konstanz with a "Z" she said, then a Bronwyn, and our hawk-nosed Kaitlyn paraded in wearing heels and heavy makeup probably for the first time. The more flamboyant monikers revealed a change in attitude among the community as if they were no longer ashamed of being born odd. They reinvented themselves. Like children playing in a make-believe world, pretending to be something different than they were born—not quite a white knight, a soldier, or cowboy—but more like a damsel in distress.

I didn't know why anyone would want to be a victim. Some of the newbies tended to revel in it like it was their destiny. They came in to challenge the gatekeepers, who tried without success to screen them out. The clinic staff found the majority of the support group were these new gender-warriors, many also in need of services.

They did not want to change their sex. Some wanted hormones, some minor surgeries to feminize his appearance, that good doctors were precluded from doing. Some wanted to have sex with a she-male. Others just wanted someone to talk to.

They disappeared at an alarming rate when they, or Canon Jones, realized the program was not designed to accommodate them.

We turned off reality. When someone was missing at the next meeting, we did not ask questions. They could be dead or just decided to revert back to the real world and hang up their heels for a while. We never knew. We'd see a newbie sitting in a chair where the recently deceased should be and we'd go on acting as though they showed up again—transformed.

I attended several meetings, twice a month, while still living at home in Vermont. But as the hormonal therapy progressed, and I began to look and feel differently, I knew I had to leave the safety of my home and family if I was to ever become the person, I knew I was meant to be.

#

Chapter 3

The Wife

A rose by any other name would smell as sweet. – William Shakespeare

Debbie was a loyal and loving wife. She hadn't done anything wrong except to fall in love with a transsexual. We were both eighteen and fresh out of high school when a mutual friend, Sue Ryan, introduced her to Roy Scott and me one night at the bowling alley.

Roy was captain of the bowling team and a Junior at the University of Vermont where he was studying Forestry. He was a foot taller and had bushy brown hair that seldom saw a comb. He would have been the perfect specimen of rural masculinity had it not been for his beaver-teeth.

We both took one look at Sue's tall, auburn-haired friend with those big bedroom- eyes staring back at us and fell in love. Roy asked her out first but he made the mistake of asking me to lend her a snowmobile suit to go to the winter barbeque. I delivered it personally and asked Debbie to a movie.

She balked at first, not wanting to come between friends, but I told her Roy was busy at college and he expected me to take care of his girl until he got home. Nine months later I proposed behind the Canadian Club and a few days afterward, at our favorite parking spot near the airport, Debbie became the first person to learn my dreaded secret.

I didn't use the T word. I simply mentioned that I felt like a girl trapped in a male body. In all fairness she wouldn't have understood the T word any more than I did. I had only learned the term a year earlier in some tabloid. I should have been more forthright and told her I was jealous of her body and hated my own.

I should have explained that I wanted to be like her in every way and had been secretly saving money for a sex change since before she came along. I honestly thought her love might save me.

True transsexuals know who they are from an early age. You don't just wake up one day and sing "Wow! I feel like a woman tonight." I knew there was something wrong with me from as far back as my memories started, but I didn't dare share my concerns, not even with my mother.

My parents were Depression-era babies and although they survived difficult times, both were fragile products of a binary world, where boys have a penis and girls have a vagina. If they knew their oldest son was really their daughter in disguise—well—somehow, I knew it would shatter their dreams. It certainly would have changed the way they looked at me. Once the alarm goes off, you are awake. Blissful sleep is no longer an option.

I shattered Debbie's dreams when I finally told her what I planned to do. She deflated, lost her smile and more than thirty pounds, and started using an inhaler. Her lungs were weak. In a perfect world, we were supposed to work together to raise our three beautiful daughters in that big house on the hill and make mad passionate love on lazy Sunday mornings. She expected us to grow old together. We never argued and I seemed perfectly happy. But that feeling that I was living someone else's life got in the way.

It was an amicable divorce. I did not have to appear in court once my lawyer explained our situation to the judge. I think he may have known me. Most people in my small town did. If not me then they knew my father, a hometown boy who came back from the war and built a million-dollar business out of old tires, hard work, and honesty. The B & L Tire Company was a mainstay in Barre for more than thirty years before my brother, Rick, and I took it over, when we both came back after our stints in the service.

Perhaps the judge visualized a bearded man wearing a

bright yellow dress rotating tires on his Lexus. Maybe he knew me as the high school soccer coach. His son or daughter may have been on my team or perhaps he used to play against me in high school, or he could have been one of those boys at Saint Monica's who used to taunt me.

His name was familiar.

Perhaps he stood in the background and watched Steve Parks and Mark Aja dunk my head into a toilet in the boys' room. He may have seen them take my pants off after school. There were many days even in the dead of winter I had to walk home without them. Whoever he was, the judge bent the rules to allow my lawyer to appear at the final hearing without me.

It could have been guilt or perhaps I really did love Debbie as I imagined love to be, selfless and self-sacrificing. For whatever reason, I gave Debbie all of the proceeds from the sale of our luxury home, the largest ranch house in Central Vermont, an almost new car and all of the money in our joint checking and savings accounts, and I left three high interest CD's in the amount of $10,000, each in the name of our three daughters with her named as the sole trustee. Custody of the children was uncontested.

I walked away from Michael's life with only the $16,000 in cash kept in a box on a shelf in the back of our closet. I had been saving up for my operation ever since I was seventeen and first learned a sex change was possible. I suspected that I would need all of that and more for the anticipated change. I kept the balloon note remaining on the sale of the family business. It would pay $1,000 a month for the next several years and $117,000 in one lump sum at the end of the term. Enough for whoever I would become to get a fresh start.

It grieved me to sell the business my father built almost as much as leaving Vermont. It was the only home I had known except for the four years in the U.S. Air Force. I rationalized it at the time. My father taught me to never get too attached to anything. Although he was referring to the 1965 Chevrolet Corvair that he let me drive in high school after I cracked it up several times, I interpreted his words in my usual way.

I took everything he said to heart: I needed a haircut or I'd look like a squirrel, men don't cry, and he was particularly fond of reminding me that I never worked a day in my life. I could not wait to get out on my own and prove him wrong. Twenty years later, I extended his advice to almost everything in my life, particularly relationships. I worked hard, kept my hair cut short, seldom cried, and I never got too close to anything or anyone including, as it turned out, my family.

I knew I should have felt remorse, regret, and all those emotions normal people had floating around in them when they walked away from all that they had ever known and loved. I should have felt something akin to shame or guilt when I broke that sacred vow to be faithful to my wife, but I didn't. There were a number of indiscretions. Casual affairs with several women in the waning years of our life together.

Debbie threatened to kill the last one, a college co-ed I affectionately labeled "Jenny O." She picked up the telephone when my lover called the house looking for me. She wasn't going to let go of her husband without a fight. She was going to keep her family intact even if it killed her.

That's when I stopped. I had been ignoring the fact that Debbie's emaciated body wracked with physical and emotional pain every night as she laid beside me. Her face had turned gray and withered like some dried fruit almost overnight, then it sucked her breath away. She carried her inhaler around after my third affair. None of them had been discreet.

One evening, Debbie sat quietly on the end of our bed watching me pack. She was wheezing and listening to Whitney Houston sing "I Will Always Love You" when her lungs gave out. It was the absence of sound that alerted me. I looked down. Debbie was lying on her side across the bed and she wasn't breathing. I picked her up, carried her out to the car, and drove her to the hospital. She had almost died. Yet I felt nothing.

It bothers me to look back at my behavior. There is no justification I can attest to. I had no motivation to cheat. There had been better opportunities in the past when I was away for months at a time on special military assignments.

At the tactical intelligence training school at Fort Huachuca in Arizona, a group of female performers were brought in to a party at the Officer's club. As I made my way through the crowd, a half-naked woman rubbed up against my body trying to get a rise out of me but to no avail. My stoic composure prompted her to apologize. My crew dubbed me the Ice Man.

Desperation sex can drive a man to chase women, where he faces the loss of his sexual prowess and gives it all he's got at the end to preserve the memory of who he once had been. I thought if other men did it, perhaps it might save me, too, but I wasn't a man. It was not lust but jealousy that drove me. It did nothing except to make me half-mad and someone I loved deathly ill. None of it was satisfying.

I did not enjoy the sex as much as I did those moments of companionship with my wife, huddled under that big, ugly, itchy quilt she had crocheted for me that first Christmas. We held onto one another in the glow of want and desire throughout most of our marriage. It amazed me how hollow and emotionless I had become at the end of our life together as though some disease had eaten me up from the inside out.

Perhaps there was some kind of survival mechanism built into transsexuals that kept some from pulling the trigger and putting a bullet in the brain. I never wanted to hurt Debbie. She was my best friend and the mother of my children. All I ever wanted was to be an ordinary woman, but to transition from male to female in Barre, a town that got its name in a barroom brawl, was out of the question. No matter how much I loved my family, I had to let them all go—for their own protection.

I was a pariah in my youth. Growing up an effeminate, sensitive male made me a target of just about everyone in my community. Between the insults and the pity hurled at me on a daily basis, I was shell-shocked.

Staying in a place where emotion was hammered out of

boys at an early age and women and girls were still considered property did not seem a viable option. I did not want my children to suffer. Jen was going to West Point and Jackie to Florida Institute of Technology after graduation.

Debbie began receiving harassing phone calls the day after I informed my lawyer. If bad news travels fast, strange news travels at the speed of light. After the sale of the house, she and April were heading to Florida to move in with my parents until they could get settled.

I packed up everything I could carry in the back of my compact car and drove off the mountain toward my new destiny early one Sunday morning. The only mistake I had made was in looking back.

The clouds were riding low on the hills. It was in that glow just before the dawn, I made out the familiar silhouette of my emaciated wife etched into the background. Her thin arm raised and entwined in the bare branches of those hard-rock maples behind our home, waving goodbye against an empty gray sky.

The memory haunts me today but not in a frightening sort of way that gives you night sweats. It is like when you stare at a red-hot sunset. The image is pressed onto your eyelids and lingers for a long time afterward. Sometimes, I am filled with that empty feeling like when you skip over a chapter in a book. Even though you know the ending of the story, you always wonder what you may have missed.

But I don't dwell on it. I suck it up and move forward the way my father taught me. There is no time to think on the past or what could have been—had I been born normal.

#

Chapter 4

Joe

"Sex is what I am, gender is who I am." – Evelyn Stone (1992 – 1994)

In the spring of 1993, I left Vermont, my wife and three teenage daughters and moved in with an aging transvestite named Joe, who liked to be called Amelia Elaine and a host of other names inspired by whatever outfit he was wearing at the time. We met at the XX Club, and although I would have preferred to live with a femme like myself, we both needed someone to share expenses with as well as someone to be available to take us back and forth to various appointments during our year of transition.

Joe was a transvestite, not a transsexual, and probably didn't belong in the XX Club under the guidelines of the DSM back then. It was a support group for persons intending to change their sex. He was married and had been satisfied with his life, dressing like a woman, but not really wanting to be one—physically.

However, as he got older, his aging maleness and diminishing prowess led him to want more femininity to feel better about himself, in the way of hormones and other treatments that were only available to those that were under the protocol of the Gender Identity Clinic. He "pretended" to be transsexual or maybe he was considering a change. He did seem confused at first, and the XX Club was a way for him to decide. Either way, he enjoyed the comfort and sisterhood of the Club and was, for me, only another step in the process.

We lived on the first floor of a white, two-story Victorian on the edge of the old New England coastal town of Stratford, Connecticut. The house squatted in the middle of a block on the west side of a quiet street. All four houses faced east towards highway 95 South, separated by a half-mile stretch of verdant scrub brush, poison sumac, wild thistle and an assortment of other weeds I never learned the name of, that Joe affectionately dubbed: "our garden."

He was a persistent optimist. He saw his glass as half-full even when it was a plastic champagne flute they pass out at cheap weddings.

We entered our apartment through the back door into the kitchen. We didn't have a key to the front. The landlady's daughter lived upstairs and came in the front door whenever she was in town. She was away at school most of the time.

We seldom saw her and when we did it was usually on a weekend, late at night, tiptoeing up the stairs with her boyfriend, Sam, the cute kid who worked at the supermarket around the corner. I forgot her name. It never seemed that important to me at the time. I think she had the same name as Joe's wife, Kathy, only spelled with a "C", but I'm not sure.

The landlady was one of those progressive types. I never met her but I could tell from the books by Virginia Wolfe, Betty Friedman, Gloria Steinem, and Joan Didion that sat idle on the built-in bookshelves in the living room that she was a devout feminist.

Joe arranged to put the lease in our femme names, Amelia Elaine Bonacorsi and Evelyn Stone, even though neither one of us legally existed yet. He paid more rent and had the larger bedroom to hold his collection of designer dresses, expensive human-hair wigs and those hard-to-find size 12 women's shoes.

I did not complain. All I had was one suitcase full of my soon-to-be-ex-wife's old clothes that fit me better than they did her and a few wallet-sized photos of my three teenage daughters.

Everything Michael owned in the world he gave to Debbie except what could be packed into my powder-blue Ford Escort. Not because I felt guilty ending our marriage after almost twenty years. I didn't feel much emotion at all when I left. Years of depression killed something deep inside where the heart was supposed to be. But it was the right thing to do. I always tried to do the right thing, even if it was not in my best interest and left me destitute.

Joe and I had different approaches to life. Where I keep everything inside festering until it burned a hole in my stomach, he exploded at the first sign of trouble. His emotions guided him. He said it was the Italian in him and reacted to the moment rather than taking things in stride. I planned and re-planned everything, over and over in my mind, right down to the last tearful goodbye. Joe hadn't told his wife yet that he was moving out of their happy home and into a ground floor apartment with me, on a street with the same name as her: Katherine. When I mentioned it, Joe looked at me and batted his big false lashes. He did not see the irony.

Joe and I came from different worlds. He changed his persona every time he changed his clothes. He had been dressing as long as I had been alive.

Admittedly, I did not know much about hair, shoes, makeup, clothes or feminine etiquette except what I observed from my mother, sisters, and others. I had always avoided such things. Not because I did not like them but because I was afraid that I could not take them off once I put them on. I spent a lifetime building the perfect man, the perfect son, and if not the perfect husband and father through to the end—at least—an attentive one.

Debbie never went without any comforts. I thought, if I pleased her, gave her everything a woman wanted it would make up for the fact I was not a real man. I always brought her to orgasm first, made certain she was pleased with her surroundings, and I gave my children the time my father did not have for me. I told each how much I loved them.

At the end of my twelve-hour work day, even when I was ready to drop, I drove to their sports field or arenas. I coached teams or stood on sidelines in rain or freezing weather. I wrapped and bandaged blisters and bruised muscles, celebrated victories and rubbed wounded egos. I held them in my arms as much as any parent could. I didn't want to ruin it all in a spurt of bad judgment. I kept telling myself over the years of anxiety, when those feelings welled to the surface, that I could sacrifice much for the wants of those I loved. It would have shown on my face if I gave into temptation. I had to be strong.

So, once I made up my mind to change, I had a lot to learn about makeup and dressing up as a girl and finding out who I really was. My lesson started the first day I met Joe at our apartment.

After unpacking and getting settled, Joe said he had a "big favor" to ask. He needed a ride home. I agreed without asking why, when he had his own truck—something I would later regret.

I didn't realize until we were in my car, headed away from Katherine Street, that Joe was taking me to his former home, not to get some things he left behind, but to meet his wife, Kathy, whom he had left without saying: Goodbye, or explaining why.

#

Chapter 5

The Other Woman

All things truly wicked start from innocence. – Ernest Hemingway

"That's it."

Joe pointed out his house near the end of a quiet street not far from the Pez factory.

We pulled into the drive next to a small fishing boat on an old trailer parked under a weeping willow. Its nose was tipped up like a big fish caught on a rusted hook. He jumped out of my car before it came to a complete stop. Joe swatted aside a broken limb and pulled a torn cover over the boat and loped toward the front door.

I reluctantly followed.

A scream ripped the air and a door slammed deep in the bowels of the house as I entered. It sounded like a dying animal then receded into the intermittent sobs of a woman. I had already been through a year of similar agony and watched love wither. It wasn't long ago that I held Debbie in my arms at night while she sobbed.

I turned to leave, but Joe caught my arm. He insisted that I follow him. I stopped and watched him from the open kitchen while he banged on a door that I presumed was to his old bedroom.

"Kathy, open the goddamn door."

The thin panels of the door rattled like a castanet each time Joe struck it with his open hand.

"Go away, Joe. I can't believe you paraded by the neighbors looking like that. What will they think?"

"Kathy, come on out. There's someone I want you to meet."

"No. I don't want to meet her. Get that hussy out of my house."

Her voice was shrill.

"Thirty years I gave you. I can't believe you'd do this to me."

"Our house," he corrected her.

"Come out, Kathy. Please, we need to talk. And she ain't a she. I mean she's a man like me."

"Liar! You get that bitch out of our house."

"Come on, Joe. This is not a good time. She's in pain."

I started to back away toward the door I entered through.

"No, please," he begged. "It can't end like this. I need you to talk to her."

"Joe, you need a professional. I don't know what to do. Have you even told her what you're doing?"

"That's all I want you to do. Just tell her who you are and that we're moving in together. She thinks I left her for another woman."

I read someplace that a man will not leave his wife unless he has someone else to run to. I had a sudden premonition standing there in some other woman's kitchen that I was in some twisted turn of fate, the other woman.

"I'm not a psychologist, Joe. She is in shock. She needs a professional—"

"No, please wait right here. I'll get her. I need you to talk with her. It's the first time in thirty years we've been apart. Please."

Something caught in his throat. He turned back to his bedroom and began banging again. Harder than before. The sobbing behind the door rose in pitch.

"Stop it, Joe. You're breaking the door. What are you going to tell our children? They are going to hate you."

"Come on, Kathy, open up. Come out or I will break it down and we both don't need that."

He banged again. After a few minutes he hurried into the kitchen and pulled out a drawer. The contents spilled onto the tile floor. He picked up a screwdriver and headed back. When the hinges fell, he pulled the door off and lay it against the wall. A small woman with short brown hair and bulging wet eyes tried to run past him but he grabbed her by the arms and pulled her into his massive bosom.

Kathy wriggled free then looked up at me suddenly. We stared at each other for a moment then she turned and punched Joe in the chest with her fists.

"Villeaco! Why have you done this? You're throwing away all our years of marriage for this bitch? I gave you everything."

"Please just talk with her. Kathy—"

"Get that woman out of here, Joe, then we can talk."

She threw a hand up toward the front door.

"I told you she's not a woman. She's like me. I mean he. Just talk with her—I mean him—then we'll leave."

She stopped sobbing and looked over at me. Our eyes met and I nodded in the affirmative. She wiped her tears with a palm and smoothed her house dress.

"Oh, my God. You must think poor of me. I don't usually swear or carry on like this. This is not me."

She looked down at the floor.

"Joe has been acting strange all week and I thought...Can I get you something to drink? We have Diet Coke, Sprite, and—"

"A Diet Coke is fine," I said.

Joe looked relieved. The knots in my stomach tightened.

I didn't know what I was supposed to say to Joe's wife, or why he felt it was my responsibility to do so. But there I was, sitting at a Sixties throwback kitchen table with a fake floral centerpiece, waiting for Kathy to retrieve a Diet Coke so we could "talk".

Joe wandered into another room but I imagined he wasn't far. He was anxious for a resolution to his dilemma. He wanted to keep part of his old life intact in case he failed at being a woman.

"Joe's been dressing up for years but he never goes outside. He has a few of his friends over from time to time. They parade around the house but..."

She got lost in mid-sentence. Her red-rimmed eyes

searched for answers in my face.

"Forgive me for staring but I've never seen anyone quite like you. You're—" her watery eyes bounced from side to side, as though a butterfly was flitting about her head. "Beautiful."

"Thank you."

My cheeks grew warm. No one had ever described me as beautiful before. My mother would grin and call me handsome at times when I dressed up for a school dance or groomed myself for church. Sometimes at the dinner table my father would glance in my direction. I wondered what he saw when he looked at me.

When I caught him, he would turn away and clear his throat or cough and call me a squirrel. Boys were not supposed to look that way. Traci said if you were an attractive male, it's likely you would become an attractive woman after transition. That was me, I guess.

"I would never have known if you hadn't said...I mean...You look like me. Like you were born this way."

"Thank you."

I stared down at my jeans and tried not to grin. Passing was important to everyone in transition. It meant you were near that point when no one noticed your existence and you were one step closer to feeling normal in your own skin. Some spend a lifetime and never blend in.

Even though I had been having electrolysis and receiving hormones for months by the time I met Kathy, I still avoided eye contact when I passed someone, either out of habit or fear. Lately, when I did dare look up, it seemed they didn't notice me. In the ladies' room, women smiled and went about their business.

I did not wear makeup except to line my eyes with a pencil and a dab of mascara occasionally, and I fluffed out my curly hair into a mini-afro when it got long enough. I had an androgynous appearance, or so I thought. It never occurred to me that I might be attractive.

Kathy's eyes watered. She may have been thinking:

Joe is fucking gay and going to leave me for something worse than another woman.

Her comfortable life that she had expected to last forever was over. She placed her head down on the table and began to sob.

"Oh God, what am I going to do? What am I going to tell the children?"

She wrapped her arms around herself and began to rock back and forth.

I didn't have the answers. I messed up with my own children. Jackie and April had sat on both ends of the divan in my study framing their older sister, Jen Rose. Their mother sat behind me in the easy chair beside the fireplace. Like Kathy, she had her arms wrapped around her, holding onto herself and rocking back and forth.

I knelt before our daughters on the floor and held out a small sword, a souvenir of some boy's life. I looked into the anxious faces of my children and said:

"Plunge this dagger into my heart. No one would blame you if you do. It would be easier than having to live through what is coming next. For this is the day that I will kill your father."

Their wide-eyed silence strangled me. I had to catch my breath before speaking again.

"You are novelties in this world, special children, unique, because you were born to two women. I have known all my life that I was different and knew that the day might come when I would have to leave you. So, forgive me please for not raising you like ordinary children. Little girls deserve to be sheltered and protected from the world. This is why I have been so hard on you. To make certain you could someday survive without—" my voice broke— "a father. Never knowing exactly when that day would come."

"No, don't leave. We will protect you."

Jen Rose reached out and grabbed me around the neck. She clung tight to my neck just as she had her stuffed bear, Bogie, when she was small. I used to think it was the bear that protected the child against all those things that go bump in the night. But it is the child who holds the bear, not the other way around.

"You mean you are getting a divorce. We're not going to be a family anymore?"

April burst into tears.

Jen Rose released me to comfort her younger sister. April collapsed in her arms. The other sister, Jacquelyn, sat immobile and stared straight ahead. She gazed off into space as though searching for answers from a God she would suddenly stop believing in.

Kathy looked frightened. Whatever had gotten into her husband was killing the man she had loved for more than thirty years.

She squeezed my hand. Her eyes shut tight as if trying to hold onto those final moments when her husband still belonged to her. A whole man. Not some hacked up eunuch but with all the parts he started out with the day he was born, and more importantly, that he possessed on their wedding night. The way God intended him to be.

Kathy's palm was warm and growing damp in mine. The refrigerator motor hummed and the clock on the wall behind me whirred and made a funny sound. One of the hands was sticking. It ticked off each second with an audible click. After several minutes Kathy sat back up, wiped her eyes with her palms, and blinked.

"Are you married?"

Kathy pulled me back from my memory.

"Yes," I said.

"What did your wife do?"

"She cried, like you."

"Now, what will she do?"

"She'll pick up the pieces and start a new life, too."

#

Chapter 6

Katherine Street

We know what we are, but we know not what we may be. -
William Shakespeare

On sunny days, light streamed into my bedroom from the
window facing the house next door. It was only for an hour after
sunrise then it was blocked by the roof-line and the air grew cold
and damp.

The heater in my room was plugged with rust. It didn't
work properly. It gurgled in those wee hours when Joe was not
stirring about his bedroom trying on clothes, he would wear the
next day, his radio purring softly in the background and the
furnace in the basement strumming like a locomotive at full
steam. I wore sweats to bed and sometimes got up and put on
my jacket, on those really cold days, when I had the urge to go
to the bathroom.

Joe's room faced the neighbor's flower garden and got
plenty of sunshine even midday. His door was usually open and
the shade up letting light stream in over his unmade bed. He was
dressed and seated at the kitchen table, coffee cup in hand,
ready and raring to go to work at his new job at Home Depot by
the time I got up. He grinned when he saw me like I was some
new doll he got to play dress-up with.

On those days when he went to work, Joe wore a plain
white blouse and faded blue-jeans with a wide cuff at the bottom
showing off his new white ladies' tennis shoes. They were not
much different from the old pair he wore to mow the lawn
except for a few stains, but he insisted they made him feel more
feminine.

The name tag over his left shirt pocket belonged to
someone named, Stanley. He put a piece of medical tape over it
and wrote in his femme name with a black Magic Marker. It now

read: Elaine. I was glad he wore one because I never knew what he wanted to be called until he told me—He had a new name for every outfit he put together.

When I forgot the proper name, Joe got upset. He had so many personas it was hard to keep track. I usually remembered Elaine because he always wore the short brown wig to work. Veronica was the long brunette wig that fell below his broad shoulders, but if he wore it with pink shorts and a button-down white blouse, it was Sandy.

The blond wig with locks that loop behind his ears was Nancy and when he wore the brown one with straight bangs, he usually asked me to call him Betty, but if he wore a red dress with black stockings it was something exotic like Simone or Carmen. Tina was a strawberry-blond and when he wore the short black wig with pumps, he was Judy.

Kelly Ann was the auburn one, I think.

There was a brassy bouffant he kept in a box that looked like a beehive. When he wore this one, I just called him Honey. In fact, that's what I usually said to be on the safe side. He smiled when I called him that, thinking I was using a term of endearment.

Like that would have ever happened.

It's one thing to be nice to somebody out of courtesy. It's something completely different to get close to another male, particularly a transvestite, who gets his rocks off wearing a dress. Sex was the furthest thing from my mind.

Transition was confusing.

I cringed when I saw myself naked. It was a little weird seeing male parts on the bottom with boobs on top. I could not wait until I got my letter recommending SRS and finally would feel normal in my own skin.

I only had one name, Evelyn, albeit temporary on my way to some other self. I would pick another one after my operation when I went stealth. No one would know me. Not Joe or anyone from the XX Club. They would be just another memory to suppress.

Joe had a calmness in his face that radiated confidence when he made himself up. It surprised me, but I kept my thoughts to myself. Everyone deserved to follow his dream. On his best day, Joe, looked more like a caricature of the woman in the photograph that he kept tucked in his wallet—some dead actress who died in a plane crash in the early 50's that used to be married to Clark Gable.

I couldn't say for certain, but I think Joe knew, deep down in his core, that he didn't pass well as a woman. His shoulders were broad, and he had a Neanderthal brow that protruded over his eyes like an awning over a pawn shop window. But he dolled up and went out every day, strutting down the street drawing stares like a dust bunny rolling under a bed.

Unlike Joe, I did not like to stand out. He wore heavy makeup and clothes that drew attention to him. He preferred flamboyant while I believed in subtle. He interpreted the directive of living a year in the chosen gender role as dressing up.

There was no guide book on how to become a woman. Fortunately, for me, I grew up in an area where women seldom wore makeup and dressed casually. I blended in. I stayed hidden behind an androgynous appearance. I wore jeans, sneakers, and a sweater most of the time. I seldom dressed up even for meetings.

When people stared at me, I panicked. My heart would beat faster and my throat would tighten making it difficult to breathe and speak, and that complicated my situation even more.

My voice wasn't bad. I'd taken several lessons from a woman in Springfield, Massachusetts, Camille, who used to teach voice to actors in Hollywood. At least I think she was a woman. She taught me techniques to sound more feminine. It was the right pitch and timbre and resonated well through my sinus cavity, until I got nervous and the muscles tightened in my throat. Then it was raspy like an old black lady singing the blues.

It took me a long time to realize that it wasn't always

amusement gleaning in the eyes of the observer. Several months of electrolysis and hormones had taken effect. It was like magic. I did not understand the trick, but somehow it worked.

Sam's sidelong glances as he crept up the stairs behind Cathy seemed to linger longer than usual, and one night, Joe asked to see me naked. It shocked me. Not so much the question but how he looked at me when he said it. I did not have a lot of experience with men who liked to wear makeup. If I had a lock on my bedroom door, I would have locked it.

Joe did not think there was anything wrong with him. He felt most men fantasized but were afraid to admit it. He contended that he was a heterosexual man despite the fact he got a kick out of dressing up as a woman. He didn't really want to become female like me. He thought I was the same as him only more extreme.

"Either that or he's an admirer," Traci had said when I mentioned it to her. She always gave me advise on how to survive, like the big sister I never had.

Some men were afraid to admit they are gay, even to themselves. Admirers liked sex with a twist. They thought of themselves as hetero-sexual and wanted the world to think of them that way.

"Look out for admirers. They're dangerous."

She would warn me every time we went out, as though she did not think it would stick. If I didn't know better, I would have thought Traci worried about me. She would point out some man in a Brooks Brothers suit and a $30,000 Rolex on his wrist staring at us and leaning against the back wall at Jacques near closing time, and give me that look. Her eyes narrowed. She looked like a cat watching her prey.

When we were at one of our support group meetings, she would look over at Laura, the big gal with the tattoo of a naked lady on her upper arm. Canon Jones makes her cover up with duct tape and sit on the old leather couch outside our imperfect circle of chairs at meetings.

Sometimes, Traci would point at Joe and wiggle her little

finger at me and wink. I would crack up and we would both get shushed and a hard look from Jennifer, the XX club president.

Joe's deep manly voice brought attention to him and me whenever we were out together. He insisted on using his normal voice, a bass that vibrated in the chest and scratched at the air whenever he spoke, and he laughed in that deep hearty way most men do that seems to come up from the soles of their boots.

"I'm never going to look like you," Joe would say.

"Lucky for me, people are more tolerant these days. The best any of us can hope for is tolerance."

"Have you ever tried to soften your voice? Maybe you'll like it."

He looked at me and shook his head vigorously.

"I don't want to sound like a fag."

I always thought a man who wore a dress was at least part gay. He wanted to make certain I understood that he was straight. To him, being gay was worse than being a tranny.

"The trannies get more sympathy from the public because everyone thinks you're insane."

It was certainly better than everyone thinking you're a pervert.

Joe insulted people at the XX Club without trying. We all knew he did not mean anything by it. It was just the way it was between the femmes and those who weren't. Being manly was hard for some.

I guess some get used to people making fun of them. I hated it. Michael worked hard at hiding his differences. He toned his body with exercise, kept his hair cut short, talked excessively loud and sometimes used profanity. At times it didn't work. I thought I was as masculine as any man but some people saw right through me.

"My, you have artistic hands" or "I wish my eyelashes were as long as yours" and some female customers would tell me about their menstrual cramps or c-section, and a woman breastfed her two-year-old in front of me while I sold her a pair of retreads for her Volvo. "Oh, I forgot you're a man," she said and tucked her breast back into her blouse like it was no big deal. Trying to unlearn all that manhood training was hard, too.

"You walk like a monkey fucking a football. How do you make your hips do that?"

Joe laughed at me but not in a mean way. He sincerely wanted to know. Everyone in our circle winced when he asked me:

"Why would anyone want to cut their dick off? That's fucking crazy."

It offended me but I said nothing. I didn't feel crazy. He thought we were men trying to be women or pretending, like him. He couldn't grasp the concept of being trapped in the wrong body. Like everyone else, he found it incredulous when I told him, "I've always felt like a woman only broken and in need of repair."

I didn't know much about, gays, drag queens, and transvestites back then or the men who loved them. The government censored everything concerning transsexualism, including educational materials, as decadent and corrupt to the public mores. If you wanted a book on the subject, you'd have to ask the proprietor of an adult book store for them. They were usually kept in a box under the counter along with the sex toys. Something no self-respecting man or those pretending to be, would ever do.

Living with Joe was, at times, a challenge. I would have preferred a roommate more like myself, however, I knew that my time with Joe was temporary. I needed someone to share expenses with, who would be available and willing to get me to and from appointments and help me navigate through all the channels required to be approved for the sexual reassignment procedure, which was the final goal. After the surgery, I knew I would never see him again.

\#

Chapter 7

The Mother Hen

Of all the ways to lose a person, death is the kindest. – Ralph Waldo Emerson

"Evelyn, Wake up."

"What is it?" I rolled over and spoke into my pillow. The lights were too bright.

"Evelyn, get up. You have to come with me, please. It's Kaitlyn. I don't think I can handle this alone or I wouldn't wake you."

I jerked my elbow toward the shadow looming near me when Joe pulled back my covers.

"Wow, you've got quick reflexes. I need your help. Kaitlyn's in the hospital."

I dressed quickly in the dark. The faint odor of my wife still lingered in the fabric of my sweater and it made me hesitate. Something warm crept over me and was gone in a shudder when I realized she wasn't there.

Joe was already dressed and sitting in his truck when I came out of the house. I didn't lock the door. It rankled him, but I lived in a small town in Vermont most of my life where crime was virtually nonexistent. He jumped out and did it for me.

"Evelyn, you need to start remembering to lock the door. We are women now, or need I remind you?"

That's the last thing I needed in the middle of the night, without coffee— a lecture from a transvestite on how to become a proper woman. Joe put his truck in gear as soon as I got in. The seat belt caught in the door, so I didn't put it on. I warmed my hands over the vent and shivered.

"What happened?" I said after we'd gone three blocks.

"Big Kathy said Kaitlyn's boyfriend got drunk. That's all I know so far except she ended up in the hospital. Big Kathy is on her way. We'll meet her there."

Like Traci, I tried not to make friends at the XX Club. I was cordial and friendly but only to the extent my newly adopted nature would allow.

Joe, on the other hand, considered it a sisterhood of sorts, and everyone knew he was a person to call if they needed help. Hawk-nosed Kaitlyn, the tall lanky blond with a married boyfriend that liked to beat on her and Big Kathy, with a gut nearly as big as Joe's, from her love of beer, were two he started to get close to. Jennifer would call them his "little chicks" that he would nurture at meetings and speak to for hours on the telephone afterward long into the evenings if any problems arose. Apparently, something had.

When we entered the highway, I got concerned.

"Where are we going?"

"To the hospital. I told you—"

"No, where are we going?"

"Chelsea."

"What? Who is that?"

"It's a place not a person. Gosh, you're a hard one to wake up. It's near—never mind—just sit tight. You can sleep if you want."

It sunk in that we were driving to a hospital, hours away, to visit someone we were uncertain was seriously hurt. Joe smelled like beer and dirty feet when he spoke.

"Joe, we're going to miss our hair appointment." I yawned. "Do you think they will charge us a fee for not canceling? I think some salons do that sort of thing. Not that they can collect it if you never go back."

He didn't answer me.

"What time is it?"

I rubbed my eyes. I barely remembered crawling into bed. I repeated the question.

Joe held his wrist out for me to study his watch. It was impossible to see the hands in the dark. He had on the wig he wore when he went to work at Home Depot—a short brown one with ringlets pulled down on his forehead that resembled the hair style Sandra Dee wore in *Gidget*, but I was sure this was his "Elaine" wig. His makeup was thick and pasty over his beard. Either he rushed to get ready and didn't shave first or he never went to bed. Some of the thick stubble showed through, and he was wearing a plaid shirt and his old lady jeans—the baggy ones with wide cuffs at the bottom. He looked like some Russian farmer's wife I'd seen in an obscure movie as a child. *Dr. Zhivago*, I think.

"I'm not wearing any makeup, Joe. I look like hell."

I pulled down the visor to look in the mirror.

"Veronica."

"What?"

Joe shook his head. I guessed the wrong name.

"Like you wear makeup anyway. You don't need it. God, I wish my face was that smooth. Did electrolysis hurt? How did you stand it?"

"Yes, I still need to cover it up. My face has so many holes. I need a paving contractor to apply my makeup. I look like shit, Joe."

Joe laughed despite his sentient mood. In a few weeks, I would go to the city to visit the patron saint of transsexuals: Dr. Felix Schiffman. He specialized in feminine facial surgery to include planning of the skin to get rid of pock marks and acne scaring and other hazards of a turbulent puberty. One dermatologist that my mother took me to called it a war of the sexes ravaging my body.

I pulled down the visor and took the eyeliner and mascara out of my purse. The road was rough and I was bouncing too much to draw a straight line, then I realized that Joe has driven onto the shoulder.

"Damn it, Joe. You want me to look like a clown?!"

He laughed.

"I should be so lucky to look as bad as you. I think I'd died and gone to heaven."

We drove in silence for what seemed a long time before I

felt alert enough to speak again.

"What's wrong? You falling asleep on me, old girl?"

"No, I was just thinking."

The light from oncoming traffic reflected into our cab for a moment, long enough for me to glimpse Joe's eyes. They were wet. I looked back out my side window.

"About what?" I asked.

"Why the Docs, don't know. Well—they know—I guess, but they don't tell us, and they use the same treatment for you and me and Big Kathy and Kaitlyn and your little bitch—"

"Traci," I completed her name for him.

"Yeah, her. And they know we aren't all the same kind of tranny. They even have different categories for us in the manual. You have a different priority than me. You get hormones faster. You and I are married. My wife has to sign off on my hormones. Yours doesn't. Big Kathy's does. I don't get it. How do they determine who is who? Who gets a letter and who doesn't? They don't really talk to anyone. Not really. All they do is see us once. We fill out a few forms. Come to a meeting when we feel like it except the regulars. When someone—" he halted.

I stared out the window pretending not to notice he stopped talking. You didn't have to be a savant to know what he was thinking. It was on the job training or learn-as-you go for psychologist and behavioral scientist and we were the guinea pigs.

"If Kaitlyn, dies—"

He stopped speaking again. I put my hand on his shoulder thinking it was the right thing to do. He stiffened under its weight.

"You don't have to pretend to care, Evelyn. It makes it worse when you do that." Joe is not mad. He is trying to parent me. "I don't understand how Kaitlyn is a cat 4 when she is so feminine while you and what's her name—"

"Traci—"

"Yeah—you and her—are cat 5's. True transsexual, they call you. Where do they come up with this shit? Like you and her are real, the stars of the show and everyone else are just understudies."

I shrugged.

"You are the real deal and so fucking unfeeling."

I rolled my eyes and stared out the windshield at the darkness ahead. He adjusted his seatbelt with a snap.

"Unbelievable. You are both like cold fish. I heard you two have a bet on who will rearrange her face first, a surgeon or her boyfriend. What's up with that?"

I didn't have an answer. It took years of depression to make us that way. I was thankful the darkness masked the anger on my face. I thought it was our secret.

"Joe, I—am as new as you are to all this. What is your point?"

"I don't know. I guess I can't get why you seem to fit the mold they are looking for and people like me, Big Kathy and not even poor Kaitlyn?"

He grew silent and slowed at an intersection as if to stop at the light but it turned green.

"She is more like you than you realize. She knew she was different from an early age. Did you know her father used to beat her every time she showed any emotion, from the time she was a child, just like you and Traci? He said he could make a man out of her. Bam! The back of his hand was stained with her blood."

He held up a fist for emphasis.

"She stayed well past her 18th birthday to protect her little sister from that drunk. Did you know after her boyfriend beat her the first time and he broke her collar bone she managed to climb up on a trash bin in her garage to hang herself with those plastic garbage ties strung together around her neck? Do know why she wears shirts with collars and turtle necks in summer?"

He glanced in my direction.

"To hide the scars--"

Joe choked on his emotion.

"How should I know?"

"And that's my point. You don't know because you don't care."

Joe shouted and threw his hands in the air before grabbing the wheel again. It startled me.

"What? I Care."

"No. You don't."

"Well, maybe next time, she'll get that nose job and it won't be an issue," I muttered and regretted saying it as soon as it slipped out of my mouth. God, I was tired.

Joe said: "shut the fuck up."

He was hard of hearing. I didn't think he had heard me. I folded my arms over my bosom and slumped down in my seat and stared out the windshield. If I'd had a choice I would have gotten out of the truck, but it wasn't an option, so I shut the fuck up instead and stared out the side window, thinking I made a mess of my life by moving in with a transvestite. I should have waited for someone more like me.

Then I thought, *what a mistake that would have been.* I hated myself more. I was a selfish bitch, willing to sacrifice everything and everyone to reach my goal—to become that ordinary woman—even it seemed, my loving family.

\#

Chapter 8

The hospital

Turn your face to the sun and the shadows fall behind you. –
Unknown

Joe knew Kaitlyn's real name. Her male name. The one
she was born with and on her security badge for work and on
her driver's license with the photo of a hawk-nosed
androgynous person with long, stringy blond hair. So, he
approached the night desk ahead of me. I didn't hear what he
said but the nurse raised an eyebrow. She knew who he was
talking about even before he opened his mouth.
"Are you family?"
The big bosomed black woman in blue scrubs behind the
fourth-floor desk rolled her big white eyes over Joe. There was
no inflection in her voice. When she asked again, she stretched
her vowels further than a diva in a Russian operetta.
"Ma'am, are you family?"
"I'm her sister," I stepped up to the desk from behind Joe.
The woman squinted at me. A fake smile stretched over
her mauve lips. I held her gaze. There was kindness swimming
beneath the surface waiting to see if it was safe.
*Either I'm a sister or something trying to be and she was
going to give me the benefit of a doubt.*
"Okay, what's your name?" She looked down at the chart
in her hands.
"Joe," I pulled on his arm. "Go sit down over there."
I pointed to a lounge in the corner by the elevator. There
were daggers in his blood-shot eyes. Neither one of us had slept
more than a few hours in the last couple of days. His irritability
slipped out onto his lined face.
"Karen," Joe whispered loudly. He looked at the nurse.
"My name is, Karen."

I nodded. I didn't want to fight with him. I softened my voice. "Please, Karen, let me handle this. We've driven two and a half hours to get here. Do you really want to leave without seeing, Kaitlyn?"

Joe glared at me and then back at the black nurse sheepishly. She was smirking behind the desk listening to our conversation. He picked up a magazine from the table and sat down crossing a heavy leg over one knee. I knew his attention would be divided between the magazine, the murmuring voices of the people on the television on the far wall and straining to listen to me.

"We, both know there is nothing on your chart regarding names of eligible family members. Some people prefer to be left alone."

I spoke low enough for Joe not to hear. The woman's gaze is softer now that Joe was not standing tall in front of her desk.

"If she has a proud family. All upstanding members of the community. She wouldn't have listed them. We both know that, too."

She caught my drift. An unconscious male brought into the hospital wearing women's clothing or even just resembling a woman but for a certain appendage is memorable. I'm certain the intake administrator's impressions were noted in the file in her hands.

"That's the only father she has ever known," I rolled my eyes toward Joe, who has his nose in a magazine.

"And as much as he may be embarrassed to list— Karen—I know he wants to see him."

When I emphasized Joe's femme-name, her smile broadened.

"God, knows it hasn't been easy on the rest of the family."
There was a long pause. I held my breath.
She exhaled audibly and said: "Room 234.
I turned to leave.
"But I need a name."
She grabbed my wrist.

"Evelyn," I said.

Her brow crinkled like crate paper as she wrote it down on her chart then looked up expectantly.

"Stone."

I would be hard pressed to produce any identification with that name other than a copy of the lease my landlady was kind enough to provide at Joe's request but she doesn't ask.

"Ms. Stone?"

I looked up at her expectantly. My heart pounded in my ears.

"You've got thirty minutes."

"Thank you, Ma'am."

"That's when my shift ends."

She pushed her glasses back up onto the bridge of her nose.

I caught her drift and nodded.

# # #

Kaitlyn was awake when we walked into the room. Her forehead bandaged and one eye completely covered with a wad of cotton taped over it. Her mouth was swollen and blood oozed from a nasty split in her upper lip. The only part of her face untouched is the one feature she could have altered that would have been an improvement. The large protruding hawk-nose rose up from middle of the black and purple flesh like a phoenix. The other occupant in the next bed was buried under piles of white blankets and appeared to be an octogenarian.

"My God, Kaitlyn. What did he do to you?" Joe leaned over Kaitlyn trying to give her a pat on the shoulder. She put a bandaged hand up to stop him.

"Ah, I'm all broken, Joe." Kaitlyn started to cry. Joe noticed her hand and backed off like she had leprosy. "Every part of me hurts."

"Oh, you poor thing. What can we do?" Joe moved closer. He tiptoed as though sound waves might hurt her.

"Nothing, right now. I'm okay." Kaitlyn's voice sounded weak. She appeared to be heavily medicated.

"I'm going to kill that son-of-a-bitch when I see him. What's his name?" Joe was suddenly angry.

"No, no. It was an accident. He didn't hit me. I fell."

A brown leather bombardier jacket was slumped over the chair by the bed. It seemed out of place. It looked too large for Kaitlyn's frame. I detected the faint smell of a familiar after shave wafting about the room. Something my father got every year around Christmas, Old Spice or Aqua Velvet maybe. The sound of a toilet flushing startled us. Adrenaline dumped into my veins when I realized who the jacket might belong to. Kaitlyn's married boyfriend emerged from the bathroom before I can warn Joe. She called him Jorge or Georgy at the meetings I thought but out of her swollen lips it sounded like she choked out: "Gerry."

"What's he doing here?" Joe looked confused. Domestic problems are unfamiliar to him. He's had a wonderful thirty-five years with Kathy. From what I have seen of Joe, he loves his wife and would never think of hitting a woman even if she stabbed him a hundred times.

"Joe, wait— Kaitlyn tried to grab his sleeve with her bandaged hand.

"What the fuck are you? The entertainment?" Kaitlyn's boyfriend was short dark and not at all handsome. His beer belly extended over his belt more than an inch and his hands and forearms were large and covered in dark fur. Joe moved between him and the bed where a one-eyed Kaitlyn waved her hand futilely in the air trying to get either man's attention.

"Who let this clown in here? You ain't family."

"Gerry, Please," Kaitlyn pleaded.

It sounded like Gerry with a lisp or something like Georgy. Laura said her boyfriend's name was Jorge, but that's what it sounded like from her swollen lips—Gerry, with a few extra 'Rs' rolled in for good measure.

"And you a married man. Shame on you."

Joe fired back.

"What kind of sicko does this? Look at her face!"

Georgy, Gerry or whatever his name was, pointed a stubby finger at Joe's. He looked over at me, uncertain of my status. The impact of Joe's statement stung him. His blotchy face grew redder.

"You fuck! I ought to slap that wig right off your clown head. I am just the good Samurai that brought her here when she fell down the stairs."

"Samaritan, you moron," Joe corrected him.

He stepped forward trying to get by me in the crowded room.

"And that ain't you."

I stood firm blocking his path. I could see a scenario where we all ended up in jail if I let him by—something that scared the hell out of me.

"Who you callin' a moron, fagot."

At the word Joe most loathes, I am unable to restrain him and fell backward and the two men, one wearing a wig, grab at each other and tussle at the end of Kaitlyn's bed. Joe was a foot taller but Gerry was equally as wide and with large bulging arms that seemed to grow larger under the strain of trying to lift Joe in the air.

"Please stop—"

Kaitlyn's voice grew hoarse. The old man next to her reeked of fresh urine.

I moved closer to the window and far away from the melee and stench as possible.

Kaitlyn looked at me with her good eye pleading.

What can I do? I threw my arms up in frustration.

Gerry got an arm loose and popped Joe in the ribs several times before Joe slipped an arm around Gerry's thick neck and moved to the side of him where his short reach made it difficult to land a solid punch. They spilled out onto the floor in front of the bathroom. There was a bang then a shrill shout that echoed through the room. It was strangely familiar and unnerving.

"Gentlemen! Cease immediately before I call security."

The black night nurse stood in the door way. Gerry and Joe released each other and leaned back against opposite walls trying to catch their breaths. The old man in the next bed remained immobile and silent.

"Damn! Give you people an inch and you take a mile."

The nurse was looking directly at Joe and shaking her head.

"What? We didn't do anything?"

"Quiet! You do not speak. Only I talk. Is that clear? Nod if you hear me. I don't want to hear a peep out of you, understand me?"

She raised her hand above her head.

"Yes—"

"Did you just peep?"

Joe nodded and Gerry laughed drawing her cross-eyed gaze.

"Yeah, this queer doesn't belong here. I'm surprised he got in. He ripped my shirt. I want to press charges—" Gerry stammered.

"And who the hell are you? What are you doing in here? I don't have you on my list?"

"Ah, I brought her in, ah, when she fell down the stairs. I was the good Sam—Samaritan." Gerry said and he automatically stood at attention.

She stepped towards him as if to get a better look.

"What the heck? Why are you still here after three hours?"

"I have a right to be here. She's my girl--I mean—

"She!"

The nurse turned her gaze and pointed a fat finger at me.

"That girl—is not injured—who are you talking about?"

"Ah," Gerry's eyes moved in every direction like a box ping-pong balls spilling onto the tile floor. He was stumped. I imagined him trying to think: *How to explain this to my wife or her insufferable family, if arrested.*

57

"Boy, who are you talking about? Which one is *your* girl? There's only one other female in this room besides me and I sure as hell ain't your girlfriend."

Her gaze swept over me then toward Joe. She made a face. It was obvious she had read both of us from the beginning. I felt done in by one of Traci's special rules. *One T might pass in a crowd, two maybe, but never three, and where one is not passable everyone is read.* The nurse was being kind to me at Gerry's expense.

"And who said he fell down the stairs. Mr. Farr's injuries are consistent with someone whose been in a fight. In fact, someone beat him up pretty good. Would you know anything about that Mister--ah, what your name again? You should be thanking your lucky stars. If it he was a female, we have to call the police."

Gerry stiffened at the nurse's provident use of male surnames. He looked over at Kaitlyn and lowered his gaze. He caught the night nurse's drift. He pushed angrily by me to reach for his leather jacket. I fell against the wall.

"Excuse me! Did you just assault that woman?" The nurse stepped forward and he ducked around her toward the door. "Now, I have another reason to call security. Apologize or you won't get out of the building before you're arrested."

Gerry gave me a double-take. There was a spark of uncertainty in his eyes and one-part fear. "Sorry."

The nurse caught his sleeve as he was putting on his jacket. "Sorry, ain't going to cut it in that tone of voice, Mister."

"Sorry, Miss," He said softer than before and lowered his eyes. He pulled his sleeve away from the nurse's grip and disappeared out the door before she could say anything else.

"You've got five minutes, dear," the nurse said then pulled Joe by the elbow, "You come with me. Your privileges are over. You can wait for your friend at my station."

"Sorry, Joe," Kaitlyn called from her bed. Her voice was low. Joe was hard of hearing. I doubt her heard her. His bass voice could be heard protesting all the way down the hall until the nurse shushed him with a final warning.

Suddenly, I was alone in a room with someone I have only said hello to in passing at a XX Club meeting. We didn't know each other well. We did not have much in common except for our malady. She-males didn't fit into the world we were born into. We both felt like freaks and belonged to the same support group. Kaitlyn looked out at me from behind her bandages.

"I am sorry, Kaitlyn." The most overused word in the English dictionary was getting a workout. Sorry, seemed so inadequate. "Fuck Me", was a better choice.

The same fate might befall me in time. No one wanted to be reminded they were vulnerable. I had a boyfriend who was homophobic. Growing up in a man's world, I had my share of beatings. So far, I had been lucky. I learned to hide my differences just as I had hidden those feminine traits over the years living as a boy. Transition was my opportunity to learn new ways to blend in. Regain that shield of anonymity that once was the key to my survival.

Homosexuality was still on the books in most states as illegal. The American Psychiatric association may have revised its diagnostic and statistical manual removing it from a class of mental illness, but it was still deviant behavior in the world we lived in that bore consequences.

The nurse was one of those tolerant people that Joe spoke about but even she was wary of our kind. All I wanted to do was get out of there as soon as practicable.

"It's okay. He'll call me in a day or two. He always does." She forced a laugh. It disturbed me that she was more worried about the one who put her in the hospital than whether her own injuries may be permanent. What price are we willing to pay for love?

"You feel alright?" I asked and moved over to the chair furthest away from the bed.

"Yeah, I'm alright. Just a little sore."

"Don't suppose you want to tell me what happened? You know, Joe, he is going to hound me after. Why didn't you ask her and all that, you know?"

"No. What would be the point?"

She tried to laugh again but it sounded more like a gasp right before someone begins to sob. We both knew the police wouldn't investigate. The victim was a male in drag that won't press charges.

Even if Kaitlyn wanted to, there was no crime, at least not a sexual assault. It was not against the law between consenting males to pound on one another unless it was for sex and neither would admit to that. Both would get thrown into jail. In the minds of straight policemen and women, Kaitlyn was a male. He consented to get beat on as soon as he put on a dress and lured an otherwise unsuspecting gentle man into coitus and thus deserved the consequences of his fallacious nature. *It's our fault. We asked for it.*

I nodded and broke eye contact. Embarrassed.

"Can we get you anything before we leave?"

There was a slight nod of her bandaged head that I took to mean, no and that strangled noise again. I patted her un-bandaged hand gently and headed for the door.

"Evelyn?" her phlegmy voice stopped me in my tracks.

"Yes?"

"Tell Joe, not to tell anyone. Please—"

I don't want Canon Jones to find out. She hadn't finished her sentence but I filled in for her. I nodded then turned back around.

It took years for most of us to find out we were not alone. That there was hope, if not to stem the disease, at least to survive its effect. Kaitlyn was worried she might be asked to leave the program. For the true transsexual that would be akin to cutting off life support. She-males like us occupied a precarious place in society.

No one wants to admit we exist. It's entertaining to read about us in some tabloid like the *National Enquirer.* We aren't real. They see us as some kind of mythological creature like a harpy or the minotaur or the one with the goat's body, an adult fairy tale about sexual deviants. Nymphs that lured unsuspecting males and some females to their astrophysical demise. People subconsciously worried that, if real and unchecked, we may lead innocents down a path of homosexuality and a life of decadent debauchery.

What practical purpose could a male woman possibly have in this world?

"Thank you," Kaitlyn said.

Silence was golden. I looked back. Kaitlyn's uncovered eye looked up at me. There was a connection. We both know she will go back to the man who beat her.

Unlike us, Joe was a man. He would not understand why someone would choose to stay in an abusive relationship or not fight back. To choose to suffer abuse when you didn't have to was inconceivable if you have a choice. The line between Transsexual and Transvestite is further drawn. We are victims in the war between the sexes. Neither side understands our position. Each gender refuses to claim us. I mean, who *chooses* to become a victim?

As I started down the hall, I heard that muffled sound again, coming from behind me. It was unmistakable this time. No doubt. It was a sob.

#

Chapter 9

The Train Ride

You can't unscramble eggs. – J.P. Morgan

The next day Joe was waiting for me at the kitchen table slurping his coffee. He greeted me as soon as I stepped out of my bedroom. He chirped like one of those annoying little brown birds outside your window at 5 a.m. and you wished you had a BB gun handy.

"Good morning, Eve. Make sure you wear your boots today. It might rain later. Did you have a good night's rest? Mine was fitful. Oh, you should have seen the dress I saw in Filene's Basement the other day that would be great on Kaitlyn. Oh, to be skinny again."

He threw his head back and dislodged his wig. I nodded and grunted a few acknowledgments. I fended off any of his questions he had about Kaitlyn simply by telling him that she was too exhausted to talk and she would explain what happened at the next meeting of the XX Club. He seemed satisfied and let it go.

Joe was in an exceptionally good mood. He was taking me to his hairdresser in New York City. A place his favorite daytime soap actress, Susan Lucci, was seen often. He found it funny that I didn't know who Susan Lucci was, and I was amused that a man who wore wigs would have a hairdresser.

We drove three blocks to the Stratford train station. We could have walked from our apartment, but he said it would not be ladylike. He parked his truck on a side street behind an old Volvo station wagon and we climbed the stairs to the platform watching our breath make circles above our heads.

There was no wind, but the air was crisp, and the sun winked at us through the thicket of small trees to the east. The ticket-master had a huge grin on his face when Joe walked up to the window. It didn't seem to faze Joe. He bought two round-trip tickets to the city and engaged in small talk about the weather and asked who won the game last night. I winced and pulled my jacket tighter around me when the ticket-master glanced in my direction.

"You, ah, ladies, enjoy yourselves," he said as we walked away.

The train arrived in a fit of wind and squeals. It took my breath away. I caught the last of my breath as the doors whisked open and Joe grabbed me by the hand and pulled me inside.

We took a seat across from two middle-aged men in suits and ties, probably on their way to work in the city. They could have been bankers, lawyers, accountants, or anything, really. Urban life was unfamiliar to me except what I'd read in magazines or seen on television.

One of the men stared out the window watching us in the reflection of the black glass, the other propped behind his newspaper. I was too excited to be nervous. I had been on a train only once in my life, if you didn't count the time at Disney World 1970, a day before I placed a razor blade against my wrist contemplating how long it would take to drain the life out of me.

Joe slumped on the seat beside me. He was wearing a frilly white blouse and long knit skirt the color of ox blood and a blond wig that he had tied in some sort of a weave on one side of his head. It resembled some European outfit that you might find on one of the villagers on the set of *The Sound of Music*.

Traci's rule of three: "One passable T gets by, two may not catch the eye but where there is three—you die. Once read there is no going back." Traci was full of little witticisms. When I told her she was overly cautious, she admonished me. "It's critical to be on guard at all times. One mistake and you can lose everything, including your life."

When one of the Ts was not remotely passable the rule did not apply. The fact I was in his company was enough. I was read. Even when Joe was not around, I had come to blame my level of discomfort on him. It was like he left his stench on me and the wolves could smell it.

Despite my rapid progress, I lacked confidence. I felt conspicuous in a leather skirt and black mesh stockings. Mr. Gray Suit continued to stare. I didn't look at him. There was something comforting in thinking, *If, you don't see him, maybe he can't see you?* Or at least, not see the fear in your eyes.

Traci warned it was our fate to always second guess ourselves. We saw a glint in someone's eye in passing or heard laughter as we walked into a room and immediately thought it was about us.

Confidence was evasive. Some never achieve any level of comfort and all of us suffered from a bout of the shakes occasionally without knowing why, and probably would for the rest of our lives. I gawked when Traci told me she got the jitters, too. It was hard to just let go of old fears and let our inner girl rule, especially when we had never met her.

Joe's eyes were closed, his lashes thick with mascara. They fluttered every so often and his mouth was agape, but he wasn't snoring. Joe always snored. It usually began five minutes after the light went out beneath his bedroom door. He was feigning sleep. Maybe he did not want to talk. He was still mad at me for something I had said, or failed to do.

He claimed I had no empathy.

"You're supposed to be a woman. What's the matter with you?"

He batted his false eyelashes in my direction. It always pissed me off, when a transvestite lectured me on how to become a proper woman. Putting on a dress and a bit of makeup did not make him an expert. It didn't evoke a feeling of sympathy for him much less the familial bond he wanted me to feel.

A teacher, Sister Mark, once told our Freshman English-class that the pursuit of love often ends in tragedy. I used to think fear prompted it. We were discussing Shakespeare. Her hands were on my shoulders after I had just read the part of Juliet in the famed balcony scene. She gave me a little squeeze when she had said it. I cringed. I guess that's what happened to me and Joe but much sooner in our relationship than I had anticipated.

We were both pursuing one of life's hidden passions but on different tracks. I steeled myself against his squeeze. He wanted to be a mother hen. I just needed a friend. We both admired the feminine life denied us for disparate reasons and would do anything it seemed to get it—even drink poison to kill off that male ego. Mine died off a little easier and peeled back a lot faster, or so I thought.

Joe used to wait on the back porch for me to come home from one of my temp assignments, hand me one of those cheap plastic champagne flutes full of beer and tell me about the indignations of his day. He finally got up the nerve to complain to Home Depot, about the badge they gave him that read: Stanley. They had ignored his request for weeks. He kept taping over it with a piece of gauze every so often and rewrote: Elaine in a black Magic marker. It bled through and looked unprofessional. But he kept asking for another. They gave him some other person's badge. "It says Ellen. They can't even get my name right."

"Well, it's a start." I said. "At least it was a female name."

I tried to sound sympathetic and cheer him up but he saw through my facade. Joe claimed he was fighting for all of our rights and we wouldn't appreciate it until we get to be his age. "If you live that long." He threatened me but he meant to warn all Ts, especially those who wanted to go into hiding after transition. At a meeting when Traci was present and within ear-shot he would look in her direction and speak louder. She would scratch her forehead with her middle finger and stare right back at him.

Joe had used the letter the clinic gave him to get some accommodation. Home Depot was one of the few progressive companies with an anti-discrimination policy protecting homosexuals—that's what they thought we all were—like everything that was not straight was bent the same way. Some of the staff and customers still gave him a hard time. The equal rights amendment didn't apply to queers, perverts, and child molesters. That's the way most people saw Joe and those like me in 1993.

"The day manager promised a new name plate weeks ago. He calls me: Betty. He knows it's Elaine. I'm Elaine, Goddamn it!"

I told him I was sorry but lately that was not enough. He seemed to want more from me. I was not the touchy-feely kind of person he needed. I was not his wife. Kathy knew how to comfort him when he was despondent or so he reminded me from time to time. Usually after he got off those late-night telephone calls.

"Kathy, wants me to come home." He would yell from his bed. I could hear him through my bedroom door. He thought it upset me. When I didn't respond, he'd say it again.

"What are you going to do?" I would say, not really caring to have the conversation to begin with.

"Don't worry, Evelyn. I made a commitment. I always keep my promise. Even if it kills me." He thought I was worried about him leaving me without support when I need it and he was right. "I will be there for you, no matter how you make me feel sometimes."

I wondered what he meant or whether it was me he was talking to. We all have demons in our heads we fought at some other time and lost. Unforgiving fathers who honed sons into men or drove them into the ground. Every time we argued it seemed he stared off into space or looked right through me as if I was not there. It reminded me of Vivien Leigh at the end of *Gone with the Wind* after Rhett Butler walked out her front door. *Tomorrow is another day!* Except she had tears in her eyes when she smiled. Joe's were dry.

I think he saw me as some discontented lover on her way out. We fought over the smallest things. I called him an ogre, especially when he made a mess. He thought me trivial. When we first moved in together, he used to joke and call me Mrs. Clean. He tracked in dirt and grass after I had cleaned and mopped floors. When he spread his legs open on the couch so I had to squeeze into one corner or when he spit into the kitchen sink, I would bring it to his attention that it was not 'lady-like' behavior. I often pointed out his male traits.

Three months later, he acknowledged that he identified as a man and felt comfortable being himself in private and that he, at times, enjoyed the thrill of dressing up as a woman. I was fairly certain that he was not transsexual but unsure why he liked dressing up.

There was no doubt in my mind from the day we met, that he was a man, inside and out. His habits were all male. I tripped over his shoes by the door as I came in at night and had to hang up his jacket or a shirt that he left hanging on the back of a chair or sometimes lying on the floor in the living room. It was like pulling teeth to get him to pick up after himself.

The state of the bathroom was a constant argument. Heaven forbid he take a bath more than once a month. He used my bubble bath once and poured half a bottle down the drain. It caused the bathroom to flood with bubbles for days. He left piles of dirty dishes in the sink before he went to bed. A colony of ants had moved in the next morning and the landlady had to fumigate the place.

Joe knew I adhered to the Harry S. Benjamin Standards of Care. I stayed in my preferred gender role and religiously sat down to pee regardless of my current anatomical anomaly. One more nightly dive into the deep would send me into hysterics and a tirade of curses and an oath to find a bucket of toilet water to douse on him while he slept but it seemed the threat was enough. He knew I meant it.

Then, there was the public flatulence—his stench caused a panic. Grown men dozing on benches beside us on a bus or train would rouse with a start, grab at their throats or cover their mouths and turn their heads towards the nearest source of uncontaminated air. I think he did this to annoy me. I had already started tip-toeing around the house at night and leaving early so we didn't have to run into each other.

Sometimes I think he did these things on purpose. Not because he didn't like me, but like that boy who sat behind you in second grade and cut off your pig tails with a pair of scissors. He wanted to get your attention.

More than anything though, it irked me when he tried to be the mother hen on those occasions when he felt like treating me like one of his chicks. I was relieved when Jennifer volunteered to allow me to recover at her stately home in Bridgeport. Joe was disappointed. He would be good in a pinch but there was no way I was going to rely on this man to take care of me. How disgusting.

Joe's large hand fell onto my lap. I pulled back startled as though stung by the thought in my head. Joe was a nuisance but a necessary one. Mr. Gray-suit laughed as he struggled to his feet. Other passengers were shuffling to the door. I was self-conscious that some were staring in our direction.

How long had I been daydreaming?

I hadn't noticed we stopped moving nor the cane in Mr. Gray-suit's left hand before he stood up. I wonder what else I had missed? Perhaps my intuition was not what I imagined it to be. The whole time, Mr. Gray-suit, the ticket-master, everyone on the train, were not staring at Joe at all. He looked like any number of oddities you might find in the city. They were staring at me. I sat frozen in place.

Joe grabbed my hand and pulled me from the train.

#

Chapter 10

Facial Surgery

Anesthesia does not eliminate the pain but merely helps you forget the memory of it. – Unknown

"Don't touch your face." It sounded like a woman—a nurse—I think. I rolled onto my side. Unfamiliar furnishings came into view, a stainless-steel sink and rows of cabinets lined the wall near the ceiling. An office. Dr. Schiffman's office. The memory began to reformulate in my brain. I remembered paying Dr. Schiffman an additional $400 to stay overnight in his office and to have someone with me—a bargain for a room on Central Park East. I never met the nurse. She came in after I went under anesthesia.

When I sat on the edge of the operating table in his office hours earlier, feeling vulnerable and scared, Dr. Schiffman had explained the procedure:

"Essentially, we use a tool that looks like a sander. It scrapes away all the imperfections in the several layers of your skin. Acne scars are deep, and you have some sun damage, and this?"

His fat thumb pressed on a wad of thick skin beneath my lower lip, the aftereffects of a snowmobile accident when I was seventeen.

"The scar may still show a little, but we can get rid of most of it."

The good doctor promised that I would be happy with the result. I noted that he used all the male pronouns in the English vocabulary while talking to me.

I managed to sit up and swing my bare legs over the side of the table. The floor was cold under my feet. I moved toward what looked like a mirror on the wall. I saw my reflection and I had to grip the side of the sink to keep my balance.

"You're brave," The nurse said in her Brooklyn accent.

"One woman freaked out and we had to call an ambulance to take her to the hospital to be sedated. I mean that's why we're here, in case you hurt yourself."

A misshapen purple football with slits for eyes stared back at me in the mirror. Hurt myself? Holy, fuck!

I had erased my face.

#

Chapter 11

The Engineer

We do not see things as they are but as we are. – Talmud

I sat quietly on a cushioned high-back chair near a fireplace in the small dark room where Joe dumped me and left. He didn't say goodbye. He said 'good luck' instead and walked away.

I was exhausted from the drive up from the city and the six hours of surgery where Dr. Schiffman and his staff reshaped my face. I couldn't respond. They used a tool that looked like a rotary sander, the kind you use to smooth rough spots out of wood. He even did my eyelids. My face swelled up and crusted over with fluids that oozed up from beneath the cracks in my facade. I had surgical staples at my hairline to hold my brow in place, sutures inside my nostrils, and thick raw scars behind my ears. Although the pain was minimal it did little to curb the misery of having my hair plastered to my head and not being able to breath out of my swollen new nose.

Andrew Lloyd-Weber's "Music of the Night" played low on a stereo-record player. Jennifer skirted around the fringes of my vision as she sang along.

A faint odor of a man's cologne rose from the cushions of the chair I was sitting in. The radiator hissed from some corner of the room. My nerves were jagged. Michael was independent. He had relied on no one for assistance. He knew his place in the world. I was still learning what was expected of me. What to say and how to act like a lady. An uneasy feeling stirred inside my chest like a small feathered creature testing its wings before it takes flight.

"Would you like a cup of tea? I was just about to make some when you arrived."

Jennifer's voice was soothing like something soft and

feathery. Traci called it creepy. She compared it to one of the old women in *Arsenic and Old Lace.*

"Yes, thank you, that would be nice."

I was exhausted. I would've appreciated it more if she had shown me to my bed but felt it would be impolite to ask. Not something a woman would do. Women were civil to each other even in pain, or so I thought. My mother harped on the proper etiquette of ladies and gentlemen all through my life. It was her responsibility to make certain we could survive in a civilized world.

"Now, when Julie comes in this evening, don't press her for information about her past. She is quite sensitive about it. We don't want to upset her now do we?"

"No, not at all."

It hurt to speak. I moved my lips as little as possible, a novice ventriloquist. The last thing I would have wanted to do was ask Julie about her past.

"I hope so. I would hate to upset her. I am so looking forward to getting to know you better."

The bird fluttered in my chest. An implication that I may be asked to leave hung in the air. Julie was that borderline personality the medical profession used to diagnose us prior to understanding transsexualism. She could go from neurotic to psychotic in seconds. My car was parked in the driveway. Joe and I had dropped it on our way to the city for my surgery but I was in no condition to drive.

"Enjoy a little ambiance while I get you a hot cup of tea. Did you know that women are like tea bags? You never know how strong they are until you put them in hot water."

Jennifer left and I pushed farther into the cushions of the chair trying to stay warm. It wasn't long before I heard footfalls coming from the kitchen to the hall outside the door.

"Oh, my, you look like a raw red onion."

Jennifer's voice preceded her as she came back into the room carrying a silver tray. It floated before me, along with the vision of her peeling metaphor, taunting me. It landed on a small table somewhere near my left. I felt a sudden warmth in anticipation of the warm nectar I would be soon enjoying and those delicious cookies. I hadn't eaten in a while. A small brown animal gnawed inside my gut trying to get out.

"Do you take sugar in your tea?"

"Oh, yes, please."

"One lump or two?"

"One, thank you."

Jennifer gingerly picked up a cube from the bowl with tongs and dropped it into a cup. The aroma wafted around my nose. In my mind's eye, I could see it dissolving under the brown liquid, a soft foam floating on top. A gnarly steady hand pouring. The thin pale skin stretched tight over the knuckles.

I think it's the most pleasant memory I have—the aroma of fresh brewed tea in my Nana's kitchen. Blue and yellow flowers on a linen table cloth that matched the saucers and cups on her tray. Steam rose from the long spout of the tarnished silver pot. The sticky sweet biscuits that tasted slightly of almonds sitting beside it and lemon drop cookies she bought especially for me. I leaned in toward the tray and tried to focus.

"Where are the lemon drops?"

Jennifer laughed. "Poor dear, you must be hungry. Julie is bringing home a pie tonight. She should be here shortly."

That flutter again in my chest at the mention of Julie's name.

"I want to pay you for your kindness."

My voice barely cleared my throat.

Jennifer sang, "I Don't Know How to Love Him." Her voice strained to reach the higher notes. After a few stanzas, she addressed my question.

"Of course, you can stay three days as we discussed. Your bedroom is upstairs and down the hall to the right. It was my son's room. Please do not touch anything. I don't need your money. However," —there was always a catch— "we expect you to perform a similar courtesy for a fellow trans in the future as agreed."

Good God! An underground railroad for gays.

"I would do that anyway, Jen. I am not poor. Let me give you something—"

"No. It's not necessary. It doesn't cost me anything to let you stay. We don't have a housekeeper. My son's room is the same as when he went off to college. It's just a little dusty. Dust never killed anybody. Um, that I know of. If you'll excuse me, I have to check the stove."

She set her cup down and left the room abruptly. If she and Julie didn't clean and there hadn't been a housekeeper since James Vandemere, II became Jennifer full-time, then who did? Her son left and never returned home after she announced in one of their father-son-weekly-chats that she was going to live full-time as a woman—several years ago.

Jennifer came back into the room and sat on a divan across from my chair. She brushed an errant blond strand away from her face and began talking. She talked about the history of the XX Club, theories of transsexualism, and spoke at length about her uneventful life as an engineer before she halted and cleared her throat. After a brief pause, she talked about the day she told her son, over the telephone in one of their weekly chats, that his father was really a woman and that she intended to free his feminine soul.

"I raised him to be open-minded. He's studying Medicine at Penn State. He calls every Sunday morning, at 9am sharp. He is always prompt. Never late. He takes after me," Jennifer said proudly. She got up, came over to my chair, and took my hand.

"Come, I will show you to his room. You can rest before Julie gets here. She said she might be a little late."

She led me upstairs and to a room at the end of the hall. "Please, don't touch anything. It's just the way my son left it the last morning he went away to school."

She reminded me again before turning off the light.

That's the way it was with shadow people. We preserved things like a curator in a living museum. We kept some boy's memories in a back room collecting dust as a reminder of who we once were. Not for ourselves but for those who loved him. We made time stand still by not thinking about it. In our world nothing changed—except maybe us—while we slept. We saw things as we were and never as they are, praying and waiting for magic to happen. We expected to wake up from the nightmare someday and start living the life we believed were meant to live.

We didn't hate the world, just the body we had been assigned to live in it. We didn't live in the present like everyone else but in some future time when we would feel normal in our own skins. All I had ever wanted was to be an ordinary woman but fate laid out a different destiny.

The bed floated just out of reach. Somehow, I managed to sit down on it and tried to remain seated while I waited for Jennifer to leave. When she was gone, I drifted back onto the fluffy comforter. I fell and kept on falling. The mattress didn't stop me. I fell through the bed, through the floor, and further. I fell right out of my body into utter darkness. That's when I heard it, a woman's scream.

It sounded far away at first and drawing closer. Growing louder, more chilling and familiar.

#

Chapter 12

The Priest

Only in art will the lion lie down with the lamb. – Martin Amis

Julie's voice pierced the air. Jennifer and Julie were arguing as I descended the stairs, or at least Julie was. Jennifer's voice was barely audible. I made my way to the chair I had previously sat in, as inconspicuous as possible. I heard Jennifer use some metaphor about a turtle crossing the finish line, just as I sat down. Her voice rose in pitch:

"I am glad you made it."

"I'm not late, Jennifer. Don't start with me."

That caged bird in my chest fluttered. Julie scared me. Borderline Personality Disorder did not begin to describe her. One minute she would be all smiles, the next, Lizzy Bordenesque.

"I didn't say—"

"I told you I'd be home after work and I came right home. You wanted a pizza. I had to wait for God knows how many people ahead of me. It's the weekend or haven't you noticed cooped up in your sanctuary all day? Still waiting for a call from your ungrateful son?"

Jennifer murmured something unintelligible.

"How long has it been now, two years? Well, tell me he called."

There was a noticeable pause and I pictured Jennifer looking pained while Julie rolled her eyes and shook off her coat.

"It was a nightmare just getting out of the city." Julie's voice was razor sharp. She sounded like the teacher who caught you napping or in Julie's case, a Mother Superior scolding an errant nun for losing her prayer beads.

"I wasn't suggesting you were late. Dear me, I was only pointing out—"

"You called to check up on me again, Jennifer. Don't lie."

A nervous laugh followed, unmistakably Jennifer's.

"Don't shake your head. I know you did. Don't lie to me. You know how I feel about lying. Maria told me you called." Julie chewed on every word and spit it out slowly and deliberately, so every syllable was easier to digest when it became difficult to swallow.

"I didn't mean—"

"Whatever! You know I work on the floor on Saturday's 'til seven. I'm busy trying to make some money so you don't always complain about the—"

"I know, I know. You don't have to say it. We have a guest. I only wanted to remind you to bring home a pie." Jennifer stammered. I saw a blur of movement through my swollen eyes and imagined her pacing in front of my chair. Her rubber-sole shoes squeaked on the hardwood floor.

"Tom called," Jennifer added. An audible sigh followed.

"What? What did he want?" Julie snapped. "Good heavens, that man is incorrigible. Why does he keep calling me? I told him I am not interested. One date was enough to know he's not the man for me. He's a triple A loser. All he did was talk about his accomplishments and ailments and his-his hemorrhoids. God, his breath—"

"He was worried. He wanted to make sure you got out of the mall before the weather turned. He was concerned that's all. He cares about you." Jennifer was flustered. Everyone at the XX Club knew she had a fragile disposition. "He didn't say he was coming over. I think he just wanted to—"

"He better not. I've had enough surprises for one day. Father Carlin was on the train out of the city this evening."

"No, no, no." Jennifer lowered her voice and stretched out the end of each word.

"Oh, yes. He sat two rows down staring at me from Central to Rochester. He looked right at me but there was no recognition in his eyes. Absolutely none. He was oblivious. Probably drinking again. He's only seen me dressed once and that was the time he caught me sneaking back into my cell at the seminary. I had on a ton of mascara and an auburn wig. I hardly wear any at all today."

"What do you think? Was he looking for you?"

"No." Through the slits opened in my vision I watched Julie pull on the fingers of the glove on her left hand. "He must have been traveling back to St. Vincent's after the winter seminar at Fordham. He always goes. Thinks it makes him appear more intelligent." Julie laughed. "Huh, good luck sounding smart with a hair-lip."

Jennifer whistled. She picked up my hand and put a cup into it.

"He's so predictable. I bet he'd die if he knew he ogled at me. The pervert."

"Maybe. I'm sure he didn't expect to see you there. It's been a while."

Jennifer's voice was barely audible.

"Argh! Are you defending him?"

Julie's voice became shrill. I nearly dropped the cup of Cola Jen had given me.

"No, no of course not. Julie, I am merely suggesting it was coincidence."

"Jennifer," Julie cleared her throat. "It's you that always says there are no such thing as coincidences only Hitsuzen. Don't be fickle."

The music of "Jesus Christ Superstar" flooded the air. Its harmonic sound lending more grandeur than the room deserved. My obscured vision made out the curve of a long divan and an elegant nineteenth century coffee table across from me. A small desk and chair sat beneath a window near the unlit fireplace. The acrid scent of dry wood, pine tar, and ash were distinguishable from other less familiar odors. Above the hearth was a granite mantle cluttered with the shape of objects too difficult to discern in the dim light except for a brass clock with the round face of the man-in-the-moon. My grandmother had one like it. Its gold hands ticked away the moments slow and steady.

I couldn't make out Julie's features, even when she crossed in front of me. I caught a waft of her perfume: *Beautiful* by Estee Lauder. My daughter, Jen Rose, wore the same one. Julie carried her coat in her arms like an infant and a purse, I think, hung off her wrist from a strap.

"Here, sweetie, have a slice of pie. I hope you like the works."

Julie's voice brought me to attention. Something was thrust in front of my face.

"I prefer plain cheese but it's all dingbat likes to eat."

Julie's mouth was inches from my face. I felt the warmth of her breath on my raw cheek.

"Oh, my God, Jennifer. Some hostesses we turned out to be. Look at her. Poor baby. She looks like one of my burn victims."

Footfalls hurried out of the room and returned minutes later. Julie set a tray with a bowl of steaming water nearby and began swabbing at the crust on my eyelids.

"Ow," I pulled back when a warm cloth touched my face. My instructions were to leave the crust to form a protective shield.

"Don't fight me, honey, it's going to help loosen some of the dried sebaceous crap—"

"Julie's studying to be a nurse. She's got another year. She's not going to be working at Macy's forever."

"Will you please stop reciting my bio to everyone you meet. I'm sure she's not interested."

Julie pushed the cloth hard on my face and I reached up.

"No, don't touch it, sweetie. Sit back and try to relax. It's good to let air get at your wounds. God, I have never seen anything like this. What did you do? It's painful-looking. Your whole face is gone. It's like hamburger."

I grew more nervous when she brushed a swab lightly against my lashes. My breaths came in short gasps. Suddenly, something loosened and my right eye opened for the first time.

Her face materialized inches from my own. Her plump lips were red. The tip of a moist tongue flicked against a row of straight white teeth when she spoke.

"They did your eyelids too, wow! Ah, I can see the possibilities. It's pink and smooth underneath some of this crust."

Julie stopped swabbing. She dropped her cloth in the bowl, picked up the tray and took it back to the kitchen. I could see Jennifer now, sitting forward on the edge of the divan nibbling on a slice of pizza while swaying to the music.

"Here, take these."

Julie's hand popped under my nose. There were two white capsules wriggling in her clean white palm.

"It will help you feel better. Just don't take them with alcohol. You're not drinking wine, are you?"

I shook my heard. Jennifer had given me a Coke.

"Thank you," I managed to say and took the pills from her as instructed.

Julie sat down on the divan beside Jennifer. She picked up a slice of pizza from the box and began picking at the toppings, popping them one at a time into her mouth. First a mushroom, next a piece of sausage, a red pepper, something green, then a paper-thin wafer of pepperoni. Each time she wiped her fingertips with her napkin. She continued the same routine until there were no more toppings left. She set the emaciated fragment of dough on the table in front of her and picked up another slice from the box and began the process all over again.

"Jesus Christ?"

Julie screamed, catching me, and nervous Jennifer, completely off guard. There was a flutter in my chest and the caged bird took flight. Julie swayed back and forth, keeping beat with the music and holding onto herself while singing:

"Where are you, who are you, what was your sacrifice?"

# # #

Chapter 13

Julie's Story

There are no facts, only interpretations. – Frederick Nietzsche

"I was excommunicated."

Julie's voice was distant. I was fading. She sounded like a child on the verge of tears. I studied her features through the slits in my vision. The fluid oozing into the corners of my eyes had slowed. I could see clearly for the moment. Her face was close to mine again. There was no moisture gleaming in Julie's crescent eyes, no tears, but she had that faraway look like each newbie had at the XX Club when she recited her story to the group for the first time. It always started out with that pained expression followed by a flood of information.

"Do you know what that means?"

Julie leaned closer to my face and repeated the question, chewing on every word.

"Do you know what that means?"

"No," I said.

"Damnation! You are damned for all eternity."

Julie was on her feet and shaking. I moved back into the cushions as far as I could go.

"I was an ordained priest. I took an oath to Jesus, the lord, our God; and I violated that oath. Now, do you know what that means?"

She hesitated waiting for my response. I nodded.

"You are from Vermont. You must have heard of me? I was assigned a parish in Newport. Way up north near the Canadian Border. My sins were highly published throughout the dioceses."

I shook my head in the negative. Everyone at the XX Club knew she had been a priest. She was the buzz when I arrived. Other than Dana, the first transsexual on the Hartford police force, Julie was perhaps the most well-known. Infamous, and not just among our group. It was rare for a priest to come out of the closet. Certainly, different than the stories of child-molester priests hitting the media.

"You must have read something in the papers about Father Julian?"

I nodded in the negative again. Her eyes widened.

"I'm sorry." My voice squeaked.

If I could have spoken, I would have told her that I didn't read the papers much, nor did I watch television. There was no time. My entire day was absorbed with work and coaching and husband and father things and trying to be something I wasn't. Depression had robbed me of curiosity. About the only thing I did was take in an occasional movie. I couldn't tell you the name of one artist on the radio or the name of a song unless it was Elvis or Willy Nelson or Kenny Rogers or someone popular in my neck of the woods. I kept busy running away from my life and blocking out everything around me that threatened to expose my fraud.

Michael's day had started at 6am. He got up, showered, dressed and was off to work within the hour. I opened the shop at 8am and closed the overhead doors at 5pm. Then I would drive across town to the old outdoor hockey rink and coach soccer to my daughters and a bunch of boys their age until 7 pm. Sometimes I would stay late if an errant parent did not come to fetch their child on time.

In later years I was the boys' soccer coach at the high school. When the boys would take showers, I would wait outside the locker room with Jen Rose and Jaq until the last boy was picked up, usually by 8pm. Then if the girls were hungry, I would take them to a restaurant of their choosing and we'd be home by 10:00 pm. I'd kiss my sleeping wife on the way into bed. I didn't have time to read the papers, listen to the local news, or concern myself with stories about a rogue priest. He had his problems and I had mine.

I'm sure that wasn't the answer Julie wanted, but I was

hurting and just wanted to lie down and forget this day ever happened.

Julie walked toward the kitchen then turned around sharply.

"I couldn't help myself. Something boils beneath our skin, doesn't it?"

Was she asking me? My face was on fire, if that was what she meant.

"It must be like the last temptation when Christ was on the mountain looking down at the world. It was an uncontrollable obsession."

In one gulp she emptied her wine glass and set it down on the corner of the table nearest me. She stretched her hand over me and I cringed.

"I kept a little black dress and stockings and cute shoes in a bag in the back of my car. On my days off... Yes, priests got days off. Don't look so surprised." She sounded angry.

Unless she was a mind reader there was no way she could read the expression on my raw swollen face. It felt like a grape skin pulled over a cantaloupe.

"One night, I drove my car down to a small town in New Hampshire where no one knew me. It was outside of Dartmouth near the White River. A little honky-tonk bar that played country music until the wee hours of the morning. I'd been there before. It was a great place because the lighting was so poor you could barely see the person next to you. I think the electricity runs off a generator and the amps from the bands' equipment drain it down. Anyway, this trucker asked me to dance. He'd been sending drinks to my table all night so of course I felt obligated. He was drunk and I was feeling the effects of the wine he'd been buying me."

She took a sip of the wine in her hand before continuing.

"Foolishly, I broke my own rules and danced with him, then another, and another. It was fun and for a moment I forgot who I was. When the band took a break, he followed me back to my table and sat down. I—"

Julie choked or perhaps she just hesitated and feigned a sob. She was an actor staying in character on and off the stage until the play runs its course so as not to lose the momentum. Some stay too long in a role and begin to manifest its malaise.

"Does it bother you to hear about someone else's tragic end?"

I remained silent. Sat stone still.

"I was quite naive. Age has no claim on naivete. I may have been dressing for several years, but the number of times would only add up to days, much less a year. You understand that I had no idea that when a man buys a lady a few drinks there is a price to pay at the end of the evening."

Julie coughed again and turned toward Jennifer fanning her hand in front of her face. Jennifer put her plate down and hurried to her with a box of tissues. Julie plucked one sheet from the box. She pinched it between her thumb and forefinger and held it out in front of her as though it was contaminated.

"I said some things at the table that shouldn't have come out of the mouth of a lady but I tried being nice and he was incorrigible. He would not budge. He sat down and draped his arm around me like he owned me. People laughed at some of the things I said to him. I wasn't discrete or cautious."

I heard slurping. She must have taken a sip of the drink in her hand.

"Wine makes us all a little more courageous than we ought to be. He got up and walked away. I thought that would be the last I would see of him, but when I went out to get in my car, he was waiting for me in the shadows. Yeah, don't look so surprised. I can be quite attractive when I want to be. It was this incident that caused me to become a little more conservative in my appearance. You thought you could get rid of me? Bitch! Come here. I'll show you where the Pope shit in the woods."

Julie dropped her voice for emphasis to mimic her angry male attacker.

"He grabbed me and said something even more crass that I won't repeat. I tried to get away from him but he had me pinned to my car door so I couldn't open it. He didn't expect me to be as strong and for a moment, I thought I could get away. He went down quick with a knee to the groin. I started to open the door. That's when he grabbed my hair—and it came off. He stared at it like it was a dead animal he had killed with his bare hands and then looked up at me. There was laughter everywhere. People were outside watching us, and it was embarrassing to hear them laughing at me and taunting him. It made him madder. If they hadn't, perhaps he wouldn't have—"

Julie stopped speaking and dropped her head. She mumbled something to herself that I couldn't make out except for the words: "Don't hurt me. Please, don't hurt me."

Jennifer touched her on the shoulder and Julie slapped it off.

"Don't touch me," Julie screamed. Jennifer moved away quickly. Julie turned back to look at me. A silence fell between us that only she could lift. I held my breath.

"He reached up under my dress, grabbed me, and squeezed with all his might. I cried out in agony and all the crowd did was laugh harder and one of them said, 'Rip it off.' He brought me to my knees and then began pounding on me." Julie stopped and shook her head back and forth trying to shake loose the fear surfacing with the memory.

"He kept pounding on me while I lay in the dirt trying to cover my face. I could only think of how I might look before my congregation wearing vestments that covered everything up but my face. He hit me, kicked me over and over while the crowd egged him on. I cried out for help—but no one helped me. Nobody. I heard women's voices tittering and laughing above the jeers. It must have been like Calvary—"

Julie got down on her knees on the floor and bowed her head. She held onto herself and rocked back and forth. Jennifer leaned down and dropped a sweater over her shoulders. Julie shrieked and threw it off.

"I was unconscious when the ambulance came. When I woke up in the hospital, I found out he had broken my nose, my collar bone, snapped two of my ribs and ruptured my spleen. I was black and blue and purple all over my face and body. But you want to know what was worse? It wasn't the beating. Not even the hospital bills that the diocese had to pay. The police had taken my identification and leaked it to the press. I guess a priest in drag is big news in Podunk, New Hampshire."

Julie's voice was no longer perfect. I had envied her for being able to speak as a natural woman, but somewhere in the course of her revelation, she regressed back to Julian.

"I know in my heart of hearts that if the newspaper had not run that story about me that there would have been another time and another country yokel and another incident. They caught me on several occasions wearing heels and makeup and once, Father Breton, he was the monsignor then not Carlin. He caught me wearing a red dress when I was coming out of a restaurant in Keene. They put letters in my file. Warnings, that if my behavior and my sinful ways continued, I would be dismissed from the order, but I never thought—God, help me. I never thought—"

Julie let out a woeful sob. She looked up at the ceiling.

"When the letter came from Rome, I was saying high mass for Christmas Eve services. Father Carlin didn't even let me finish. He dragged me behind the vestibule to show me the sealed letter. He made me read it aloud to him. I wailed and cried so loud that the whole congregation could hear me, but I didn't care. My life was over. It was as if I'd been cast into Hell at that very moment when I read the word: Excommunicated."

Jennifer and I remained immobile. We froze, hoping it would be over soon. My face was drying out and stretched tight from the swelling that my entire head ached.

"Do, you know what that means?"

I nodded slowly. It hurt to move.

"It means that I am cut off from His holy church, the congregation, and all believers. My mother, father, anyone I had ever known are forbidden to speak to me or even look in my direction. I am a pariah for all the remaining days of my life on earth and thereafter. I cannot go to heaven. I am damned for eternity."

Julian faded and Julie's returned. Her voice had noticeably softened. Suddenly, she got up off her knees and left the room without uttering another word. The stairs and floor above us squeaked a few moments later and I presumed she went up to Jennifer's bedroom. The show was over.

"Transsexuals are devils in some cultures."

Jennifer spoke as soon as she was certain Julie was out of earshot.

"They gave her no mercy."

Jennifer headed for the stairs.

"Now, she'll be morose for days."

She clucked her tongue against her cheek. Before she ascended the first step, she stopped and turned towards me, shaking her head as though somehow, I was to blame.

"Like peeling an onion."

I nodded. My eyes burned. I wanted to go home.

These people were crazy!

#

Chapter 14

The Crone

From where the sun now stands, I will fight no more forever. – Chief Joseph

In the morning, I sat up and threw off the covers. A boy's room unfolded around me. A room built around the turn of the century with a full-size bed tucked in the corner where two windows converge, a nightstand and lamp with an embroidered shade, and a large desk at the foot of the bed. On the corner of the desk was a photograph in a brown frame of a smiling boy and man that looked a lot like Jennifer with short hair and chin stubble. He had his arm draped over the boy's shoulder. The model plane that took up most of the desk was in the boy's arms and he smiled up at his father adoringly. I shuddered. Another memory haunted my thoughts.

Sometime in the night I made up my mind to drive back to Vermont. Debbie and April were still there. I could recover in familiar surroundings and feel safe. I remembered the warning the nurse gave me: stay out of the sun for the next few weeks particularly while the new skin was forming to avoid hyper-pigmentation, a browning of the skin or more likely a mottling effect similar to a mulatto. The damage could be permanent. It would be tricky driving in the sunlight, but I had to try. I wrapped my silk scarf around my head and brought it across my face like a hijab.

Julie stood by the front door watching me carefully descend the stairs. She was dressed in a black suit and her nun-shoes, the dull black heels with the blunt toe. A velvet black ribbon held her hair back behind her ears accentuating her near perfect round head. Her pony tail lilted to one side like a ragged animal's tail. She studied me for a moment then pulled on her black leather gloves, nodded almost imperceptibly, and left without saying a word.

The eerie sound of Andrew Lloyd Weber's "Phantom of the Opera" rose up to greet me as I entered the study. Jennifer sat in a chair by the small desk under the window at the far end of the room. The drapes were closed shut, but she stared out, envisioning a scene in her mind from long ago when they used to be open and the sun felt warm on her face. Her thin speckled hand gripped an oversized coffee mug. The other rested near a silent black phone. I cleared my throat. Jennifer looked up. Her eyes washed over me. A shiver ran up my spine.

"I want to thank you for your kind hospitality. I appreciate you letting me stay here while I recover."

"I thought you were staying a few more days?"

There was no inflection in her voice to show she was surprised.

"Ah, it looks like the swelling went down."

"I feel good this morning. Better than I thought I would. Julie will make a great nurse someday."

"She will," Jennifer agreed.

"Please, be careful. There's a lot of snow and traffic out there."

"I am more worried about the sun."

I pulled on the end of the scarf partially covering my face.

"The rays can be intense." She said, then took a sip of her coffee.

"Well, you are certainly welcome to stay longer."

"I feel okay. I have a lot to do. No need to inconvenience you and Julie further."

"It's no trouble on our part. You pretty much have to fend for yourself. Of course, we expect you will still honor your obligation to assist with someone in the future when we call on you?"

"Of course. I am more than happy to help out."

I reaffirmed my commitment, but it couldn't be further from the truth. All I wanted to do was get as far away from anything and anyone that reminded me, that I was or had ever been remotely like them.

"I have to leave to get ahead of the traffic. It's a three-hour drive—"

"Oh, you're going back to Vermont? Not staying in your apartment with what's his name?"

"Joe," I finished for her.

"Yes, I have some unfinished business to finalize back home. I can take a few days rest and maybe catch my daughter's school play. No one should recognize me now."

"No, I guess not."

Jennifer forced a laugh then settled back in her chair.

"Family is important. Blood is thick, water is not."

She clucked her tongue. Her eyes wandered toward the black telephone on the corner of her desk.

"Yes, it is."

I agreed absentmindedly.

"Are you expecting a call?"

It slipped out before I realized what I had said.

"My son."

She paused as though she wanted to say more.

"Oh, I see."

An awkward silence settled between us.

"Well, you should get going then if you are going to beat the traffic."

Jennifer took a loud slurp of her coffee and turned back to stare at the fabric of the heavy curtain in front of her desk.

I pulled on my gloves and started for the front door. I didn't look back.

As I crunched across the frozen yard towards my car, a new version of Traci's warning played in my head: *get in, learn all you can about becoming a woman, and get out.* Otherwise you'll be some old crone wrapped in a worn shawl and sitting in the dark by a phone that never rings.

# # #

Chapter 15

Safe Haven

Nothing is more sad, than the death of an illusion. – Arthur Koestler

Four hours after I left Jennifer's old Victorian home in Bridgeport, I arrived at the place I used to call home. Debbie ran outside as soon as I parked in the driveway. There are no windows on the south side of the house. She must have been looking out from the big bay window in our kitchen and seen me coming up the road. I never called to let her know that I was coming. I just drove to the only safe place I have ever known.

Debbie helped me out of the car and into the house. She undressed me and settled me into our old waterbed then fetched a tray with a mug of warm cocoa. She applied a new coating of salve to my wounded face. The last thing I recalled was seeing those big brown eyes and wondering how long the dark circles had been there.

The next morning Debbie sat beside me on the bed with a pan of warm water and balls of cotton on the nightstand. She gently patted my eyelids and face until the crust loosened and flaked off. When she was through, she left and came back a few minutes later carrying a tray of buttered toast, bacon and eggs, a glass of orange juice, and a single red rose like the one I used to lay on her pillow.

"Hi," I said. My voice cracked. The tears started flowing as soon as I saw her and realized the purpose of her earnest gesture of kindness. I turned my head away. She was trying to woo her husband back.

"You slept a long time. I let you sleep. I think your breakfast is cold." There were tears in her eyes, too and I knew it wasn't the stale breakfast she was tearful about.

"I'm sorry, Deb, I didn't know where else to go."

"Shh," she hushed me. "It's okay. We are here for you. The kids and I still love you."

"I know." The words caught in my throat. A hard silence fell between us and she looked away almost at the same time as I, then she turned back and patted my cheek tenderly. Most of the crust had been washed off. Her touch was soft, familiar, loving.

"It looks really good and smooth. I almost don't recognize—" she didn't finish but I could read her thoughts. She missed her husband. She no longer saw him when she looked at me unless she looked into my eyes.

"I'll run you a hot bath. You stink." Debbie wrinkled her nose, got up and headed toward the master bathroom.

"How are the kids?" I asked when she came back into the bedroom. I was not inquiring about their health. She knew what I meant.

"Fine. April is adjusting to it well. Jackie, not so much but she'll come around. She was close to her dad...um, they love him and they'll love you, too." She went silent, lost in thought. Her smile had disappeared. I suspected our children would blame me for their mother's unhappiness soon enough. I understood Jackie's reluctance to deal with her feelings. She was the most popular kid in her school. Her father had just become infamous and the brunt of cruel jokes and innuendo. She would be pitied to death.

"Jen is struggling at West Point."

An appointment to the United States Military Academy had been no easy feat. The candidate had to be near-perfect. Not just one of the top 15% of the entire country academically but a well-rounded individual. In short, leadership material. Jen Rose was fifteenth in a class of 430 students, an athlete with accolades in softball, bowling, basketball, track and a superstar in soccer. She was second trumpet in the school band, wrote and choreographed a dramatic production, attended church regularly, organized social functions and sporting events, and performed community service without compunction.

"She'll make it," I said. "She's strong."
My hair was flat and plastered to my head with sebaceous goo. Debbie laughed despite the sadness in her eyes. She helped me up out of bed, stripped off my pajamas, and settled me into a warm bath. Debbie took off her own clothes and eased down into the tub. She leaned back in that familiar way with her head tipped back on my shoulder. I wrapped my arms around her and we sat there in silence listening to the warm water slap against the walls as it swirled around us. Debbie was quiet. I thought she was sleeping until she said,

"Are you going to miss us?"

"Yes, I already do," I said. "I miss us terribly."

"Will you miss me?"

Her voice rang out like a child. The exhaustion lashed at me.

In our final days I spent more time with our daughters and my friends than I did with her. Soccer, basketball, softball, bowling, track, watching plays, helping with term papers, snowmobiling in the Laurentian Mountains, and trekking half way across the country to watch NASCAR races. The time I spent running away from myself and hanging out with my friends, Frank and Frenchy, in bars, picking up lonely women and drinking myself into oblivion was her nightmare.

But in the early days before my malady overtook our life together, we were happy, I think. It seemed so long ago. My heart would swell just thinking about getting back home and holding her in my arms. There were times I came home from work, walked by my family at the supper table without saying a word and went directly into our bedroom. I would leave a single red sweetheart-rose on her pillow like I did on our wedding night. I wanted her to remember that she was once loved.

"Yes." I squeezed her gently.

"Are you sure you want to do this?"

She reached behind with her hands, searching. Her voice eerily reminiscent. It belonged to that teenager lying in the back seat of my '65 Corvair, arms and legs spread open for me to come to her. We lay there in each other's arms making promises in the dark that we were both too young to know that we would someday break. There was something oddly comforting, if only for a moment. Her naked body resting against mine with my arms wrapped around her in a hot bath, and thinking this was the way it should have been, had I been born normal.

I was silent. I didn't answer. I lingered wearily in that listless state where bliss may have been hiding all of my life. Could she ever be with another woman? How easy it would have been not to sell everything and start over. Debbie stared up at me with those big, brown, bedroom eyes like I was her hero and she a damsel in distress.

It's the way I always saw Debbie when I closed my eyes, the perfect picture of innocence and want. Especially in the service, after I came home from those long sorties where some Russian MIG tried to blow us out of the sky. She would saunter into the bedroom after settling the kids, remove her clothes and lie there waiting for me to come out of the shower. Sometimes, she would climb atop and straddle me, if I was lying there first. Her long hair draped over her pale oval face. She let it fall over me and shut out the world. Those loose auburn ringlets swayed like a soft curtain above me as we made love.

Then emptiness, cold and dark crept into our lives. Her husband became unrecognizable. I shook the thought. Deb's naked body next to mine reminded me how much I hated my own. Jealousy crept into the tub. The water was tepid but it chilled me to the bone. I couldn't change who I was nor could I reshape her nature. She was heterosexual and wanted something I could no longer give. We always knew the day would come. She cupped my testicles in her hands.

"Are you going to miss these?"

"No," I said.

She let go and pushed herself up out of the tub. She hesitated for a moment, turned and looked at me over her shoulder. There was a vacancy in her eyes. A thought flickered in the tears. She wondered where her life had gone.

Holy, fuck! so did I.
Except for our children, it was like *we* never existed.

\#

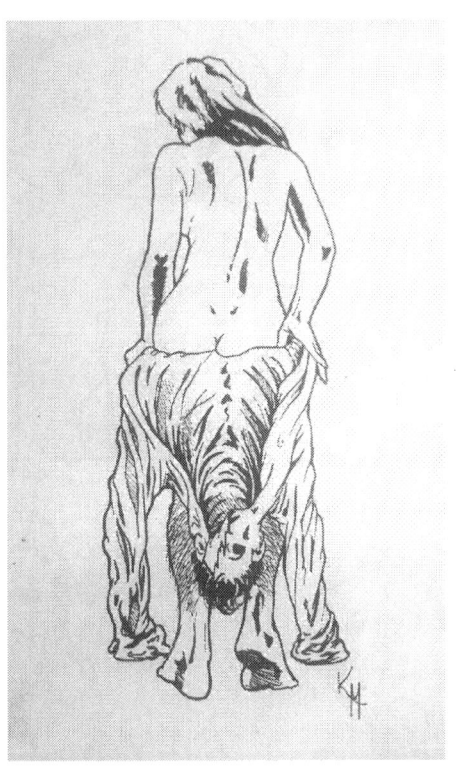

Chapter 16

The Boyfriend

Love, as the poet has said, is a woman's whole existence. – Virginia Woolf, *Orlando*

Shame is a piece of food stuck between your teeth up under the gum-line. If not removed it begins to decay. Even if you can't detect it yourself, everyone you come in contact with can smell it on you. People avoid you like some disease. To cover up the shame of my existence I had to transform myself into something less contemptible. I had to convince myself that I had a right to exist and then convince others that I was like them even if I wasn't. Possessing the heart and soul of a woman was not enough. I had to be beautiful to create the illusion that I was normal. Having breasts and a penis made it a little more challenging.

It wasn't long after I recovered from my facial surgery that I returned to Stratford and the apartment I shared with Joe. I decided laying around the house with an old transvestite was unproductive. The black hole I had somehow crawled into over the years was beginning to close around me. I found myself staring up at the spider cracks on the ceiling of my room and trying hard not to think about Debbie and the kids. My old facade as the stoic male was beginning to crack. I got a job with a temp agency and enrolled in a night class on expository writing at Norwalk Community College. I wanted to meet the normal people, attempt to blend in, and begin my new life.

At night school the girls shared their secrets freely in front of me. We often went out for drinks after class. Each spoke about those discrete things only women talked about with each other: who was suffering from menstrual cramps, an uncomfortable bra, or how it felt when breastfeeding a child after he grows teeth, when to douche and what products were best to hide those embarrassing odors. And we did a lot of male bashing: whose husband was lazy, not good in bed, or was cheating on her.

It was with the women of my writing class that I told my first white lie.

A white lie is almost the truth but not quite, like an alternative fact—some plausible assimilation of an experience that could have been but wasn't. I assumed the role of my wife, Debbie, in our failed relationship and presented myself from her perspective.

I explained that my 'ex' and I had met and fell in love in high school and divorced nearly twenty years and three kids later. It implied, and was naturally assumed, that I did not have much experience in dating men—which was true—but not for the reason anyone thought. Whenever I said or did something that was out of the ordinary, they would laugh politely and say: *Oh, Evie!* Like I was a child who got caught doing something naughty.

My method worked with Paul, my first boyfriend. He forgave my ignorance and odd behavior. My Jamaican classmate and friend, Pauline, introduced us or actually she just gave him my telephone number without asking me. Before she had met her "Lazy-assed" husband she had been dating this blond-haired, blue-eyed editor of some trade magazine she had temped at in New York City called: *Beverage Aisle.* She thought he would be "jus' purrrfack for the wannabe writer."

Paul was thirty-six years old and saw his ten-year old daughter, Alison, every other weekend for four hours. He usually took her to the park for a cook-out or to the movies and sometimes to the library for story-time. After he met me, I was always invited along. I became part of his little extended family.

Even though he was my first, Paul was a man I never loved and often feared. It wasn't long into our relationship that I experienced Paul's temperament. After several dates he had arrived late one night and wanted to take me out but most restaurants had closed.

We caught an all-night Perkins nearer the highway and when he headed for a booth near the window overlooking the damp street outside, a waitress stopped me.

"That section is closed," she said.

I halted. Paul and Alison were already seated. When he noticed me talking with the waitress, he called to me.

"Don't listen to her. I know the manager. We sit where we want. Come on, Evie."

The waitress reiterated: "It's closed."

She spoke louder for Paul's benefit. He got out of the booth and started in my direction but stopped half way and demanded I come sit down.

"Get over here. You like booths. This one is by the window. They have to serve us. That's their job. Now."

People in the crowded restaurant were staring at me. I froze.

"Go ahead, sweetie," the waitress whispered in my ear, "I have one of those at home I have to deal with."

Paul took me by the hand and we sat down to an uncomfortable meal just the three of us in a closed-section at Perkins.

Paul suffered from migraine headaches as a result of a head injury he received in an automobile accident several years before I met him. He claimed it was the cause of his violent temper, something his ex-wife disputed vehemently. She contended that he had always been a man with an intemperate disposition. He kept his temper in check with me, most of the time. He lived in a studio apartment in Stratford, Connecticut, with his pet coy fish, Mabel.

It was obvious after our first date that he believed I was just some naive divorcee from Vermont who had very little experience in the real world. It would do for now, I rationalized. Paul was merely an experience. Practice for the future when the day came that I wanted to fall in love—with a good man.

Paul was horribly homophobic.

He did not like Joe. He would taunt him whenever he

came to the house to pick me up or if he saw us out. Whenever Paul teased him, Joe looked at me suspiciously as though I gave his secret away. I was in a constant state of heightened awareness whenever we were together. I knew that if I didn't alert him about Joe, Paul would be onto me in seconds.

To avoid any problems, I told him that after my divorce I wanted to be near Jen, my daughter, a new cadet at West Point and moved from Vermont to Connecticut where I could be supportive. I answered an advertisement in the Hartford Currant and moved in with someone that turned out to be a transvestite, who after years of dressing, decided to go through the process of becoming a woman. I told Paul that if he wanted to continue dating me that he would have to be kind. He knew what I meant.

"You need to be nice when you meet him, Paul. He-she is a really good person."

I purposely misspoke Joe's gender then put my hand over my lips as though I caught myself in a faux pas. I used to ask myself:

What would a real woman do?

"It's a transvestite, Evie. What the fuck? A fag is a fag."

"Be nice."

I held up my finger to show him that I meant it. He gave me that grin that men give women when they say something incredulous like love is forever or men and women can have a platonic relationship or Santa Claus is real.

After he came into my life and our first kiss, I almost forgot my origins. Not unlike when a horse is broken. She still yearns to be free but becomes so used to the saddle, reins, and bridle that she forgot why it was necessary. My survival mode kicked in.

The first time was an awkward moment.

It was the Fourth of July and Paul had come home from work in the city late. It was half past seven by the time he got to a Mexican restaurant somewhere near Stratford shores where we were meeting. After dinner, we sat out on the sidewalk to watch the fireworks burst over the harbor, then he walked me to my car.

He stood close with one hand on my door and the other on my hip, trapping me between the car and his warm body. I couldn't bend to get in without bumping my head into his. Then he leaned closer and tipped his head toward mine. His eyes were closed. As soon as his lips parted I could smell the chili-peppers he had had at the restaurant earlier. I panicked.

"Is this when we kiss?" I asked.

Paul's eyes snapped opened. His lids fluttered for several seconds. My heart was a runaway train when he grabbed hold of my shoulders. I thought he was going to throttle me to an inch of my life, then he burst out laughing and kissed me hard on the mouth. His tongue probed my lips looking for a way in, but I kept my mouth shut and held my breath. I told him I married my high school sweetheart and did not have much experience dating men—which was true. It must have worked. I guess he saw me as a naive little country girl.

I have always weaved in elements of truth to create my illusions. I talk about my daughters as any mother would except, I use the word spouse instead of husband. I assume the role Debbie would have had if she were in my place. Paul never caught on. No one ever did. He appeared amused and assumed that it was innocence and inexperience that prompted my irregular behavior, or so I thought.

It never occurred to me that he might have suspected someone living with a transvestite might also be one, but for some reason he was afraid to ask, almost like he was afraid to lose me. A real conundrum for a someone who thought he was secure in his own sexuality and suddenly finds himself attracted to someone of the same sex.

Regardless of why, he was always a gentleman with me. Or perhaps as my daughter, the social worker explained to me years later, there was another person living with me and Joe in that apartment even though we never saw her: Paranoia.

A certain amount of fear, albeit in the right dose, was

healthy for a member of the XX Club. Someone coming into the light from the shadows of prejudice and ignorance back in the early 1990s had to be cautious or she didn't survive. It was a time when anyone who was not straight was a threat to public decency.

Although the medical community had recognized homosexuality as a natural human occurrence for nearly twenty years, the laws and mores of the world we lived in were slow to change. Our survival mechanism, inherent in all humanity, was to fight or flee. As a male to female transsexual I interpreted that to mean: hide among them, and if caught, run.

By late summer, I had fallen into a routine. My trips to Vermont to see Debbie and the girls and settle any unfinished business had slowed to once a month. I began receiving more temp assignments, and I kept busy going to my college classes, club meetings, and the occasional lunch or outing with Traci.

Paul was a busy editor and made that awful commute from Stratford to the city in his small Ford pick-up truck during the week and was usually too tired when he came back to his studio apartment to do anything but call and whisper sweet nothings in my ear before he fell asleep. We would see each other late in the evening occasionally but Friday night and Saturdays were our time together. He never questioned what I did when he wasn't around, but he continued to nag me about moving out and warning me how dangerous it was to be living with a transvestite. His disdain for Joe was apparent.

The tension between Joe and him began to spread to me. I feared it was only a matter of time before he cracked and told Paul, I was like him. I think that was when my paranoia began to escalate. I knew our living arrangement was temporary. I had one more operation, the big one, before I could walk away from this life that left me looking over my shoulder and that nagging fear of exposure knotting my stomach. I kept my eye on the final prize and focused on absorbing as many experiences as possible.

People made assumptions about our kind—they could

recognize a man in a dress—no matter how good the makeup. Despite sensational stories in the papers over the years about Christine Jorgensen or Rene Richards, who were both tall and arguably passable, there was a certain look to them. Notwithstanding, Carolyn Cossey, aka "Tula", a beautiful international supermodel exposed by the media in the 1980s, they did not anticipate someone who had been born male and lived as a man for years could disappear among women.

No one, not even the staff of the gender clinic believed it was possible for a male body, once it had passed through puberty, to alter so quickly, and blend in so seamlessly. I had become female in appearance after only a few months of hormone therapy and some minor surgical intervention. The hormones and surgeries had made rapid changes in my appearance. I was on my way to achieving that dream I had since I was a small child, to feel normal in my own skin and become an ordinary woman.

What I had not anticipated was becoming attractive to the opposite sex. It had a deleterious effect on me, my plans, and on my possessive boyfriend, Paul. For someone used to living in the shadows, I did not enjoy being stared at—like I could be devoured at any moment—if I let my guard down. It would take me a while to sort out the leer from the curious stare and dissect the fear of exposure from the want and desire of lonely men, and too long to realize that both could be dangerous.

#

Chapter 17

The Mystery Girl

Reality is an illusion, albeit a very persistent one. – Albert Einstein

Black suede boots with two-inch heels, the kind the hipsters wore that crawled all the way up the calf and stopped below the knee, appeared in the four windows that line the ceiling. The top of a skirt swayed back and forth, dusting the powdery snow off the top of the boots. Although I couldn't see anything else from my perspective, I knew she was a wannabe like me, unseasoned and uncertain of where she was going but determined to get there, nonetheless.

My mother used to tell me that I never lacked for imagination. My daughter, Jen Rose, said it was a part of my illness—to imagine such things. It was some form of PTSD. Years of living in fear of being read makes one hypersensitive, she said. I saw a pair of boots on the sidewalk in front of Christ's Church at 9 a.m. on a Saturday morning on the deserted streets in downtown Hartford and automatically I assumed the cautious steps belonged to some new girl coming to our meeting.

When the door didn't open at the top of the stairs after several minutes, I was not disappointed. My premonitions were often correct. It just took time for some to materialize. I knew it would happen eventually. She would walk through that door in those black-suede boots, maybe not today, but someday. I settled back in my chair and listened to Cindy chat about the misgivings she had when she'd first met Dr. Menard. "He's too prim and proper," she said. "Never trust a man who has no dirt under his fingernails."

That was precious coming from an automotive technician.

Cindy's little-girl voice broke when she got to the part about her botched operation. One of the newbies with bright red hair and a bridge full of freckles tried to console her. Joe nodded off in his chair. Big Kathy was reading something she picked up off the back table. Traci filed her nails. The hairs on the back of my neck stood on end and my skin still tingled like before when I saw those black boots. I looked up and there she was, head down between her bare knees, hair dangling down nearly to the frozen walk. She stared at me like a monkey behind the glass at a zoo exhibit, her tongue black from sucking on licorice. I laughed out loud. Everyone stopped what they were doing to stare in my direction.

"What's so funny?" Cindy asked, her voice no longer quivering on the verge of tears.

The radiator hissed noisily from its perch in the corner of the room. I felt the heat rise in my face and then the heavy oak doors at the top of the stairs opened with a distinctive clang. As the iron latch fell into place the room went silent. Footfalls sounded in the hallway above us. The mystery girl had arrived.

Everyone strained to hear the hollow thud of bare feet padding down the tile floor that halted outside the door to our room. It creaked open and the world under the street, as Traci called us, all turned and stared at a tall thin girl standing in the doorway wearing a mousy brown sweater and a frayed purple scarf that looked like it found its way off one of the throwaway racks at the neighborhood Goodwill store.

She was older than I had first thought. Dark brown hair sprinkled with loose strands of gray. The corners of her mouth curled up into a smile as she pattered barefoot across the damp tile, carrying her boots in one hand and a mustard-colored purse in the other. The edge of her long maroon skirt swept from side to side as she made her way into the center of our imperfect circle of chairs. She stopped before Jennifer—and curtsied. A laugh escaped my lips before I could stop it.

"So, who wants to talk next?"

Jennifer's voice went up one octave. When no one answered her, she looked up from her book at the new girl standing before her, posing with the purse hand on her hip as though she was on a runway of a New York modeling agency. Her eyes sparkled playfully as she looked around the room before pausing in my direction and pulling me into her orbit.

Jennifer waited for the silence that followed the scraping of metal and withering voices before speaking.

"Can we help you?" Jennifer's button nose was red. She looked tired. Big Kathy tapped her bare toes nervously on the tile floor while she sketched something on her pad. She was an amazing artist.

"No, I don't think so." The new girl looked more amused than nervous. "I seriously doubt it."

"Can we help you?" Jennifer repeated.

"No, I don't think so." Her voice was soft and nasal like a gay male. Each word carefully chewed and swallowed before trailing out through her nostrils.

"Ah," Jennifer looked down at the notebook in her lap as though there was an answer somewhere in the tattered pages. She repeated herself, "Can we help you?"

"I seriously doubt it." The girl laughed. She drew a few nervous giggles from some of the members.

Jennifer blinked and pushed her wire-frame glasses back up her nose. She leaned forward to study the intruder more closely. "Um, Miss, are you sure you are in the right place? This is a support group of the Gender Identity Clinic of New England."

There was a slight smile on the girl's face and her fingers twirled the strap of her purse.

"Are you here to join our club?"

"No."

Jennifer blinked. "What do you want?"

"I just came to watch."

"No, that's not possible. You can't just watch. I mean, this isn't the kind of meeting where the public can just come in and sit down to watch. You have to be screened first by Canon Clinton Jones or Dr. Higgins. Then you can come—but not to watch."

"Why?" the girl asked. Her eyes darted around. An

uncomfortable silence filled the room. Everyone rolled their eyes down to their laps when her stare alighted upon them. The ones who didn't, like me, were awed to find something behind the mischievousness mask she wore that shone from within. Jennifer had spoken once about our kindred spirit. How it could root out and sense another like us—desperate for companionship—when others missed it.

"Because it's...uh, just not done that way. It's a support group not an episode of Geraldo."

Jennifer looked over at me.

"Let her watch. It's no big deal. Maybe she's here to see if she wants to join and needs to be certain it's safe."

My voice erupted with more confidence than I felt. There was something intriguing about this girl. She was like us, yet different. We could always tell a kindred spirit from a real woman. The spread of the shoulders, contour of the body, protruding Adam's apple, size of the hands, or that irascible timbre in the voice.

Perhaps, as Laura suggested, the aura that a person projects gives a careful observer the edge. Trans people are spiritual creatures. They have more energy than others, Laura insisted. I could not tell whether it was a line with her or if she was serious. I didn't really believe Laura, but I noted that he did not include himself in the analysis. I was uncertain whether male-women have secret powers as unique as they are, but I did agree that most are superstitious. We were desperate creatures grasping for an answer and would look anywhere to find one even if it's absurd.

"No, she has to follow protocol." Jennifer's voice was stern. "All the chicks must follow the mother duck. A stitch in time saves nine."

The mixed metaphor made no sense except there were nine of us in the room that day. Traci rolled her eyes and I stifled a laugh.

"Jennifer, you are not going to find the answer in your book. There is nothing in there regarding an observer. Maybe she's just someone who wants to get some answers like the rest of us. Reporters, writers, and therapists visit all the time and they aren't screened. Canon Jones allows it. What's one more observer? Besides, if it's something she wants to pursue, then she can go through the process and follow protocol as you say. The rules are made for us, not the outside world," I said.

Jennifer looked around the circle. Everyone held their breath waiting for something to happen and as if on cue, the radiator started hissing at us from the corner. I was glad Julie was not there. Jennifer was a sweetheart most of the time. Confrontation bothered her, but Julie thrived on it.

"Okay, if no one objects." She looked around the room. "Alright, she can stay but she can't participate until Canon Jones screens her when he comes back from Ireland."

I was about to argue further when Traci's hand slipped across my mouth.

"Take a seat," Jennifer instructed the mystery girl and then asked, "what's your name?"

"Candy," the girl said. It was not her real name. Not the one on her license and certainly not the one on her birth certificate, but no one cared. No one used her real name at the XX Club. Names were unimportant. Especially during transition. We tried on more than one before we were done, not unlike the way Joe used different femme names depending on his outfit. Candy was the name the mystery girl wanted us to call her and the one I would use until I learned her real name.

# # #

I had waited so long for my life to begin that I had some unquenchable thirst for experiences, my own or someone, I thought, was like me. Perhaps I saw something in Candy that foreshadowed my destiny or maybe she was me in another life. Had I chosen to leave Vermont after graduation and not gotten married I could have ended up on the street, like Candy. Would our lives have intersected sooner or perhaps gone in a similar way? I was odd like that, always thinking of possibilities, could-have-been-scenarios, and counting my blessings.

Candy came up from New York, a place we simply referred to as "the city." She lived in an apartment on the lower east side, closer to the Village than the river, on the top floor of some low rise that used to be a garment factory at the turn of the century. She came to Hartford at the behest of a friend—whom she didn't name but I suspect was Sarah.

The moment she walked in, Sarah began staring at her hands in her lap and only looked up from time to time to peek in Candy's direction when she thought no one was looking. We didn't get much further in our hushed conversation before Jennifer shushed us. That's when I suggested we go to lunch. "I know a great place."

Candy nodded in the affirmative. I had been thrilled she had accepted my invitation. Typically, Traci and I always went to lunch after a meeting, but when I turned to her to let her know we would have another, she was no longer in her chair. I spotted her in the doorway.

Traci's eyes narrowed in my direction. She'd been studying me or perhaps, Candy. She didn't want any part of her. I think she saw her as a threat. In a few weeks she was going stealth. Perhaps she was worried about me. If I connected to another tranny, even a passable one like Candy, she would never see me again. Traci compared us all to rabbits trying to blend into our surroundings for survival. She lived by her rule of three. "It's critical to be on guard at all times. One mistake and you can lose everything, including your life."

Joe thought Traci was stuck up and anti-social. I told him it was about survival. He was not fond of her and she couldn't care less. The femmes intended to leave those who were not, as far behind them as possible. If you didn't look like you belonged in the natural world after a few weeks, Traci stopped talking to you. She was cordial at meetings but didn't go to lunch with a group.

Prior to my facial surgeries and hormones, she had made

an exception. I had the shine on me, whatever that meant. I took it to mean I fell into some gray area. I passed or got less scrutiny than others because I was attractive. Notwithstanding androgynous persons, it never occurred to people that some males could look like women without applying makeup. She had many rules but none as harsh as to never look back. She sounded like my father: *never get too attached to anything.*

From the start, I had the feeling our relationship was as tentative as meeting someone in chemotherapy. You never knew how long you had before they were gone. I think she and my father would agree—the last rule would apply to Candy as well.

#

Chapter 18

Candy

I've come to hate my body and all that it requires of me in this world. - Lou Reed, The Velvet Underground, *Candy Says (1969)*

At the edge of town, a few blocks from where Mark Twain penned his last novel, *A Connecticut Yankee in King Arthur's Court*, there was a quaint little strip mall with an Italian diner in the middle of the block, between an antique store and a closed shop that used to be a beauty parlor. Inside the restaurant, several wobbly-legged wooden tables and chairs were scattered haphazardly about the narrow space.

A large picture window faced the street just as you came in the front door. It was where most of the XX Club members liked to sit and enjoy a non-threatening meal and talk about things, like where to get falsies, gaffs, makeup, and clothing that fit. Hard-to-get things, from people who cater to our kind.

Where to get the best styles to hide that receding hairline, or a scoop on a plastic surgeon who does noses and boob jobs or someone who injects silicone in the behind. Like the main character in Twain's novel, most felt out of place and time. They came in made up like a mannequin in a secondhand store. The staff greeted us with courtesy and tried to hide their amusement.

Although patrons and staff stared and whispered amongst themselves, no one had ever been mistreated or cajoled into leaving, except maybe Joe.

Once, three young men followed him down the street to the restaurant door hollering insults and clucking like hens. He wore a bright orange wig and a red dress with a bow tied behind him. He looked like a giant rooster out for a stroll. For the most part though, we were a welcomed novelty that brought students, artists, writers, and curiosity seekers into an establishment that otherwise served the same stale sandwiches and tasteless spaghetti as any small diner with an artsy name.

"We have better places in the city," Candy said. "I will show you the best pizza in town."

Did she just invite me down to the city?

Joe and the others had left after lunch, cackling about a new wig shop that had just opened. Candy and I were alone except for a few patrons sitting at the counter. Her eyes were unfocused. She stared in my direction, but she was not there. My premonition told me it may be dangerous to become intimate with her but there was a reckless haste inside of me, anxious to absorb every experience I could before completing my transition. I was drawn toward the mysterious woman across from me.

Perhaps I saw in those dark mysterious eyes an oracle that would foretell my future. We all wanted to know, albeit with some trepidation, whether there was a life on the other side of our transition or more importantly whether after we survived what was to come—would we be happy.

I told her a little more about myself. How I spent time in the military working for a special branch of government and flew secret missions during the Cold War over Russia right after Viet Nam then came home and bought out my father then brother and ran the family business until it sold. I was trying to impress her but I left out the part where I got married to a beautiful girl right after high school and we had three dynamic daughters and lived in a big house on a hill overlooking the city that I grew up in. I was not sure why.

Candy was not impressed. She sipped her Coke while I talked. Her stare never wavered. She seldom blinked. I decided to turn the conversation. I wanted to know more about this phantom boyfriend of hers.

"So, what do you do in the city? And who is this guy you mentioned? Is he your boyfriend?"

She had left a series of simple questions unanswered earlier. She remained evasive. There was no polite sidestepping, no change of subject or pretense that she didn't hear the question. She simply stared directly at me as though looking into a mirror, smiled and said nothing. She wasn't going to tell me. I was a game to her or worse yet, I was game. Like some scared rabbit in the brush she had a bead on. It was then I realized my fascination had been more illusory than real, as the magical word suggested.

It was not purely sexual in nature but more curiosity. Her allure, if at all, seeped up from the 14th century meaning of the middle French word *Fascine,* to bewitch. I was under some spell, uncertain whether it was emanating from her or some other more nefarious source from deep within my psyche that was starting to awaken but instead of taking evasive action—I shrugged it off—and zipped up my jacket.

When we left the restaurant, the sun was an orange ball over the rooftops of the gray colorless buildings along South Main street. We drove in awkward silence to the train station in Stratford, not far from Joe and my apartment. Candy pulled on her gloves and opened the door. She got out and I panicked.

"Aren't you going to say goodbye?"

Inside I was dying. I thought we had made a connection, yet I knew the way of our world, and it was possible we would never see each other again.

"What for?"

She shook her head. Her smile was gone, replaced by an expression I could only describe as despot—that sublime look one gets when they sit on a bridge contemplating the water temperature before jumping off—somewhere between desperate and lost.

"I hate goodbyes, don't you?"

The door slammed shut. I sat and pondered what she meant. Did it mean she would be back or what? Before I could put the car into gear the door opened.

"Have you ever wanted something so badly it hurt just to think about it?"

She described how I had felt most of my life until I found

the XX Club. Instead of breaking away from her stare, I fumbled around for some trivial thing to say and stared back, trying to mimic her blank expression. An old English professor of mine once quoted Andre Breton, a Fourteenth century philosopher, before opening his discussion of European literature, "All my life I have yearned for something I cannot have."

There was yearning in Candy's eyes that scared the hell out of me. It once belonged to me. She got back in the car and I drove.

We went to a hole-in-the-wall bar on the edge of town. One of those long narrow rooms where the closet drunks felt right at home. It reeked of stale beer, whiskey, urine and cheap perfume. Two men in green work uniforms sat at the counter hovering over their long-necks like seagulls over a piece of garbage on the beach. A young couple in their twenties sat beside each other in one of the booths across from them. We chose a table farthest from the bar and tried to shrug off the curious stares—the ones that wondered if we were a lesbian couple, professionals open for business or merely available— before sitting down. The waiter was a pimple-faced boy barely out of high school. Candy made eyes at him while he took my order for a whiskey sour.

"And you, M-m-miss?" he stuttered. His pencil shook as it hovered over his pad.

"Can you make Sex on the Beach?" Candy's voice was sultry. The boy's eyes were silver saucers under some imaginary moon, his mouth agape and tongue knotted. He couldn't speak. After a few moments I decided to wake him.

"It's a drink with—" I tried to save him some embarrassment. His face glowed pink under the florescent light overhead.

"I-I-I ca-can ask, Martin." The boy-waiter looked over his shoulder toward the tall man at the bar.

"Never mind. I'll take a draft."

"Ah, what kind?" he asked.

"What do you recommend, Slim?" She stared down at his

crotch. His jaw went slack. "We will have whatever is popular. Just give me what you sell the most of. I hate stale beer."

"Um, we don't s-se-sell s-s-stale b-beer, M-m-miss. Our b-b-beer is f-fresh every, Monday—"

"It's Saturday," Candy interrupted him. "Isn't it?"

The boy blinked rapidly as though his brain was misfiring as he walked away. He returned several minutes later with our order and grinning from ear to ear.

"Martin says you're f-funny. He says to tell them b-b-bitches that b-b-beer doesn't go s-s-stale in the k-keg that f-f-f-fast."

"Oh, okay," Candy raised an eyebrow. She tipped her glass to him.

"B—b-b-but, if-f-f-f you d-d-don't like it. He s-s-s-says he'll b-b-buy you anything else 'c-c-cept the good s-s-stuff on the top s-s-shelf."

"I d-don't think he meant for b-boy-wonder to share that last tidbit," Candy said as the waiter walked away. "He is cute though. Nice b-butt." We laughed. "He wouldn't last a day in the city. S-s-s-somebody would eat him up."

I laughed out of politeness. She looked down into her beer and stared into the foam a long while before taking another swig. When she looked up there were tears in her eyes. "He is adorable though, don't you think?"

"Yes," I said.

"I knew someone who was like that. A long, long time ago."

I waited for her to go on. She seemed lost in thought for a while with her glass raised to her lips but she didn't drink. She put it back on the table in front of her, leaned forward, and looked me dead in the eye.

"What do you think we'd find, Eve, if we could walk away from ourselves?"

This was how the conversation, or lack thereof. It continued throughout the evening. Candy not really saying anything that made sense but alluding to a past that was sad and intriguing. Taunting me. Pressing an ethereal connection beyond a commoner's comprehension.

As I dropped her at the train station late that night, I wanted to know more about her—pierce that inner veil of trust. But it would be several months before I saw Candy again—at least in the physical sense.

#

Chapter 19

Traci

Life is like a bicycle. To keep your balance, you must keep moving.
– Albert Einstein

There are many suburbs around Boston. Small towns that spilled inland from the harbor and were mopped up into a larger city by some invisible metropolitan sponge. Distinct little middle-class neighborhoods that kept their charm. Built from sleek ranch-style single-family homes of the early 1950's, with a few three-storied older Victorians at its edges and a spattering of narrow Cape-Coders of post-war Americana laced in between. Their pitched roofs all folded together like praying hands pressed into neat blocks buried under a verdant veil in summer that grew more colorful in the fall.

I turned down a street shaded by gnarly oak, eloquent elm, and hard-rock-maple. Their broad twisted limbs reached out over the street like the fingers of a benevolent old matron. When the wind blew, the remaining dry leaves still clinging to the pitted branches made soft rustling sounds like those freshly starched taffeta skirts old women wore to church on Sunday mornings.

By late afternoon, dark shadows moved stealthily over everything below. Traci's family home was a two-bedroom modern ranch situated midway down the block on the high side with a driveway that pitched up a bank at a 45-degree angle and curved along the side of the house. I didn't attempt to drive up it.

Traci had asked me to meet her here after a meeting, not at her house near Wilmington. We usually went out on those weekends we had XX Club meetings but this time she asked me to come down later in the week. Her time was close. She would be leaving soon. Likely, we would never see each other again.

She had her SRS letter and a date with Dr. Biber in Trinidad. She didn't say it, but I think she was going to miss our time together. We had grown quite close. I think she may have wanted to talk to me about something before she disappeared forever. Stealth was a bitch. Unlike, Candy, maybe good-by was still part of Traci's vocabulary.

I parked in the street as Traci had instructed, behind a small steel-blue Chevy Cavalier that I presumed belonged to her mom. I wasn't quite sure why Traci wanted to meet at her parent's house. Probably to collect some things that belonged to Parker. She had said her two brothers and father had disowned her when she had come out to them. It wasn't pleasant she had said. She chose Thanksgiving dinner while they were all there with their families gathered in the dining room around the table. They verbally abused her until she broke down in tears and she ran up to her room, but her brothers and Dad followed her.

She was short. They were all over six feet tall and broad shouldered and weighed more than two hundred pounds. One of her brothers was a quarterback on the high school football team growing up and the other a track star. Her dad had been a marine. They dragged her back downstairs and tried a family intervention or some form of therapy run by one of the brother's wives who was a therapist at the local hospital. Traci had been a wrestler in school and when she broke free of her older brother's lock around her neck, they let her go. It was over. Love was gone. She was free to leave and never look back.

That had been a year ago, before she began her year of living dangerously or perhaps, not entirely in Traci's case. She had been dressing up long before joining the XX Club and creating the life she had always wanted on the streets of Boston. At night, she became the girl she always wanted to be leaving Parker far behind. She had even been back to her parent's home by herself several times before. She had a good job, her own car, house, life reimagined, so as I carefully negotiated my way over the ice and snow toward the front door, I wondered why she would ask me to meet her here. Why now—where it all began to go wrong. Traci was a loner. She didn't need anyone. She got by on her own. But she asked me to come while she packed up belongings from a former life that her mother wanted to discard to make room for something or someone else. Some things make no sense at all.

It seemed odd to think Traci had once been a boy, growing up in a household of burly men and a stoic mom. I couldn't imagine anything from my former life that I would want to take with me unless it was some old threadbare tank top that I fell in love with before I turned seventeen because it had once clung to a sleek feminine form before puberty decimated it.

A tall, severe woman opened the door. Except for the dark circles around her bulging eyes, she had left middle age gracefully and was still attractive. She was in a long gray skirt, white blouse, and black sweater with a colorful scarf tucked around her neck. She didn't smile. Her eyebrows went up a notch when she saw me on her doorstep, shivering.

"Hi, is Traci here?"

"Who?" Her brow pinched together. I ran a quick hand over my hair to be sure it was in place.

"Is this the Schultz residence? Traci told me to meet her here." I hated my raspy voice. It didn't sound feminine.

"Oh, please come in." Mrs. Schultz eyed me quickly then turned and shouted up the stairs. "Parker, your friend is here."

I was startled when I heard Traci's birth name. She said her two brothers and father disowned her when they found out but that her mother was somewhat okay with it.

"Come in, come in." She closed the door behind me. Traci emerged at the top of the stairs.

"Hey, Eve, take off your boots and come on up."

"Oh, you don't have to take off your shoes. Those look like a pain to lace back up. Just brush them off if you don't mind."

"Yes, ma'am." I reached down and knocked some of the snow onto the rug I was standing on.

"You are fine." A hint of a smile appeared on her chapped lips.

I trotted up the stairs and moved carefully down the dark hall. I must have been the first shadow person Traci had ever invited home. Our kind were not known to have a lot of friends even before we begin our journey.

Traci's old bedroom was not what I imagined it would be. She was the youngest of three boys growing up in suburbia. I pictured cool blue with thick, tartan curtains and posters of football and hockey jocks all over the walls. Sunshine and lollipops slapped me as I walked in. The room was pale yellow. Off-white curtains trimmed in lace adorned the windows. A yellow comforter with blue patchwork covered the queen bed. On one side of the room, a poster of New Kids on the Block was tacked above the bed and on the canary yellow door of a closet, a full-size poster of a man in goggles skiing down a steep white slope under a bright yellow sun set against a pale blue sky. Traci sat quietly on the edge of her old bed staring into a box on her lap. She didn't look up.

"Wow, Traci, I need my sunglasses to come in here." I wasn't certain if all of the décor was Parker's or the nephew's weekend hideaway at Nanny's after he had abandoned it. It seemed clear the portion important to Traci sat in that small cardboard box.

Traci grunted something under her breath that sounded like: "you're late," and continued staring into the box as though looking for something that was missing. I stood back, giving her space.

It is hard to confront the memories of the past even those you intended all along to discard. When your mother calls and tells you to come home and get the rest of your junk, you obey her. I didn't ask whether this was all there was, and I didn't offer to carry her box. It's personal. I remembered that feeling. Like your whole world shrunk and fit into a small leather suitcase. I set it on the front passenger seat beside me like some mortally wounded friend when I left home.

"Thanks for coming."

I nodded and stepped back. Traci stood, hugging the box

against her chest. She looked up at me. Her Adam's apple bobbed twice, then she moved past me out the door and down the hall. She halted suddenly at the bottom step and I almost ran into her.

A tall gray-haired man blocked the hallway at the bottom of the stairs. He pushed his glasses up onto the bridge of his nose. Furtive grey eyes fluttered over Traci's bare knees that peeked out from under the hem of her little black dress, then rushed over me as though I was not there, to stare at some space above the ceiling as if looking for an answer from the Almighty Himself.

"Hi, Dad." There was a noticeable shake in Traci's voice. The two stood and stared away from each other. Him at the ceiling, Traci at her box.

"This is, Eve."

Her father's head nodded almost imperceptibly. I nodded back. Didn't she tell me that if I met her at 4:00 p.m. no one would be home? What had happened? I am thirty minutes late and both parents seem to have broken some tacit truce that Traci had counted on for discretion.

Mr. Schultz stood back to let us pass.

Traci's mom, a worried look on her face, watched from the kitchen behind her husband. Whatever was left of Parker was leaving. The remnants of their son's life carried away in a small cardboard box on a cold winter's day, in the wiry arms of a girl they never formally met.

She held open the door.

There was no goodbye. Only the sound of a dented brass tea pot hissing from atop the kitchen stove as the door shut behind us.

#

Chapter 20

The Admirers

Between two evils, I always pick the one I never tried before. Mae West.

Jacques was humming past nine o'clock. Wannabe Cher was belting out an old tune from her days with Sonny in a voice oddly reminiscent of the rock diva herself. Traci sat down on an empty chair at a table by the make-shift stage and I plopped down beside her. Two wannabes at the far end of our table appeared to be heavily invested in the performance and didn't seem to mind that we had joined them.

"Be careful."

Traci warned me every time we went to Jacques. She noticed me staring in the direction of two men leaning against the back wall. Both were wearing Brooks Brothers suits with expensive watches on their wrists. Perhaps they belonged to the same accounting or law firm and ventured down town after work from the financial district for a little fun. I toyed with the idea of letting the shorter cute one pick me up—or at least try. Traci shook her head and raised a finger and I nodded in the affirmative, acknowledging her warning, and cracked up.

"Stop staring back. It's an invitation."

"Well, he's cute. Don't you think?"

"Cute and dangerous. These guys will hurt you, Eve. Stay away from that temptation."

The music was too loud for my voice to carry on a conversation. It was too low and throaty. I hadn't learned to resonate well through my nasal passages. We sat alone in silence, huddled in our own thoughts until there was a break then Traci would lean forward and share something profound that she had been dwelling on or tell me she was going to the bar to get us something to drink.

When I leaned back up to tell her what I wanted, I nearly knocked over a bottle of beer someone left had on the table earlier. A hand shot out and grabbed it before it could fall. A Rolex gleamed in the overhead light. I was startled to find the diamond smile that I had been watching from across the room radiated down on me from over my shoulder. He picked up the bottle, put it to his lips and took a big swig. His face collapsed into a grimace.

"Gads, this tastes like piss. What are you drinking?"

I detected a trace of an accent but couldn't decide if it was Swiss or German.

"I don't know. It's not mine. It was on the table when we sat down."

His face contorted and he sat the bottle down as far away from us as possible. He recovered his smile and I realized it was the taller man from the back wall. The short cute guy was talking with Traci, who was suddenly coy. She liked the attention but pretended to be annoyed.

"Well, I hope whoever it belongs to is as beautiful as you. I wouldn't like it if—perhaps she would not forgive my indelicate intrusion."

He was an educated man. I guessed Harvard. We were not far from the campus and a lot of foreigners attended the school. He picked up my hand and I let him hold it in his large warm palm.

"I'm Bernard Reinhardt and this debonair gentleman speaking with your friend is Conrad Richter, soon to be Dr. Richter, and one of the foremost scientists of the world."

I wondered if the name and its accompanying accreditation were real. It certainly fit each man's character. Harvard or BC Preppies. Trust fund babies setting out to fit into the shoes their fathers bought for them.

"And you? What are you going to tell me you do? Accounting or law?" I challenged him.

He had one of those controlled laughs that seemed to come from a place where children are taught not to put their elbows on the table, to address others politely as sir or madam, and keep faces expressionless. His thoughts must have always been under lock and key.

"Neither. I work for his family." Short stuff looked over at me and winked when he said it. I didn't know how to respond so I looked away toward the newest performer dressed like a hippie and singing "It's Too Late" by Carole King.

"What kind of work is that?"

The words slipped out. He intrigued me even though I was not overly attracted to him. His interest in me drew me in.

"Ah, let's just say I do anything he asks."

My eyes narrowed at him suspiciously.

"Sounds sinister."

"It's complicated."

"I bet."

"You sound doubtful. You don't believe me?" He didn't wait for an answer. "What is your name and what brings you into a place like this?" His eyes rolled over the wannabe woman next to me with the broad shoulders of a former high school linebacker and her exaggerated blue eye makeup. She looked like a transplant from the 70's. Traci shot me a warning look.

"You don't want to know." I looked into his eyes. He smiled and nodded, and his dark eyes never left mine.

"Hungry?"

He glanced at Traci, then back at me. My stomach was growling under the table.

"I know a nice quiet place."

"Um, look Charley, you and your friend are very nice and normally we'd be charmed by your attention and kind offer—" I looked at Traci and she was shaking her head.

"We have to decline. My friend is leaving tomorrow and—"

Traci frowned. I'd given away too much information. There was some unwritten script that I was still not privy. Learning to navigate the precarious relationships between single men and women was a game I hadn't quite gotten the hang of. Don't mix reality with imagination or it could explode in your face. Traci had warned me several times, but the scenario never formed until now.

"Conrad comes from an old respected family in Switzerland. He wants to take you both to a fine restaurant this evening. We are new to town and unfamiliar with its—how you say—its night life or best places to go after hours. We were hoping you would show us around."

He addressed his last comment to Traci. Conrad's eyes sparkled when his name was mentioned, or perhaps it was his pseudonym. If this was an act to set up women, it was quite good.

Traci pondered the invitation for a moment then leaned towards me and whispered into my ear.

"Alright, stop with those puppy-eyes. As long as we can stay together and not get separated."

My eyes gave away our answer and Conrad grinned at Bernard before Traci could sit back up.

"Good, shall we go?"

Bernard pulled out my chair and helped me up by the arm.

Gee, he is strong!

# # #

Chapter 21

The Magnum

A true man wants two things; danger and play. For that reason, he wants woman, as the most dangerous plaything. – Frederick Nietzsche

It's was early December and cold. The Hyatt Regency Hotel was only a few blocks away from the club. Normally, we walked when the weather was nice. It was her go-to place after a long night of partying. Traci had had several guys buy her dinner and drinks there in the past. She would make up some emergency and split before they got too cozy afterward. There was a restaurant on the roof with a great view of the city, a place I had always wanted to go since seeing it in the glossy pages of some magazine.

I pictured myself as some eloquent lady in a long sleek black dress similar to the one Traci was wearing. I would sit by a fire in a room full of elaborately dressed couples at one of those white draped tables with a single red rose in a crystal vase at its heart. A tall dark handsome man in an expensive suit would stare longingly at me from across the table while I tipped back a glass of a fine claret, perhaps a Mouton Cadet '94. We'd stare out the wall of glass at the twinkling lights of the city below. I always stared back at my reflection in the glass. I looked happy.

Conrad offered to fetch his car parked not far from the club, but Traci adamantly refused.

You can play around. Let them buy you drinks or dinner but never, ever, get in the car.

Traci's warning words echoed in my brain as we shivered on the near-deserted sidewalks of downtown Boston. The wind bit my bare skin and nipped at my ears and nose. I allowed Bernard to put his arm around me. He smelled of expensive cologne and tobacco and another odor that I was familiar, having spent many years in male locker rooms. After a block, Conrad stopped suddenly and pulled on Traci's sleeve.

"It's fucking bitter cold out, tonight. If you won't let me get my car, let's take a taxi at least."

Conrad was smiling but he didn't look happy. He was a man used to having his own way and Traci was his anomaly. For the moment, she was in control.

Traci nodded her approval. My teeth rattled noisily in my head. Her nose was bright red when she looked at me. I felt lightheaded. A new experience was about to unfold. I don't know why I have always felt exhilarated around the unknown.

For some reason she agreed to let them take us to the Magnum instead of the Hyatt Regency. I didn't think much about it at the time. It was cold, we were going to have a nice dinner in a fancy restaurant with two handsome young men. It seemed harmless. Only later would I understand how dangerous admirers could be to women like us.

The law did not protect shadow people—only real women.

# # #

In the ladies' restroom of the Magnum hotel the mirror behind a row of sinks ran the length of the wall across from the four stalls. It was angled so that you could look into it and see if there were feet beneath the stalls before trying a door. A pair of black boots pointed in an odd angle despite the sound of urine falling into the toilet.

"Traci why if you're worried did you let them take us here instead of —"

My voice echoed in the near empty room.

"Don't be so naive. We are not here for the food, Evelyn. We ate earlier. You can't be hungry."

She sounded angry. In the taxi she kept looking at me then at Bernard's hand or arm. Bernard's watch rode up higher on his wrist revealing a tattoo of what looked like the business end of a bull whip that encircled his thick wrist. The whip was black except for a red "S" signet in the center of a small shield. I didn't know the significance but I made a mental note to ask her what it meant when we were alone.

"What is it with that weird tattoo?"

Traci did not answer. She came out of the stall. Her eyes darted left and right. She put her finger to her lips.

"What?" I whispered.

"We don't have much time. For any reason if we can't ditch these guys—"

"Ditch 'em? Why?"

I thought the idea was to get them to buy a few drinks then leave.

"Keep your voice down."

She waved a hand in my face.

"Don't ever step out of your role whatever you do. Stay in character. No macho bullshit. It is not likely we will be in the same room."

"Room—what are you saying?"

"Shh, listen. Just play along and pretend you have to use the bathroom then sneak out and meet me in the stairwell on the next floor above us. Wait until I get there. Do not use the elevator."

I wanted to ask why or if we were in danger why we wouldn't just leave but the look on her face silenced me. There was something wrong. She was genuinely scared, and her fear started to infect me.

I wished I had paid more attention to what her and short stuff had been talking about instead of listening to Bernard's baritone voice lure me into a false sense of security. He had kept a firm but gentle grip on my shoulder and neck, pressing my head against his massive chest on the ride. His musky smell and warmth were intoxicating, and I felt a connection to that feminine persona that had been denied me for years. It was like I was one of those orchids that opened up every seven years and only in the dark. I nodded in the affirmative, afraid to speak, and she moved quickly for the door.

"Hey, I almost sent the Calvary in there to look for you."

Conrad's joke fell flat. Neither Traci nor I laughed. He was leaning on the wall next to the door when we came out and he shot his arm around Traci before she could turn around.

"What? We were only gone six minutes," I said as I looked down at my wrist then remembered Michael's watch was sitting on the nightstand by my bed.

"Where's Bernard?"

"He's taking care of some business. He'll join us in the lobby."

What kind of business? I wanted to ask, but Conrad had Traci by the back of the neck and was pushing her down the hallway toward the lobby. I tried not to show my alarm. Bernard stood near the elevators with one arm extended inside.

"Aren't we going to get something to eat?"

I pointed toward the entrance to a restaurant a few feet away from the concierge's desk. There was no one there. Only the clerk behind the counter on the far side of the room busy with another male guest. He glanced at us and went back to his business. I hesitated before the elevator doors. I heard about places used by gays to conduct their business in private.

Homosexual conduct was still illegal in most states including Massachusetts, although not as enforced as consistently as in the past, it could still cause problems for someone if caught, particularly those in high profile positions. It was well known in our circles that certain hotels catered to gay organizations and groups, some that may not be as licit as others. This may have been one of them. I wondered if that tattoo symbolized some gay or other more sinister organization and this was their meeting place. Worse yet, no one would be coming to our rescue. As far as the world was concerned, we were male prostitutes. If curiosity killed the cat, I hoped our spirit animals were not felines.

"It's after ten. It's not open, silly."

Conrad laughed and Traci was strangely silent.

"But I'm hungry," I said even though it wasn't true and tried to look pained. I wasn't certain I wanted to go any further.

"I thought we were going to get something to eat. I—"

I didn't want to go to a room. My imagination began to show its ugly side. What kind of organization uses a whip and an "S" as its symbol? Why did Traci get on the elevator?

"Baby, come on," Bernard's voice sounded impatient.

I responded to his term of endearment and stepped onto the elevator. It would have been a good time to have ran. I kept asking myself, what am I doing? When the doors closed, I fought off a strong urge to pee. I noticed the tattoo of a whip with a red crested "S" on Conrad's finger pressing just under Traci's jaw in the soft part of her throat.

"I don't know why you're worried. We order something when we get to room. What you like? Caviar and champagne, a cheese fondue, or chocolate covered fruit?"

"Strawberries," Conrad added.

"American women love chocolate on strawberries."

They spoke about us as though we were real. They picked us up at Jacques. They knew what we were. Was it to appease us or themselves? What was their game? Did we impliedly consent to playing as soon as we stepped out with them or when we get onto the elevator? And what was with Traci? She appeared reticent and complacent. Like she was being submissive. There was an ache in my head beginning in the back of my neck and throbbing at the temples.

"Why are we going to a room to get something to eat? I don't understand."

Both men laughed and Traci smiled albeit weakly despite her apparent nervousness. She and I grew up in an age of dominant men and submissive women. A world where there were few women in the work place and fewer in leadership positions or in authority. We knew we would surrender our male privilege when we become female. It was expected of us— women—are docile and compliant, aren't they? I noticed Traci played the role of submissive quite well. Speak only when spoken to. She hadn't said a word since we came out of the bathroom.

Having grown up in an above average home ruled by a man with an iron fist, I learned to man up and fall into the role my sex reserved for me in order to garner respect. I took over a business, became a husband and father and a military officer.

As a male, I was expected to run the world someday and not be one of its servants. I was not certain if I could adapt to my new role and bow down to lesser men and other women but I was willing to try. If threatened, I visualized a punch to the meaty throat or the paunchy midsection. If Bernard gripped my neck in the manner Conrad locked onto Traci's I wondered. His fingers almost completely wrapped around her throat. I was only just learning that the role we play dictates the reaction. Bernard rested his hand on my shoulder. It was huge and meaty. I tensed up.

"Relax. You will have a great time. I promise."

Bernard's smile appeared easily on his face, as though it was painted by some great Italian master. He leaned down towards me and I turned my head away. He buried his face in the crook of my neck. The warmth of his breath caused a tingling deep within me and then he drew me up on my toes when the soft pad of his lips sucked the soft flash in, gently at first then harder.

A gasp escaped my lips when his hand probed my buttocks through my dress. A strangled sound of a woman moaning stirred me into sudden silence. Bernard stood erect and I stared into the grinning faces of Conrad and surprisingly Traci. Her nervousness aside, she appeared lit up with amusement in a Hitchcockian sort of way.

"See what I mean, baby?" Bernard crowed.

The bell dinged and the doors to the elevator slid open. The lighted panel indicated floor 21. I wondered how many floors spanned above. Outside of one visit to San Francisco, when my Uncle took Debbie and I to the top of a pyramid-shaped building for a view of the city, I had never been higher than a fourth floor. It was when I learned that I was afraid of heights.

Bernard handed a plastic room key-card to Conrad as we got off the elevator. Traci's eyes met mine as we passed. Her message was acknowledged with a slight nod of my head.

Meet her in the stairwell one floor up as soon as I break free.

I understood but wondered how she was going to slip Conrad's grip on her neck. It appeared unbreakable. Then it occurred to me as a former intelligence analyst, something I should have caught earlier. How did Traci know we would be in separate rooms? She emphasized:

"Wait for me".

Why would she think that I would escape first?

How did she know we would need an escape plan?

\#

Chapter 22

The Escape

I know well what I am fleeing from, but not what I am in search of. – Michel de Montaigne

Bernard's fingers dug into the upper flesh of my arms. He grabbed and pushed me forward as soon as we entered the room.

"Ow, that hurts."

He pinned me face down on the bed. I caught a quick glimpse of his face in the mirror as we passed. His demeanor had changed from amiable into something more feral. "I thought you like it rough, baby?"

"What?"

I searched for answers but nothing came to me. My high school sweetheart popped into my head as his hands rolled over me. We had the same equipment. Was he searching for something? A gun, or a wire perhaps?

"No, I mean—what are you doing?"

His large hands seemed to be everywhere at once. I had only had a few homosexual experiences, most prior to puberty. When I was twelve my neighborhood friends, Mitch, Sandy, and I, used to lay in the snake grass in a clearing in the woods behind my house. We took turns whacking each other off. Later that summer, I gave them each a blow job behind the bar in my parent's basement. When I was sixteen, I seduced the neighborhood homo, Donny Demers.

I wanted to see if I was gay. He was the only kid in school taunted worse than me. One hot summer evening, I took Donny by the hand on a stroll in the woods behind my house. I took off my clothes and lay down in the grass. He tried to enter me several times but failed. I kept yelling at him to fuck me, but he couldn't maintain an erection. It shocked both of us. He screamed, "You're like a girl with a dick. I'm just not into girls." He avoided me after that.

Bernard's sudden change in demeanor jolted me. There was no real fight left in me other than wiggling around. I was almost paralyzed with fear.

"Will you lay still, or do I have to tie you up?"

His voice was nonchalant but firm. I lay with my face down in the comforter as still as I could to show him compliance, but as he released his hold I rolled over.

"No."

I managed to squeak out the word. He pulled me back onto my stomach and leaned his knee into my lower spine. It hurt.

"Okay, okay." I gave in.

Bernard let go of me. I didn't move. I pressed my face deep into the comforter and held my breath and didn't notice the fan in the bathroom come on until it began clattering.

In my former survival training I learned that the best time for escape is at the behest of any engagement. I rolled over and slid onto the floor and began to crawl toward the door as silently as possible. The bathroom door was open, and I could hear the splash of his urine in the bowl. Bernard stood with his back to the door, looking in the mirror beside him. Thankfully, I was out of his scope of vision. I crawled toward the door and reached the handle to pull myself up. I unlatched it, careful to hold the chain from falling.

The hall was empty. I remembered Traci's instruction to head for the stairwell and wait one floor up. I sat on the landing catching my breath. Footfalls sounded in the hallway outside the door. I inhaled then held my breath. The door slammed open and I froze like in some silly child's game: One, two, three, red-light!

The heavy breathing was familiar. It was Bernard. My heart was a runaway train. I laid back against the wall on the landing above him and waited—perfectly still—holding in my breath—afraid to let it go. Would I be able to get up and run if he walked up the stairwell? in my mind's eye, I saw him leaning over the rail and looking down waiting—and being very silent.

He was waiting for a sound—any sound—of my ragged breath to give me away but I didn't let it out. The door creaked as it opened. I lay still and waited. Something was missing. There were no sounds of footfalls. Nothing to indicate he was gone. I waited in the blackness of my fear and held my breath deep inside my tight chest. After a few moments, I was floating. Stars fell through the darkness. Tiny flashes of light sped by, the fringe of its bright tail fluttering. Oxygen deprivation to the brain was not good but I was afraid to breathe.

How long had I been out?

I didn't have a watch and there were no windows to indicate whether it was still dark or daylight, only a bright light bolted into the ceiling. I didn't hear movement or uneven breathing. If Bernard was there, he would have found me already. I wondered where Traci was and whether she had tried to find me.

She said to wait. I knew she wouldn't have left without me. Perhaps she saw me lying here and thought I was dead and ran. But that seemed implausible even for her. We had spent so much time together that I can't imagine she had not formed some bond to me as I had her.

My heart ached. This was supposed to be our last escapade together. In a few weeks she would be going to Trinidad for SRS and into deep stealth. We likely would never see each other again. Somehow, I felt responsible for putting her in danger. She had always been so careful and teaching me how to stay safe. She went along with this tryst because of my overzealousness. It was to be my last experience—the last lesson before her little chick went free—as Jennifer would have put it.

I sat up, shivering nearly uncontrollably, and realized I didn't have my coat. It was still in the room where Bernard shucked it off me before grabbing my arms. My purse had gone down to the floor with it. My keys were in my purse. I was beginning to panic. How would I get home? No money, no keys. Where was Traci?

A parade-of-horribles passed through my head. I saw her tied to a bed and both Bernard and Conrad were taking turns with her. I shuddered and pulled myself to my feet. I had to wait. She had said to wait. But for how long?

There was no heat in the stairwell and my muscles were stiffening. The door below opened and I froze again. I squatted back into a sitting position. I felt helpless. It angered me that all those years of special survival and martial arts training in the military did nothing to improve my confidence when real danger loomed. I wondered if it would kick in when I needed it.

The footfalls began sounding up the stairs and this time I heard breathing. It was labored and fast.

I will kick and put up some resistance, surprising Bernard with my unanticipated strength, I thought. *I might be able to fight him off for a while but in the end, I know he will overpower me— and be very angry.*

Screaming never entered my head.

I saw Traci's face and was relieved.

"Traci," I gasped. "Are you alright?"

She looked pale and a bit discombobulated. I suppressed the urge to hug her. I thought she would have been more scared. Her finger came up to her lips to silence me, and she pointed to the door. I stood up and pulled it open and followed her down the hall to the elevators.

The doors slid closed and I pushed the button lit up with an "L" and turned. Traci had leaned against the wall and was looking down at the floor, holding herself, bobbing her head in the way I had seen my mother do, in that slow rotating motion, right after my Nana had died.

I remained silent. There were no visible signs of damage. No torn clothing. No black eyes or cut lip or broken nose, but she told me without saying a word that something terrible had happened to her. Nothing I could say or do would make her feel better. It would be futile to try. I was glad she was alive.

We were part of the world no one wanted to know existed.

People felt those who lived in the shadows had no right to complain. The police would laugh, shake their heads and say we brought it on ourselves. Hospitals would turn us away. Medical staff in emergency rooms were indifferent once they found a man under all that make up. If he was able to walk, no harm was done. The only crime was in that dress he was wearing.

Laura claimed that Morgan, another passable tranny who joined the XX club before my time, was arrested for male prostitution. The police were called to the hospital to investigate a mugging. She had suffered an awful beating one night at a straight club. Once they found out she was a he, all charges were dropped on both sides.

I recalled what Julie had told me about her own experience. *I was broken and they—the police, the onlookers, nurses and doctors, everybody—laughed at me.* Even if you died, they would call it a suicide and save the cost of investigation.

The girl leaning over a newspaper at the front desk did not look up as we made our way outside to the street and huddled together on the sidewalk. Neither of us had our coat. The air was frigid. It was the hour darkest before the dawn, which means Traci had been in that room with Conrad for the past few hours. I did not know my way around the city and Traci had shut down. She did not speak. We were lost and wandered around for a while until I found an all-night diner near the ball park. It was almost deserted.

I pushed Traci into one of the booths furthest away from the lunch-counter and slid in beside her. We sat shivering, legs touching under the table, trying desperately to steal each other's warmth. When I looked up chattering, a tall, frilly-haired waitress was staring down at me. A yellow mushroom with the name: "Shirleys" was stitched above her right breast. I ordered two regular coffees and a cheese Danish.

Suddenly, I remembered we didn't have any money. I

took some change left on another table and called the one person I thought might help us from a pay phone in the corner by the restroom doors. When Joe answered, I choked.

"Joe—" Something caught in my throat. The last man I had left in the world that I could rely upon wore a dress.

#

Chapter 23

The Diner

Joe walked into the diner an hour later looking like something out of *Transvestia*, an old magazine for crossdressers that went defunct sometime in the 90s. His eyes were darkly painted with brown and black liner and he was wearing a yellow top with a black pleated skirt. Everyone in the diner stared over their breakfast platters of runny eggs, burnt sausage and French toast as Joe strolled by their tables.

"Good grief!" Traci muttered under her breath as Joe slid into our booth. Joe smiled, but I knew she was not going to talk to him or even me. I wondered if she even knew where she was.

"Evelyn, are you okay? You look like hell. I was worried when you called me. Kept thinking the worse on the way here. Oh, Traci, you look like death warmed over, too, by the way. Hello? Earth to Traci. What's up with her?"

Traci looked up at him at the sound of her name then turned back and stared out the window. Neither of us had keys to our cars and even if we had I couldn't recall what lines to take on the metro to get back to where we had parked her car at the Alewife station unless she helped. Her eyes were glassed over and vacant. My car was still near her parent's home.

"Did you find the spare key where I told you?" I let Joe take my hands in his and forced myself not to look around to see if anyone was staring. Joe handed me the spare key, looking from Traci to me and back again.

"Wow, your hands are freezing, Evelyn. What have you guys been up to? I mean, what happened? Is she high on something?" Neither one of us volunteered an answer and were relieved when the waitress hovers over Joe. She was not as nice to him as she was to Traci and me.

"Ok, pops, what will you have?"

"Excuse me?" The happy expression on Joe's face sunk.

"We don't have any money, Joe, everything—" my voice caught in my throat. I tried to hide the desperation in my eyes and looked away.

"I'll pay you back."

Joe looked up at the waitress.

"Just bring the bill, Sunshine."

"I have a name."

The waitress frowned and pointed to the name plate pinned to her frock. It read: "Shirleys".

"Okay, Shirleys," Joe laughed. "Bring the goddamn bill so we can leave."

His emphasis on the plural made her look down as though noticing the mistake on her nameplate for the first time. She shook her ponytail from side to side as she walked away.

"You guys have to be more careful. Didn't I teach you anything?"

"It's crazy, Joe. Let's just go. It's been a long night."

I looked at him pleadingly. He handed the exact amount of the tab to the waitress and left a penny on the table for a tip. Before he got up, he slid it into some spilled syrup.

"So long, Tootsie," The waitress taunted Joe.

Laughter rose up behind us and Joe turned and whipped the long strands of hair from his wig over his shoulder. He looked straight at Shirleys, and raised his middle finger before he turned back toward the door. My face burned. I didn't dare look up as we passed under the windows of the diner.

Joe stopped his truck a block from Traci's house. It's where she had told him to park. I am pretty certain she did not want to go back to that house again to get another key to her car but sometimes, we have to return to where we started, before we can get to where we are going.

When she got out, there was no goodbye, no keep-you-chin-up advice, not even a nod to say I'll miss you, and like her father earlier, Traci showed no emotion. It's funny what we took away from the men we fought hard not to emulate. I sat and stared at her slight frame ambling slow and steady down the street. She was draped in the early morning light as it filtered through the stark branches of those ancient elm and oak.

In a blink of an eye, Traci disappeared into those eerie shadows waving overhead.

Joe pulled a little further down the street where I had parked and I got out. He nodded and I said thanks, see you at home or something to that effect. Driving back, my mind was on Traci. I was uncertain if I would ever see her again. I felt hollow inside and wanted to cry but my tear ducts were dry. I had hoped at least for that final chance to say good-by, but I knew that chance was slim. There was one more meeting before Traci was scheduled to leave but after tonight, I doubted she'd show. Why would she? She used to say the only reason she showed up at all anymore after she got her letter was for me. I think I botched that, but I only hoped that someday she would learn to forgive me and maybe look back on our time together fondly.

All we have in the end are the hurried chapters of our unplanned lives, some arranged haphazardly for another time to be remembered, others dogeared and worn from being read and reread over and over again until we tire of them, but the ones hardest to forget it seems are the ones left unfinished. I don't think I will ever forget what happened on this night.

#

Chapter 24

The Last Goodbye

There are no strangers here; Only friends you haven't met yet.
William Butler Yates

    I tried to contact Traci several times in the days after the incident at the Magnum hotel but to no avail. She wasn't much for returning telephone calls. I knew she was scheduled for her surgery at the end of the month and hoped the night at the hotel wasn't the last time we would ever see each other.

    When I descended those stairs into the basement of the Christ Church the meeting of the XX Club was already in progress. I hadn't expected Traci would show but I looked around for her anyway. I didn't see her until I looked back at the table in the back where all the goodies were usually stacked for the break. There she stood surrounded by a crowd of groupies wearing a white faux fur coat with gloves to match. She was decked out and made up like she was going to some uptown interview afterward. It was so different than her usual repertoire no wonder I missed her on my first pan of the room. Traci took her usual seat beside me and politely nodded but didn't say anything, like I was some newbie she was meeting for the first time.

    I went up and asked if she was okay. Traci smiled at me and nodded. It was as if we were meeting for the first time. I barely knew her. So, this was it. She was ready to leave everything behind, block out everything from her past, the pleasant with the unpleasant, Conrad and Bernard, the XX Club, her brothers, father, mother and me were just a few more mementos to be put in that box next to Parker's items and left in the back of some closet.

    Some photos were being passed around by a senior member that I met only once. Laura had a wry grin when she put them back down on the table after reading through them.

A black and white photo showed one of the Silicon Sallies, a black Tranny or drag queen that Laura had known from the city. She injected silicon directly into her body at an illegal party back in the 70s and ended up a quadruple amputee, with no hands or feet when it all went awry. The gross photos were left on display on the table in the back of the room as a warning. They usually showed up there whenever someone was 'ready' to leave the nest. A sad reminder of our brief trans history but it didn't affect us. Not really.

We had lived so long without a future that it was hard to picture anything we did as real. We saw only what we wanted to believe and hoped what Dr. Higgins said about the ones that never came back was true. That they made it. They blended in so well they forgot who they once were. Our focus was on the prize at the end of the rainbow—the sex change—on becoming the dream girl we always wanted to be.

We didn't think much beyond that or about the complications of a new life afterward. We blocked out the past, our families, friends, acquaintances, and people we never met but who judged us anyway as the unacceptable. The pictures were there to inject a dose of reality, but for us, it was a case of "that won't happen to me," which I'm sure most of those on the table had once said, too.

"Okay, people, let's take our seats. It's time to expose our soul." Jennifer's voice was soft and hoarse but carried over the hubbub of excited members and guests gathering in anticipation of a big coming out party to be held at the end of spring. Supposedly an uplifting subject to balance the nightmares that lay on the back table.

Jennifer picked her notebook up off her lap and started reciting the rules as she does at every meeting, but only after she reminded us who we are: The XX Club is the support group of the Gender Identity Clinic of New England. And she never forgot to remind us, "This is not a place to make new best friends."

"Here we go again." Traci smiled and rolled her eyes at

me as she always did, and I stifled a laugh.

"Due to popular request, we are going to host a coming out party for late spring and we'll need help on several committees to make this happen." Jennifer looked around the room. "The party will be held outside."

No one had to ask what outside meant. Everyone looked around the circle to see how to react. Joe, Big Kathy, Kaitlyn and several newbies were beaming. Cindy and Sarah nodded sheepishly. Traci breathed uneasily. When the rumor of a party started circulating last month, she had told me about the club's summer picnic the previous year in the beginning of her transition. She had made several trips to the hospital to convince staff to provide services for some of the club's bleeding members who were less than passable in a swim suit. Everyone was afraid of HIV and AIDs back then as though the mere presence of some gay male would contaminate you, your family, and your next of kin in another state.

"So, Evelyn, any ideas for the party?"

Jennifer caught me off guard.

I looked around at all the expectant faces and felt my stomach sinking. I was dumbstruck. As the club's new secretary, it apparently fell on me to make things happen. When Julie nominated me to take her old position, I hadn't realized all that it entailed. I wrote articles, letters and solicitations, produced the newsletter, mailed clinic correspondence, and coordinated with all the new faces that showed up at meetings. It was my job to provide them the rules and information about the screening process.

"I'll help," Joe jumped in. His enthusiasm sparked others to raise their hand to volunteer.

"Count me in," Hawk-nose Kaitlyn said. She wore a hat, tipped at one side, trying to hide her current black eye.

"Sounds like fun." Some other male voices chimed in.

"Are you taking names?" Jennifer asked.

I sighed and reached for the notebook inside my purse. "They can be our decorating committee."

"Don't worry, Evelyn. I got it."

Big Kathy lifted her pad and flashed me one of her famous deep-dimpled smiles from across the circle. She was writing down names or more likely sketching again. She had given me several of her drawings for the book I intended to write someday.

"Thanks." I exhaled.

I didn't dare look at Traci. She thought a bunch of wannabe women parading around in public was an invitation to a disaster. I liked the idea of a party.

Some of the members, perhaps most of them, could use something to bolster their transition, but in another way, I agreed with her. I had been out with Joe enough to know that people could be cruel to him in the daylight. I could only imagine what would happen late at night in an unfamiliar city. He may have been strong enough to fend off an attacker but what about some of the others in our group?

Out of the twenty-three members, only two or three might have been what the DSM-IV terms as true transsexual. The others were some variation of dysfunctional person not yet listed in the gender manual. Traci called them "freaks and geeks," as most had jobs in the newly developed IT field working with computers.

"Any job that avoids being around people is a good one for something that resembles a refugee from the *Rocky Horror Picture Show*."

She was incorrigible.

"I will be happy to help you. Just let me know. I miss our chats."

Cindy reached over and grasped my hand. Hers was frail and cold. She had been starving herself again. A row of yellowed teeth peeked out between her thin dry lips as they peeled into a smile. She smoked like a chimney. I shrugged off a shiver and smiled back. First impressions can be misleading. Cindy had issues. The least of which was her lack of hygiene, sexual perversions and poor confidence.

"Evelyn, make certain you get Kathy's notes after the meeting and I need to coordinate a time to go to the city next week. Julie found a place that would agree to host our party. Let me know your schedule so we can set up a time to meet with the hotel manager."

"What? I have plans—"

"At your convenience, of course. He said he would meet some evening to accommodate our schedules. Julie may have to work so I will need you." Her voice was close to pleading.

Disappointing sweet Jennifer was difficult.

"Perhaps on a Friday?"

Jennifer checked off something in the notebook on her lap.

"Wonderful," someone said.

"You can't imagine how important this is to us."

I really can't. Big Kathy waved and everyone around the circle seemed to nod in unison. Everyone except Traci. She grinned like the cat that swallowed the canary. If I could have heard her thoughts, *I told you so*, would have echoed in my brain. I dipped my chin to acknowledge my defeat. I always gave in to their demands. My new role, Traci claimed, was Joan of Arc. The patron saint of the social lepers.

At break, we used the bathrooms upstairs, the one that said "Women" in faded black letters on the door. It made us feel we were moving toward our goal. We milled around in the hallway outside the room waiting for Jennifer to call the meeting back to order.

"Looks like you have a date on Friday with Jen and Julie," Traci said.

"They need my help, Traci. Can you imagine Jennifer trying to negotiate on her own? I can't say no."

She rolled her eyes and mocked playing a violin. She was being a real bitch today.

"Jen and Julie and the other rejects need you. Not because you are a good negotiator but because you're a femme. They can't tell us apart from the real thing if we keep our clothes on.

We blend in and don't threaten the natural born," Traci said.

"You are there to show management they have nothing to fear."

I shrugged. Helping the people who helped me arrive at the doorstep of my 'dream come true' seemed appropriate. The right thing to do. I was assurance that our kind—whatever that is—blended in so well the likelihood of an incident, however possible, was remote. If only I believed that were true.

An article cut out of some newspaper lay on the back table near a paper plate of Julie's 'Come-to-Jesus' chocolate chip cookies and a bowl of stale Cheetos. It was about Morgan, who the Club knew as Monica. His wife found him hanging from a beam in their garage. The previous week there was one about Wanda, found naked in a tub of her own blood.

The article spooked Traci. Morgan was a promising passable trans. In drag, she looked like a model in Cosmo or Mademoiselle magazine. She and Traci hung out before I came along and then she suddenly stopped coming to meetings. I could see it in Traci's eyes she was bothered. It was okay for people to drop out suddenly, never to be heard from again, just not learn what happened to make them disappear.

We took our chairs in silence. The articles left on the back table were meant to intimidate the ones who were leaving. A kind of final test. She had her letter of referral and a date with Dr. Biber in Trinidad, Colorado. Everyone knew this was her last meeting. Traci took it personally.

"It's a sick tradition," Traci said.

"Someone said Laura is trying to rattle your chain."

Traci shook her head vigorously. "She wouldn't dare fuck with me. Canon Jones put it there."

The small Episcopal priest smiled as I looked over at him. It was a confident smile. A man of the cloth unafraid of anything of this earth. His eyes only revealed kindness.

"Why? Why would he do that?"

Traci shrugged and twisted her lower lip.

"Whatever." She stared up at the windows above our

heads. She folded and refolded her feet up under her on the chair.

"I thought he liked you."

"He wants to be sure when we leave her that we don't get into trouble. It drives home the underlying purpose of the clinic. Why this support group was formed."

"To save our immortal soul?" I asked.

She scoffed. "They only care about the survival of the clinic. We are just part of the research for their next paper."

It didn't make sense. Traci passed easily. No one would even know she had a penis. Those who passed well enough to fit in generally moved on without resistance. Stats for survival were dismal. Several of the newbies and one of our regulars would be gone by the next meeting.

"What the fuck!" Joe's voice boomed from behind us. "Did anyone see this? Poor, Morgan. Who would think she'd do a thing like that? What a waste. She had so much potential. I would have killed to look as good as her, even when she wasn't dolled up."

Traci rolled her eyes when she heard his voice. Kaitlyn was standing near Joe but refused to look at the article when he tried to hand it to her. Her right eye was bulging and blueish-black.

"Oh, God, I can't believe it." Cindy whined. She trained her eyes on Traci. "Morgan and I used to hang together."

Traci had told me that she and Cindy passed as teens when they went out but were nothing alike. I understood that they were both petite and cute—at least at first glance—or when Cindy opened her mouth. She sounded more like a five-year-old the way she carried on. Besides Traci, they were the only femmes in the club until I came along.

"I am so sorry, Evelyn." Cindy put her hand on my shoulder.

"I didn't know her."

Her statement was not directed at me. She had leaned on me and looked straight at Traci when she said it.

"Oh, my. Another chick fell from the nest."

Jennifer's soft voice interjected. She clucked like a hen as she walked away.

Traci was still staring up at the world above us. Another pair of shiny black boots passed by the windows as I looked up.

# # #

When the meeting ended, Jennifer turned to me and said she needed ten minutes to consult with Canon Jones. She reminded me not to go too far. She wanted to coordinate with me the details of our meeting at the Magnum hotel and to discuss the other committees' responsibilities for the party. Joe and Big Kathy were already leading a coalition of volunteers toward the goodies table in the back to discuss their interest in doing the decorating.

The Magnum? Wasn't that the hotel Bernard and Conrad took us to? My stomach turned. Traci was amused. At least that's how I interpreted the strange look she gave me when they announced the location of the party.

"How can I refuse?" I said. It was exasperating. Traci shook her head. She unfolded her legs out from under her and began pulling on her boots that she had tossed under her chair.

"Where are we going in such a hurry?" I made mental note of her attire. Traci usually dressed casually for meetings but today, he was all decked out. Ready to "fly the coup" as Jennifer would have put it. Girls stuff.

"Aren't we doing lunch today?" My heart picked up steam. This would most likely be our last meeting together. I still needed her guidance. I was not ready to be on my own. "It's my turn to buy."

"Can't today, Eve I've got to be somewhere by three." She didn't share where or with whom.

I hid my disappointment behind a frozen smile, the kind I imagined natural-born females wore when they didn't want you to know what they were thinking. As though she could read my expression, Traci reached out and touched my elbow.

"Hey, keep that smile. It looks good on you."

"Thanks," I gasped. It was barely audible. I didn't think she heard me.

Traci moved toward the door. She glanced up at the four windows that lined the ceiling. A pair of hipsters, those boots some women wear that creep half way up the thighs, passed by. It was an omen. She had always said she wanted to jump in a pair someday and walk away from this place. Her back was to me. I sensed more than saw her smile.

"Hey, kiddo!" Traci shouted as she turned around at the door. Everyone went silent, including Jennifer. She hesitated then pointed at me.

"Don't forget the rules."

"I won't." I nodded. That's when the tears came rolling down my cheeks. I had to touch them to be sure they were real.

"Excelsior!" Traci shouted and raised her hand up.

The door swung shut slowly behind her. That was it. Our last goodbye. I stood staring at the closed door a long while before feeling someone standing behind me. Joe draped his arm around my shoulder. I wanted to shrug it off and walk toward the bathroom to be faithful to the rules but I left it there and let him try and comfort me knowing it comforted him. Inside, I made a vow: I'd never forget those rules again.

The XX Club was not the place to make new best friends.

#

Chapter 25

The Catalyst

When you expect things to happen—strangely enough—they do happen. – J. P. Morgan

Paul and Joe did not like each other. Paul taunted Joe whenever he came to the apartment to pick me up. When Paul teased him, Joe looked at me suspiciously as though I gave away his secret away. I denied it of course but I did. I told Paul that he wasn't real. I had to keep up my image as the naïve country-girl-divorcee from Vermont who innocently moved in with a transvestite. I told Paul to keep my own story intact. But Joe didn't need to know that.

Like Paul, Joe was homophobic. I tensed up every time the two of them came into contact with one another. I feared exposure and was trying desperately to preserve the illusion that I was a natural-born woman. I had an ulcer when I was young. At fifteen, one of my bile ducts had malfunctioned from a long night of binge-drinking. It damaged my liver. My mouth filled with a foul bitter taste whenever I became overstressed.

There had been subtle changes to Joe and my relationship since I had met Paul. Our girly-girl-outings became fewer and fewer and Joe became more withdrawn and morose. His smile waned. He no longer sat on the back porch sipping beer in a plastic cup waiting for me to come home. He stayed in his room longer each morning and he was on the phone more often with his wife or Big Kathy late into the evenings. He no longer shared the tales of his day with me. I was either running to a class, working another temp-job, or out with Paul.

It worried me when I found Joe sitting at the small wooden table in our kitchen one evening. His thick arms folded over his phony bosom and frowning. Joe always frowned when he wanted me to know that he was displeased. He knew I had a date with Paul and was rushing from a temp assignment that ran late.

"If he says one nasty thing to me, Evelyn, I swear I am going to punch him out."

"Joe, calm down. You can't stop someone from being prejudice."

"How did he know? Did you tell him?"

"Of course not," I lied. Credibility was my illusion. It was self-preservation.

"I swear if I find out that you gave me up, I am going to tell him you are like me."

My heart thumped. I touched Joe on the shoulder, feigned tears, and softened my voice.

"Joe, you wouldn't. You know me better than that. Haven't I included you in our outings? I invite you along with us to the mall and restaurants."

Joe looked up at me. His false lashes bounced when he blinked.

"He brings those Jalapeno poppers you like, remember?"

Joe shook his head. We both knew Paul carried them up to the door because he was looking to dispose of his garbage. Joe turned and stared out the kitchen window.

"And he paid for your lunch several times—"

"Yeah, right," Joe moaned.

"Don't I always chastise him whenever he says something derogatory in front of me?"

Joe smiled. It worried me when he smiled during one of our arguments.

"He's dangerous, Evelyn. You are going to get hurt."

"I am a big girl. I can take care of myself."

"He'll kill you if he ever finds out you still have a dick."

I didn't respond. It was late and I had to get ready. Paul was picking me up in an hour. It was his birthday and he'd made reservations at some fancy restaurant. I was more apprehensive than usual. We had only kissed. He hadn't tried to do more. I was still uncomfortable whenever he pressed his lips to mine and tried to get his tongue into my mouth.

We had been dating several months and I worried that he was expecting more than the paisley tie that I bought him at Filene's Basement. Perhaps, he anticipated a different kind of gift commemorating our anniversary. Something more intimate and personal. It worried me more that he was picking me up at our apartment where he may run into an angry crossdresser. So, to appease Joe, and have some kind of interference if Paul wanted more for his birthday, I invited Joe to go with us to dinner.

"You'll have to hurry, Joe. No dilly-dallying. He'll be here in an hour."

Paul arrived at quarter-past eight and I was not completely ready.

"Tell me you didn't invite that fagot along."

Paul's voice was purposefully loud. He wanted Joe to hear him.

Joe stood quietly behind me all dolled up and dressed in his best fifties-diva outfit complete with a beehive, natural-hair wig and a pink sweater and frilly skirt. I think he was trying to be Sandra Dee.

Paul raised his hands when he saw him.

"Come on, Evie" —that's what he called me. Like I was some pet spider he kept in a box when he was a boy— "it's my birthday. I want it to be special. I don't want to drag the circus around tonight."

I slapped his arm.

Paul's face split into a grin and he pulled me into him. His thick fingers locked onto my upper arms and he kissed me hard on the mouth. I felt like he was going to swallow me.

"Evie," Joe mimicked Paul behind me. His voice was dangerously guttural.

I was suddenly warm.

"Don't," I gasped. I pinched Paul's arm again to remind him to be civil.

Joe's eyes were burning into my back. Paul was overly passionate. I opened my mouth allowing him to insert his tongue. As long as he was kissing me, he was not taunting Joe. I think he was doing it longer to piss him off.

Paul's hands moved down and squeezed my buttocks. We both knew Joe was watching. It caused a stirring inside of me. I heard the moaning and I pushed him away.

"Please be civil," I said when he let me up to breathe. "Don't taunt Veronica."

"Veronica? I thought his name was Betty."

Paul laughed.

I winced. *Shit.* I'd forgotten which name Joe had told me to call him this week.

"Use the proper pronouns."

I punched Paul in the upper arm. It came across more playful than I had intended, and he laughed heartier.

Joe hands clenched and unclenched involuntarily. I feared he was about to expose me to get even with both of us. Panic poured into my veins.

"Go wait in the car. I'll be right out," I said to Paul in a hushed voice.

When I turned around to face Joe, a red raisin stared back at me.

"Joe, I know I told you that you could come with us but—"

"Don't worry, Evie," Joe mocked. "You don't have to explain. I was right here. Remember?"

"I'm glad you understand. We'll do something this weekend. Maybe go to the city shopping."

"Oh, Evie, I understand. More than you think I do."

It had taken him a long time to get ready. He'd been singing something from *West Side Story* and dancing around in front of the bathroom mirror for nearly an hour. Disappointment hung on his face.

"Joe, I'm sorry." I tried to sound sincere. Inside I was seething. Hormones crashed into one another fighting for control.

"Don't pity me. I don't have to tell him what you are. It won't be long before he reaches into your pants and finds out on his own."

I tried to keep from looking at Paul when I climbed into his truck, but he saw the fear in my face and opened his door.

I grabbed his arm.

"No, Paul, please let it be. He's just upset. You were mean."

"He puts my girl in a funk on my birthday and you want me to let it go?"

"Please," I said.

It sounded like begging. I let my hand brush his thigh. I gazed into his eyes and let my lower lip fall open. I was already learning those lessons lost to me when other girls learned to be coy and I was trying to be a boy.

"Be the bigger man."

Paul stopped. He looked at his watch then glanced toward the house. We were late. They would only hold a reservation for so long. He shook his head and climbed back into the truck and slammed the door shut.

He sat quiet for a moment. He didn't look at me. His hand was shaking, perched over his key like a bird over its prey— waiting, wondering.

We drove away into a Godiva evening like the night we first kissed. My stomach squeezing and churning into chocolate knots.

Bile tastes like liver.

# # #

It was late when I got home. I removed my shoes at the door and tried moving stealthily to not awaken Joe. As soon as I entered my bedroom, his voice boomed from behind his closed bedroom door.

"Your wife, Debbie, called. She wants you to call her in the morning."

I pictured Cathy, the landlady's daughter lying upstairs under the covers in her bed with her boyfriend next to her listening to the odd conversation and smothering fitful laughs under a downy pillow. *Holy cow! Evelyn is a man. She has a wife. He-she-it is a freak, too. Ha, ha, ha.*

"Did she say what she wanted?" I shouted back as silently as I could.

"Something about your house. There was trouble with the financing and the sale might fall through."

I let out an audible sigh. All of my plans depended upon the sale of our family home, and moving Debbie and April safely away from the fallout. I shook my head, and went to bed.

# # #

The house my father built sat at the top of Beckley Hill, one of the seven hills in Barre. It had six bedrooms, four baths, a kitchen, formal living room, a den that doubled as my study, a formal dining room, modern kitchen, a laundry room, storage room and numerous closets, some lined with aromatic red cedar, a finished basement replete with a full size wet-bar, a billiard table, and a Steinway baby-grand piano.

The outside was nearly as grandiose. It had a patio with an outdoor kitchen, large above ground pool, a lighted basketball court—built for my baby sister—a two car garage, and a detached out-building that stored two snowmobiles, a John Deere riding lawn-mower, a small outboard boat with trailer, various tools and the things found in most garages including boxes of junk accumulated over the years.

At 4500 square feet, all on one floor, the house was the largest ranch-style home in Central Vermont and perhaps in the entire state at the time. It had a view of New York to the west, New Hampshire to the east, and on a clear day, Canada could be seen looking at a point just Northwest of Mount Mansfield. A grove of hard-rock maple behind the house lined the Eastern border of the property while the remainder of the lot was surrounded by pastureland and bordered the Martineau farm to the west.

Debbie was in tears when I called. Rumors had circulated around town that I was planning to change sex and she was receiving sympathy calls from family and friends. After the sympathy calls, she began receiving threats—to her person—not mine, from people she didn't know. Men were volunteering to show her a good time. People were attempting to make me pay for my deception and her for still loving me.

April was sexually assaulted by three boys at school citing my condition as a reason to "check her out." They said they wanted to see if she had a dick like me. The principal suspended them for three days. It's all she could do. Protocol, she said. It was the boys first infraction

Debbie agreed, after some coaxing, to take April and move in with my parents in Florida until she could get employment, prior to the house sale. It would give her a chance to recover from her loss. Debbie was relieved but worried about me.

"Are you going to be okay?" she asked.

"Yes," I lied.

I missed her and the kids terribly. I was living with an aging transvestite and dating a homophobic misogynist editor from the city. I was part of a support group of wannabe women waiting for a letter that would allow me to get a costly operation that I needed in order to blend into society. It would take every penny I had saved but I couldn't take anything from Debbie. I had already robbed her of her future and broken every promise of our marriage. I had no idea how I would earn a decent living working at Dunhill Temporary services but there was no need to worry her. I hung up the receiver and went back to bed.

If I prayed hard enough, God would answer me. I was certain He would.

#

Chapter 26

The Invitation

The most wasted of all days is one without laughter. – e. e. cummings

At the next XX Club meeting, Candy sauntered back into the basement of Christ Church arm and arm with a tall black woman. They entered like two statuesque models strutting down a runway. Candy had on a black blouse with a green ankle length skirt carrying her white sweater on one arm and her friend, Sherlyn, an ebony-skinned woman, was dressed in a yellow empire-waist dress with a white sash that draped loosely from one shoulder across her shapely bosom and narrow waist. She was so tall in her stilettos that her big brassy hair nearly touched the ceiling in the basement room at Christ's Church.

Sherlyn, addressed the group about a parade down in the city, some celebration of Gay Pride—if there was such a thing in '94. They wanted a trans contingent to be there.

"The public gots to be educated. There is more than just gay and lesbian. If yous don't come and speak up, they just going to define you the way they always do, like a bunch of pervs and sex fiends. Now's your chance to tell people what you all about."

Not many people appeared interested. Everyone, including Julie, looked away. You could hear the radiator hissing from the corner of the room as soon as she asked for volunteers, but afterward, the group surrounded her and showered her with attention. Everyone wanted to add their two cents but not commit.

Trannies are not the proud type. Most are too shy or too busy planning their own funerals to march in some parade. Or perhaps the XX Club members that year were too busy planning their own show to get interested in someone else's cry for attention.

Candy introduced me to Sherlyn before they had to scoot away to catch an early train back to the city. Sherlyn was a drag queen who worked as a bouncer in an after-hours club near the village and sometimes crashed at Candy's place.

"Come on down to the city," Candy said. "We'll show you a good time."

"What?"

Sherlyn seemed surprised as much as I did. I pretended to be my usual noncommittal self.

"Why don't you go?"

Jennifer came up behind us.

"We need to find alternative places for the party and you might make some inquiries while there and learn something we can use to enhance our own party."

I knew she was talking about security. Jennifer had already let her worries be known to me.

"We are a small group. Our little chicks don't know how to fly yet."

I wanted to add: *a stitch in time saves nine,* as she was fond of saying but there were more than nine members at this meeting.

"Not to worry, Jen. The Tiffany Club has been having parties for years in Boston and there have not been any reported incidents." Julie sounded nonchalant. It was just something to say to downplay the importance of my role.

I wanted to add, "because no one reports them."

The year was 1993. One year after the highest murder rate in the city's recorded history. Most were transient. Like our little gay population. The world was hostile to shadow people, particularly the authorities. No one cares if we get hurt. Ordinary folk don't want to admit we even exist.

But I kept silent. I did not want to commit to going to the city, but I was curious about Candy, and with Traci gone, I had no other femmes to hang out with, so I made a date for the next weekend, and agreed to meet her at a bar in New York.

Life was beginning to get interesting again.

Chapter 27

The Rumors

History is nothing but gossip about the past, with the hope that it might be true. Gore Vidal

With Traci gone, and Julie settled into a job at a Bridgeport hospital now nearly full time before her surgery date, I feared most of the gossip circulating around the XX Club was about me. It looked like I was next be that "chick about to fly the coop"—as Jennifer would likely say at some near future meeting. She'd wipe a faux tear from the corner of her eye with her sleeve and then read her rules that were meant to dissuade everyone from getting close to each other.

At lunch time, the regulars and some newbies met at Biscotti's as usual. I followed the crowd feeling lost without Traci or other femmes to keep me company. I sat at the end of the long table in the back where a group of newbies mixed in listening intently to Laura speak about her exploits and experiences and conquests. Storytelling was her forte.

Laura loved attention almost as much as she loved she-males. It amazed me that she was allowed to stay a member of the XX Club. She violated every rule in the book at first opportunity. Whenever Laura was out of Canon Clinton Jones view, she appeared to thrive.

"Looking back, it is hard to recall exactly what happened. What I do remember about her just before she disappeared is that she was—what's the word? —forlorn. The word has no meaning unless I see her sitting in that bar listening to some song playing on a radio in another room. She kept slipping under the table playing Saigon suicide with these suits—"

"What is that?"

Kaitlyn had too much to drink.

Laura laughed, took another swig of her beer, and leaned

across the table toward Kaitlyn's wide-eyed stare.

"In 'Nam the chicks and lady-boys were a dime a dozen. Literally! Ten bucks would get you laid, less if you just wanted a blow job. They'd surround you when you walked in and you couldn't tell tit from tat, if you know what I mean. After a few months in country, they all looked alike. Cute as hell and if you got drunk enough you didn't care. There was this game we played when one of them would slip under the table. The first GI to smile bought the round."

"Huh?"

Sarah looked up from rubbing a file over her nails under the table.

"The trick is to not let anyone know—"

"I don't get it."

Kaitlyn's eyes narrowed.

"Kaitlyn, darling, you were still in diapers when—"

"Don't patronize me, Laura."

"Anyway, when a bitch slides under the table, unbuttons your trousers and pulls your dick out, you best not smile or you buy the rounds and the entertainment."

"Fuck you, that never happened."

"Every pay day, sweetie."

Laura held up a wad of bills in one hand and pinched Kaitlyn's lips together with the other. Everyone except Kaitlyn laughed.

"See what I mean?"

Kaitlyn slapped Laura's hand away.

The laughs grew louder. Kaitlyn's cheeks flushed bright red against her pale skin.

"So, what happened to Candy?" Joe asked, he leaned in next to Laura's other shoulder. His voice was low.

"Who? Oh, yeah, her, well you know that's not her real name?" Joe nodded but looked quickly at me. He had no clue.

"She went by Rachel then. Her eyes were glazed over and not from alcohol. Those were days people shot shit up their veins right in public. No one cared."

Laura had our attention and played it for all it was worth.

"So, that's the Candy that came to our meeting with that black drag queen? She's a druggie?" Joe leaned in towards the center of our table. His booming voice carried through Biscotti's. It was not that big of a place and the waiter smiled at me then nodded to someone at the next table as though pointing me out.

I was the novelty. The one that stood out. Other than skinny Kaitlyn, the others at the table were thick-waisted, broad across the shoulders, and had large arms and hands. My features and movements were more feminine. The waiter whispered "hombre" in the ear of his friend, and I felt my stomach knot.

"Absolutely not--"

Laura stopped when she caught Sarah's expression.

"Why would anyone pretend to be some dead tranny? Who the fuck does that? It is embarrassing enough being a live one."

Joe laughed. No one laughed with him. They didn't think he was funny. Tranny's love legends. Especially one about their own kind.

"Hey, big guy—"

"Margaret," Joe corrected Laura. He distinctly told everyone before we sat down to lunch what name to call him.

"Okay, Maggie, think about it. You never saw an auspicious visitor or some wannabe that came in and claimed to be someone else? Ain't none of you bitches who you say you are." Laura laughed. Several patrons stared. I stifled a laugh. She ought to know. Every other word out of her mouth was usually some lie to get some she-male into bed. A trick of the trade, Laura was fond of bragging.

"But why someone famous if nobody really believes who she says she is anyway?" some newbie with long dark eyelashes and a whisper-soft voice inquired.

"Remember Skinny Marie?"

Laura looked over at Sarah. Her head tipped slightly forward like she had nodded in agreement.

"She took that name from the movie *Pretty Woman*.

Ironic that she ended up in a dumpster herself or at least tit's up in some alley."

"I don't believe that."

Kaitlyn appeared upset by the conversation. Perhaps she remembered Skinny Marie or heard that she had a married boyfriend who used to beat her, too. When we last saw Kaitlyn in the hospital, every part of her face was purple except her nose.

"Fuck."

Joe waved his hand in front of his face as if to dismiss Laura.

"Why not? Joe, I mean, Maggie, are you going to eat that?"

Laura pointed to an onion ring on the blue chipped plate.

"Call me Margaret. No, go ahead."

Joe leaned back to let Laura grab it off the plate.

"Who is she then, do you know? I mean she seems to have the confidence of a real girl. I never would have guessed she was like us until she opened her mouth to speak. She sounds like a fag."

"We are supposed to be talking about the party and coming up with a theme, guys. We shouldn't be dissing one of our own, especially, Rachel. She has never said an unkind thing about anyone. She is a real friend to the community. Not like some people here."

Sarah's voice was loud. It surprised everyone, especially, Laura. All eyes turned in her direction. She looked down at her plate unable to meet anyone's gaze.

"What the fuck?" Laura laughed. "The peanut gallery speaks. What do you care?"

Sarah shrugged.

"She didn't care about you when—"

"Did too—" Sarah's face was bright red.

"Okay, but she's not a saint. You idolize her but she's no—

"She's the most generous soul on this earth and you have no right to talk about her like that. You promised."

"She fucked you over."

"She did not. It was him. He didn't like me."

"Fuck him and her. That bitch was dead. She OD'd. He dumped her on the street. You both did time and she let it happen."

Sarah got up and ran away from the table toward the bathroom.

"Oh, poor baby. Did I hurt your feelings?"

Laura yelled after her and several patrons turned to look over at us.

"Okay, she's gone. Tell us. What happened?"

Joe prompted Laura.

I had a feeling there was a lot of things in Candy's past I did not want to know about. Learning about her other name was one of them.

"Joe, we don't need to—"

"When she got out of prison, she had to pick up tricks to stay afloat."

Laura cut me off. She held out her empty glass and Joe poured more beer from the pitcher into it.

"She was at some dive in the Village. A song came on the box. It was not one of those syrupy love songs that she was listening to but some guy moaning into the microphone. You know that kind of song, —not really singing as much as talking—I never liked that kind of shit music. You have to be on drugs or drunk to appreciate it but at the end of the song there was this dedication by the singer—or talker—he said, 'I'd give it all up for Rachel' or some such shit like that and she bolted."

"What? Why?"

Joe was curious as were the others at the table.

"She got up and left without saying a word. I mean, one minute she was slouched in her seat with her head on the table and her hands over her head and not moving, then she sat bolt upright, looked at some photo on the back wall behind the bar, face white as snot and ran out. Bam! Gone, just like that."

Laura clapped her hands together for emphasis.

"Shit," Joe said.

He looked over at Laura then toward me. We each looked away from his gaze for different reasons. Laura was bored. She was ready to leave. I felt uncomfortable exposing Candy's secrets. It was like walking into a room while someone was undressing and trying to shake off those raucous feelings that rise to the surface provoked by a disquieting lingering image.

Laura lowered her glasses to the edge of her nose and stared over at me.

"Sarah thinks she is some kind of queen, but she's whacked out of her mind. I think the syphilis rotted part of her brain and not just her dick off. She is soused most times. She falls asleep on the kitchen floor. Shits herself. I have to drag her out on the patio to hose her off before I dare let her sleep on my couch."

"Oh, that's gross. I think we've heard enough."

Kaitlyn covered her mouth with her napkin. She was probably wondering if we spoke about her similarly when she was not present. We did, but not like she thought. It was her future that we speculated about, not her past.

"What do you think, Eve?"

Laura persisted.

"You two appear cozy."

I shrugged. I didn't want to talk about Candy.

"She's not half as pretty as she used to be. Time has not been kind to her. What did she say to you?"

Laura was probing for more gossip.

"Nothing."

That was the truth.

"She doesn't talk much about her past."

I had more of the puzzle that was Candy or Rachel or whatever her name was and some of the things Laura mentioned seemed to fit but still there was some lingering doubt. I didn't want to violate her trust. I owed her, if not loyalty, at least silence on matters of confidence.

"She says she is an actor or something like that and lives near the Village."

Laura grinned and sat back content with himself.

"The old Kansas City Grill and the Factory are old hang outs of Andy Warhol. It's near the Village."

Laura was smug.

"What happened to her—is Rachel still with her famous boyfriend? That would be worth some coin."

"I don't know, Laura. She says her name is Candy and that's who she is until she says otherwise."

"And if I said I am Mother Theresa?"

Laura folded her napkin over her head and drew it in around her face. Joe and Laura laughed. The waiter gave our table a wary look. He did not look happy. Our kind made him nervous. Laura picked up the tab and looked back over at me then Kaitlyn.

"Hey, wanna play Saigon suicide for the bill?"

Kaitlyn and I moaned our disapproval and Laura belted out another hardy laugh.

#

Chapter 28

The Call

A man usually has two reasons for doing a thing, one that sounds good and a real one. – J.P. Morgan

The telephone rang as soon as Joe and I get through our kitchen door. Joe answered, still lighthearted from the early festivities. His face was ashen before he hung up.

"Kaitlyn?" I asked. Her swollen and bruised face popped into my head, the way I had seen her several weeks ago, when we had received another late-night call.

"Sarah," Joe said. "If it ain't one of you, trannies it's another freak. I don't know why I get involved with you people. I have my own troubles." He mumbled as he headed for his bedroom without saying more.

"Joe, what happened?" I followed him into his bedroom. His head was down and Joe was leaning into his closet. He threw aside several outfits that had fallen onto the floor.

"What's wrong? Who was on the phone?"

"Nothing," he said, then sighed aloud. "I hope."

"What?"

"Laura says she is gone."

"What do you mean, she's gone."

"Sarah packed up her things walked out of their apartment and left. They had a fight. He thinks she went to the city to find what's-her-name."

"Candy? Sarah went to look for Candy? What on earth for?"

Joe didn't answer. He picked up a blouse and held it up to his chin in front of his mirror. Sarah knows Candy enough that she thinks she could find her in a city the size of New York? I made a mental note.

"Joe, you are scaring me. Why does Laura think she went to the city to look for Candy?"

"I don't know. Laura didn't say." Joe shouted.

"You're not telling me everything. What's going on? Why are you upset?"

I followed him around his bedroom.

He threw another blouse back into his closet without hanging it up. Joe turned quickly and started to say something but stopped.

"What? Joe, tell me what's wrong? Where are you going?"

"Laura found a lot of blood in the bathroom and a razor in the shower. Sarah's cutting herself again and some of her clothes were ripped to shreds on the floor of the closet."

The XX Club lost another regular. It happened all the time. I was one step closer to being that one in six who made it through the process. It was a wicked thought, but survival meant adopting an unemotional posture. Cold, hard to the core, and unforgiving.

Like that day when I left my family, I felt nothing. I was numb. This was not my life. It was someone else's. Evelyn wasn't me. She was not real. She or he, whatever a she-male is, didn't really exist. It was just a vehicle to carry my spirit to somewhere else. There was little time to grieve about someone you barely knew but I was shaking and didn't understand.

"Why?"

Joe shrugged and pushed past me towards the bathroom.

"She thinks this Rachel is some kind of hero or saint among Ts."

Joe was pulling on the sleeves of his bathrobe. It was too short to cover up his thick forearms.

"We have to find her."

"No, we don't. I have a job to go to in the morning and so do you."

I was tired. I couldn't deal with this situation or Joe. I just wanted to be alone.

"We shouldn't get involved. Remember what Jennifer

and Canon Jones said? It's not our job to save each other."

There was too much drama living with him. Joe frowned and folded his arms across his chest.

"She and Laura had a fight and Laura threw her out. Big deal. That shit happens all the time. It's none of our business. People disappear from the Club. It's a part of our world, Joe. It's a fact of life for our kind. Get over it."

"They also say it's not a place to make new best friends." Joe smiled down at me.

"For your kind maybe, but not me. Don't worry, no one expects you to help find her. You don't have to pretend to be concerned."

Joe's voice wafted around me in the dark. I tried to reconcile what he meant by "your kind". Did he mean transsexual or a femme? Those who can, blend into the world of women without being detected or did he mean something more sinister? Heartless?

I ignored the implication. I was not that selfish. Not really. He didn't understand that I had waited all my life for the change. I couldn't let anything or anyone interfere now that I was so close. The DSM-IV separated us by a number. I was a five, he was a three. The later was supposed to be more stable. Sometimes, I wondered.

He wasn't smiling when he left. Could I trust him? Would he leave me when I need him most?

# # #

Chapter 29

The Uninvited Guest

God never uses anything until he first breaks it. – Adrian Rogers

A thump at the door awakened me.

Not a knock like you would expect to hear late morning when the mailman raps twice to deliver a certified letter that requires a signature, but a single thump, like when a bird flies into a window or some dead body slumps up against it.

A blast of cold air hit me in the face and sucked my breath away as I pushed the door open. I squinted at the dark slim form shrouded in the yellow glow of the porch light. Sara was wrapped in a threadbare sweater pulled over her head. It covered most of her face. She clutched what looked like a small plastic bag, presumably a change of clothes or underwear. It'd been almost a week since she disappeared and no one had heard from her. Until now.

"Come in, honey, out of the cold."

I should have asked her, "What's happened? What's wrong?" but I already thought I knew. The image of Kaitlyn's face in the hospital was all too fresh in my mind. When she entered the kitchen, I noticed raw pink legs and ankles and it looked like her feet were wrapped in two small dead fuzzy pink rodents.

"I like your slippers."

There was a gasp that only slightly resembled someone trying to laugh. Behind her mask I imagined Sara smiling.

"Sit, please."

"Do you mind if I crash here for a while, Eve?"

Her voice sounded strained and lower than I remembered. The hair on the back of my neck rose. I noted she said, "a while", not overnight. A while could be a day or week or—whatever. It was indeterminate.

Traci's rule of three popped into my head and I saw Paul's face when he came to the house. No matter how good I looked even my thin excuse for living with a transvestite would not stretch that far if there was another one that suddenly moved in, but I couldn't turn her away. It wouldn't be right.

I reached over and pulled out a chair from the kitchen table. She slumped slowly down into it. Her face squished into a grimace and she moaned as soon as her bottom touched the hard surface. She leaned to one side.

"Of course. You are welcome here anytime. You know that. Joe and I are happy to help you—"

"Thanks."

She choked out.

"You are a good person."

I pulled an old jacket of Joe's off the rack by the door. It was a thin windbreaker that he wore while mowing the lawn. I put it over her shoulders and brushed off some dried grass.

"I'll make you some tea. You like it white or black?"

She looked up and nodded. I avoided looking directly at her. Her eyes were blackened and purple. One of them bulged out of the socket unnaturally.

"Or would you rather have cocoa?"

"Anything warm. Thanks."

She sounded breathless.

There was a bright flash as the overhead light clicked on. One of the four bulbs popped and spit above our heads as it went out.

"Oh my God, Sarah, are you alright? What happened?"

Joe rushed over and threw his arms up as if to pull her into his arms. Her hands came up against his freshly shaved bare chest defensively. Joe stepped back to assess her as he pulled his robe closed.

"Oh, my God, Sarah, your face."

He pushed the sweater from the top of her head and my eyes were immediately drawn to the angry purple bruise on the side of her right cheek and the red gash across the bridge of her broken nose. A tangle of blackened and knotted hair was matted to the side of her other cheek from dried blood. It was coming from a deep wound in her scalp.

"You belong in a hospital. I'll get my keys."

"No, Joe, I can't. Don't. No hospital. No—"

"Sarah, have you looked in a mirror?" I added.

"You need a doctor."

Joe finished for me. He sounded angry.

"Who did this?"

Sarah looked down at her lap.

"Was it Laura? That fuck. How could she hurt you like this? I'll beat that fucker senseless. It's—"

"No."

Sarah's eyes opened wide. I didn't believe her. There was something feral in her eyes and the way she stiffened when Joe repeated Laura's name.

"Who then? Who did this to you?"

Sarah was silent and Joe plopped down in a chair beside her and kept asking: "Who?"

He was shaking and not from the cold. He shuddered every time he looked at her and I recalled his reaction when he first saw Kaitlyn lying in her hospital bed, broken. Joe had a strong paternal instinct that invades some men.

I got ice out of the freezer and wrapped it into a small towel and handed it to Joe. He placed it on the open wound on the side of Sarah's head. She winced and moved away instinctively.

"You need stitches. That gash is big. It's—

"No."

There was genuine panic in her voice.

"No, please, no. I'll be okay. I've had it worse."

"It's still bleeding." Joe looked over at me.

"Don't place it directly on the wound. I read someplace if you have a nose bleed place ice on the back of the neck and it slows the flow of blood. Maybe it will work."

I pushed Joe's hand lower.

Joe put it against the back of her neck and Sarah let him.

"Here, hold this in place," he told me.

"Don't be such a wimp. Use more than two fingers. You hold that towel like it is poison. You really are a femme. It's not going to hurt you."

Joe got up and went back into his bedroom. After some rummaging through his closet Joe returned with a bottle of alcohol and a small first aid kit. He put it on the table. Several items fell out as soon as he opened it.

"Maybe this will work. I've got a couple of these butterfly stitches."

He finds a metal pin and holds it up for her to see.

"It's going to hurt. I don't have any anesthetic."

Sarah nodded her approval. I put the towel with the melting ice on the table beside the kit and moved away while Joe wiped the dried blood and hair away from the wound.

It was the early 90s and AIDs was the new plague sweeping the civilized world. My brother Rick said the government should round everyone known to have the disease up and quarantine them, like a type of concentration camp, and don't let them leave until they all died off. It was the only way we could eradicate the gay disease.

"But some are women and children and other men who aren't gay who caught the disease in other ways, through transfusion," I argued.

"A consequence of war," he said. He was a Captain in the Special Forces and wore a Green Beret. I wanted to ask him: *what if it was someone you loved?* But I could see in his eyes, it did not matter.

I wanted to run my hands under the hot water and scrub them with a bar of soap until they turned bright red. Especially since it was Sarah. They said she came from the streets of the City before Laura took her in and even spent time in prison somewhere in upstate New York. It was a hotbed of AIDS. Joe gave me a sour look as I backed away.

"I have to get some rest or I won't be worth a damn

tomorrow. I mean today."

My excuse sounded lame under the circumstances. I avoided looking at Joe and hurried away.

I scooted into my bedroom and jumped into bed. I didn't see the irony in leaving a homophobic man to tend Sarah's wounds while I worried about catching some gay disease and how long Sarah would stay afterwards. I feared what Paul would say when they met. I rehearsed the excuse I would tell him if he saw Sara—As long as I didn't try to lie too much, I remained credible in his eyes.

"But Paul, how can I say no?"

I whispered aloud to myself.

"If we didn't take him in, what would happen?"

I pictured myself placing my hand over my breast and feigning sympathy like I had seen my mother do countless times. I always ran things through my head first, measuring one scenario against the other. It was the standard I lived by, what kept me alive.

I always prepared for the worst. I had to be ready in case Paul came to the apartment early for one of our dates. It worried me that Paul might think I lied to him, that I may be one of the shadow people once he saw me living under the same roof with another one, that is if Sarah survived the night. People have died from concussions. I recalled Julie telling a story about one of her mentor's wives who was out riding her bicycle when she fell off, hit her head on the concrete and died from head trauma three days later in the hospital. I mean, it was possible.

#

Chapter 30

The Awakening

Sometimes good things fall apart so better things can fall together. – Marilyn Monroe

I peeked in the living room before rushing off for work. Sarah was curled up in a ball under one of Joe's blankets on the couch. At least I think it was Sarah. She appeared to be breathing but she was much longer than I thought. Her legs dangled over the arm and her form seemed fuller. It occurred to me as I closed the door that it may have been Joe stretched out in the living room. It wouldn't surprise me. Joe was the kind of person who would give up his bed to a sick friend. He was the mother hen, always trying to take care of somebody.

The moment I moved in, Joe became my tutor and protector. He encouraged me when I stuttered and stammered at drive-thru windows and at store counters trying out my new voice. He bought me ice cream after someone laughed at me. He greeted me on the porch on those hot summer days with a bottle of chilled wine. It became our habit to sit outside drinking wine and sharing our day. He showed me all the best places to buy makeup and to get my hair and nails done.

We used to parade around our living room wearing some new fashion that he designed for me out of the tons of clothes in his closet. We would sing and dance to the sounds of Cindy Lauper or Madonna and singing songs like "Girls Just Want to Have Fun" or "Like a Virgin."

"Let's go out," he would say after he made up my face.

'Now?'

I would stammer trying to think up some excuse, but Joe insisted I try.

"No one knows you. Take a deep breath, let it half out, and breathe—"

"But I—"

"You look amazing. They are only looking at you because you are the most attractive woman in the room. Let them bitches be jealous. Shake that ass and shake it like you own the ground you walk on."

Joe was relentless.

After I gained confidence in myself, I began making changes in my appearance that irked him. I didn't think sexy was my look. I dressed more as a mature woman. Someone like she was coming back into the workplace years after raising her three children.

"It's too matronly for you. You're still young. It doesn't become you," he'd say, but I got the temp job at Dunhill and after I started working, we saw less of each other. I began to think of him, not as my mentor, but as a nuisance.

We stopped going out for ice cream to Pirelli's on those hot summer nights dressed in colorful sun dresses and flip flops that he'd pick up from Filene's Basement after work. Our shopping trips to the city and hair appointments at Vitelli's became rare and not merely because of me. People were rude to him.

One manager of a bar refused to let him use the Ladies' bathroom. He showed her his letter, the one that said he was transitioning to another gender under the care of a licensed physician. It irked him more that after she told him no, she let me use it.

My appearance was softening, becoming more feminine. I was twenty years younger. Joe had been too long under the bombardment of male hormones. When he grabbed my arm in public it made me nervous. I feared someone might think we were together or worse, that I was the same kind of freak or pervert as he. His attitude changed. He began criticizing my appearance instead of building me up and questioning my taste in wearing a particular outfit and asking me why I came home late from work. He sounded like the jealous husband or lover.

At some point I forgot what it was like not to pass every

day. I was beginning to get absorbed into my new gender role. Emotions were hard to control. They pushed themselves up to the surface when I least suspected it.

When we watched some show on TV or I read a novel and the protagonist died or simply seeing a child run into the arms of his father, I broke down. The hormones made me timid. It was subtle at first.

When I caught people staring at me, I used to think it was because of Joe but when they continued to stare, especially men and I was alone, I realized it had to be something else. The smiles of women became less acidic and more genuine, particularly when passing in bathrooms. They saw me differently, like we belonged to the same exclusive society.

Men came up to me on the street or in stores and began to flirt. Once while shopping at Walmart one of the managers asked me out. Another time some handsome young man, a little older than my daughter, Jen Rose, followed me around the store until I confronted him. He stuttered some lame excuse like I reminded him of someone he knew then blurted out that he was afraid he would never see me again. He gave me his business card and asked for my number. I ran away from him.

When I told Joe what happened, he laughed and took me by the hand and walked me back into the store. He hid behind a wall of detergent while the man fumbled for a pen. I had one of the new flip-type cellular phones by Motorola, but I gave him Joe's number at the apartment instead and we had a good laugh. We stopped by TCBY on the way home and each broke our diets with a frozen strawberry yogurt. It was a celebration. I had graduated.

I think we would have gotten closer as roomies had it not been for my insecurity and later my choices in friends. First it was Traci with her implacable rules and then hard Candy came along. Each taught me more than how to dress but how to act and how to use my new gender role as a weapon. I learned from each of them how to manipulate men who found me attractive. They warned me to keep away from people like Joe or he would give me away.

I wasn't convinced it was completely necessary to avoid the shadow people.

My experience with Paul and others caused me to think differently. There had been too many times while standing in line beside Joe or Sarah or Laura in some ladies' room and when each went into a stall some women would smile over at me and nod with empathy. Some would whisper: "You are a dear. You are a saint. Your husband is brave" and another felt sorry for me. One waited until Joe went into a stall to tell me that I was the most open-minded and kind woman in the entire world to show him the ropes.

They began to see me as one of them and not like him and that secretly thrilled me. It meant I was blending in and becoming the ordinary woman I always wanted to be.

#

Chapter 31

The Tenant

I'm bored with knitting. I've taken up arson. – Audrey Niffenegger

A tenement had sprung up in the living room virtually overnight. One corner of the room looked like tent city with a blanket that ran from the banister of the staircase leading to the upstairs apartment down to the floor in front of the closet door. Sarah's clothes and some other stuff was rolled up in another old blanket and tossed behind the sofa during the day. I realized as I was leaving for a job one morning that it had been a month and she was still there, sitting quietly in a chair by the window staring out at me as I passed by. She smiled. I waved. It took me by surprise. It shocked me that I had not spoken or noticed her in all that time and Joe had not spoken to me about it, albeit we hadn't really spoken much about anything. We had become roommates in name only.

I hadn't sat in the living room watching television with Joe in quite some time. My life had shifted direction. I decided to try a little harder at being more human. More like the woman I wanted to become when I set out on this journey in the first place. I would talk to them when I returned. Maybe skip class or at least the night out with the girls and come home to have that glass of beer in that plastic flute on our back porch and share stories about our day.

It was dark when I arrived, and I could hear their voices murmuring like two bees buzzing over a garbage can.

When Sarah was a little boy, her mother moved into a double-wide with a pedophile who had an intemperate disposition. He used to sneak into Sarah's room whenever his mother passed out for the night and do "bad" things to her, she had said. Sarah's mother was an addict and her new boyfriend supplied her with crack and stayed at their trailer in a small park on the outskirts of Binghamton, whenever he was out of prison. He had served time somewhere in upstate New York for a botched robbery where the clerk of the convenience store that he and two other men had attempted to rob was killed.

Ironically, it was the same prison Sarah would eventually go to several years later, for setting the man on fire. She had found him on her mother's couch passed out and couldn't resist the temptation. She broke open a lighter she found on the kitchen counter and poured it over his beard. She woke him before lighting the match. He was too drunk or stoned to realize what was happening until after his face was on fire. "He had it coming. He hurt me. Bad," she had said. Her male genitals had to be removed because the syphilis had gone unchecked for too long before her mother took her to see a doctor. Joe poured a little more wine into her plastic flute. His hand was shaking.

Thereafter, Sarah had a problem. She hated homeless men. She and several other boys relocated to the City where they made their way on the streets. Deep into the bowls of the city she and her friends would find some poor sot in an alley and douse him with gasoline while another lit him on fire.

"I burnt my hands trying to put him out. Never meant to kill 'em only make them pay for their crimes."

"Good, God!"

Joe stood and brushed off his leg.

"Spider. Damn!"

We both looked at him. Joe had a case of the creeps.

"If it wasn't for Rachel, I never would have survived another stint in the pen."

Sarah continued. She took a long swallow and blinked up at me.

"She found me hiding on the stoop by the back door to her apartment building and invited me in. My friends were all caught. I know they would have given me up for a deal. Not sure whatever happened to them, but Rachel kept me there in her flat for two weeks before helping me find work at a bar down the street. Some dive named Brick's Parlor. I swept floors at first then they taught me to tend bar. It catered to the gay crowd. Some dudes that came in had money. I pulled my share of tricks before getting out. Didn't want no clap again."

"So, Evelyn, how was your day?"

Gay talk made Joe a little nervous. He was visibly shaken. He must have seen me standing on the bottom step in the dark.

"Not as interesting as yours, I'm sure."

I stepped up into the light. Joe's expression was unsettled. He looked alarmed by her admission to arson and murder. Shy quiet little Sarah who seldom talked or even made eye contact with anyone at meetings. Who would have guessed?

"You think that Candy is the same person as your Rachel?"

I asked the question that had been plaguing most of us since the first day we met the mysterious woman from the city.

Sarah laughed.

"I don't have to guess. I know."

"What makes you so sure?" Joe asked.

"Joe, she just said she knows her."

I chided him. Joe was a skeptic. I don't care.

"It's okay if you don't believe me. Rachel doesn't want anyone to know who she is."

"Why?"

I was genuinely curious but not because of idol worship. I wanted to know her connection to all of this gossip.

"For the same reason you don't tell us who you were." Sarah stared into her flute.

"But I am not famous. Never was. I am just an ordinary person trying to start a new life. I value my privacy."

Sarah looked up at me from her lap and smiled. I answered my own question.

"But if she had all that fame, why not cash in on it. Use it to her advantage."

Joe was aroused by the change in topic.

"If she knew Andy Warhol, met a bunch of celebrities and had this relationship with a Rockstar, why not? I mean she would be well off by now. Why not bypass the XX club and gender clinic and go punch her own ticket? What is she waiting for?"

Sarah grew quiet. Night enveloped us on the back porch. The air was damp and chilled from an earlier rain. She moved the blanket Joe had given her up over her shoulders.

"Sarah, you don't have to tell us if you don't want to. I understand."

Confidence and loyalty have always been sacred to me. I have kept my own share of secrets of friends and family and even acquaintances, strangers who felt safe enough around me to entrust their secrets.

"Rachel never really said much. She was quiet like me. Kept pretty much to herself. I learn stuff by being still. Her friends talk about her. Everyone was afraid to speak about certain things around her."

Joe sat back down in the wobbly chair next to her. Somewhere nearby a hoot owl began his prayer to find a mate. My feet hurt. The heels I wore to work dug into my swollen feet. I should have gone inside to take them off, but I didn't want to while Sarah was talking.

"They were happy for a while. Then they would fight like a married couple, but they were still happy. She'd go off and be quiet after he'd smack her around and then he'd go mad trying to find where she'd run off to. Those magazine people didn't like her much, too, I guess. There were articles calling Rachel a fagot or homo. He didn't like that. I think he thought of her as a woman until they said she ain't."

She paused as if pondering, not so much what to say but whether to say it. She glanced in Joe's direction.

Joe balked and stood suddenly and exclaimed: "I have to hit the little girls' room."

The gay talk was getting to him. When he had gone, I turned to Sarah.

"So, Candy came to our club—" I hesitated, "to see if she can get an operation. She wants to change?"

I was thinking aloud to myself more than asking her.

"Don't know. Maybe. She—"

"Why not go to some place in the city? Its bigger than here. I'm sure she could get help there."

"Don't know. A lot of doctors do nose jobs and silicon injections but not the full operation anymore. Not sure it's on the up and up. Nothing like what you have up here in Hartford. A clinic and all."

"Oh," I said and started towards the kitchen door to our apartment.

It was late. I was still in my dress and heels. I was suddenly aware how much they pinched my swollen feet.

"Coming in?"

I asked her to be polite.

"No, I think I will sit here a while and finish my wine. Thanks."

Sarah put the flute to her lips. I passed Joe going back out as I went into our apartment.

"Don't forget to be here early tomorrow," he reminded me.

"What for?" I asked.

"Committee meeting. I got Big Kathy, her roommate, and Kaitlyn coming over after work and Sarah of course will be here."

"What?" I didn't hide my surprise.

"You said we could help, so we organized a decorating committee to set up the festivities for the dance party."

"Dance party? Joe, what are you saying?"

Jennifer only said it was a coming out party. She never said anything about a band, D.J. or a bunch of faerie queens dancing in public at a crowded hotel that caters to a secret organization that practices S & M and who knows what else.

"Evelyn you are so naive. Jennifer asked some members of the Tiffany Club to come assist us. They have many members. Hard to say how many will be there but it's a party. Music and everything. Isn't it great?"

I knew the Tiffany Club. Its members were a fun-loving group of men who liked to explore their feminine side. When I decided to search for some help with my dilemma, I found an ad for a transvestite group that met at a private home near Walden Pond. I drove three hours after work one evening to attend one of their gatherings. I found a bunch of men in high-heels and dresses made up to look like women. They sat around a tiny living room, drinking beer and watching a ball game on a 19-inch television. I arrived in my jeans and sweat shirt and socialized in the kitchen with their wives until it was time to leave.

"I don't like it, Joe. It doesn't feel right."

"Oh, don't be a spoil-sport. You've never done it so how would you know?"

People laughed and rolled their eyes when they thought he wasn't looking. It was an embarrassment just being around him in public. The Tiffany Club membership was made up of people like Joe, transvestites of varying ages and similar tastes, who have had plenty of practice dressing up as women for kicks over many years. Most of our members had very little experience presenting their feminine side. Most transsexuals had spent the whole of their existence up to that point trying to hide it.

"Who else will be celebrating in that hotel on the same evening?"

"Who cares. We are having a party. Lighten up."

I started for the door.

"What if it's a policeman's ball, or the fraternal order of Elks or some such male group?"

"You worry, too much."

Joe got up and followed me inside. He was not through arguing his point.

"You know, Joe, this party thing is not going to end well." I insisted.

"Why do you say that?" he snapped.

"I mean, they shouldn't do it in a public place. If they want to have a private one at the church then—"

"It's not for you to decide that, Evelyn." He was angry. "We all voted on it and you will just have to live with that."

Perhaps picking a time when he was more rested might have been more prudent. Joe really wanted this party, as did several other members who I suspected were more crossdresser types than transsexuals.

"Isn't Kaitlyn an example—" It slipped out before I could shut my mouth.

"Fuck you. Not everyone can be a size 8 or 10 or whatever the fuck you are and wear pretty clothes. You and that little fairy, Traci, go out to clubs and can party any damn time you want. You even have a boyfriend, who may or may not know how unique you are, but the rest of us are doomed to spend the rest of our lives in a closet. So, we're having a party. Deal with it."

I shook my head vigorously from side to side and kicked off my shoes in the direction of my bedroom door. I wished it was over. I couldn't wait for my operation to be completed and I could leave. Disappear like Traci and go into stealth and forget I ever met him and all the clowns at the XX club and that's when I felt a sudden chill in the middle of my rant and turned around.

Sarah was staring at me. Her eyes affixed on mine as soon as I lifted my head. Something I said had angered her. She looked like she was about to light a match.

#

Chapter 32

Ruminations

It pays to be obvious, especially if you have a reputation for subtlety. – Isaac Asimov

An early morning mist clung to my clothes and caressed my face as I stepped out onto the front porch and loped across the street. I left quietly so as not to wake Joe and certainly not Sarah. I did not dare look up at the window as I walked toward the truck parked down the street. Paul was waiting with his daughter. He came early and parked in the street as I instructed.

"Evie, you need to roll your window all the way up, Alison has a cold and I don't want her to catch a draft."

"Oh, sorry," I said and followed his instruction. Alison stared up at me and smiled. She looked cute in pig tails.

"What's gotten into you lately? It's as if you are someplace else these days. Am I boring you?"

"Oh, no, no. I am just worried—" One day was all that separated me from my sanity. Jennifer and Julie would be picking me up tomorrow to go to Boston. We were the committee that would meet to set a date and secure the facility for the big party—as everyone called it now. Julie had picked the Magnus or Magnum or whatever it was called. I knew it was the palace of fear and pain Traci and I had escaped from. A foreboding had crept over me as soon as she'd said it. Why on earth would she pick that one?

"Worried about what?"

"Ah, Joe, he's—" I said the first thing that came into my head. It was a bad habit. It usually got me into a different pot of hot water.

"Let's not bring up that sicko with Alison here. We'll talk about it later."

"Who, Daddy?"

"Never mind. Adult talk. Look to the front. I don't want you getting car sick. Your mother will blame me if you ruin that nice dress. Isn't it pretty Evie?"

"Oh, yes, it's very pretty."

"That—," Paul hesitated. I knew what he was going to say and so did Alison. "She always blames me for something."

Paul gave me a wary look and I was nervous. I tried to stare out the side window most of the time, but Alison pulled on my sleeve.

"You look pretty today, Evie." Alison smiled up at me.

"Mommy says you must be weird—"

"What? Why is that, sweetheart?" Paul interjected.

"Because you are the most beautiful woman Daddy has ever dated. She's thinking you might marry him, and you would have to be weird to do something weird like that. Are you going to marry my daddy?"

"What?"

There was more surprise in my voice than I could suppress. I worried it may have hurt Paul but when I looked over at him, he was grinning.

"Ah, thank you Alison. You honor me with your flattery. Tell your mommy, Daddy hasn't asked me to marry him. No worries."

Paul shot me a strange look. Alison laughed at my choice of words. It sounded too formal or archaic. I have been told by many that I was born out of my time.

"Mama says you are smart too. She doesn't know what you are doing with my daddy. She calls him a pretentiousness mother-humper."

"Your mother is jealous," Paul said and put his arm around his daughter. "And don't repeat everything she and I say to each other, okay, kiddo?"

He winked at me, then Alison vigorously shook her head up and down. Then as an afterthought Paul added: "Tell her I haven't asked her yet."

He looked straight at me when he said it. I suppressed a

shiver.

Alison giggled. I diverted my eyes to my lap and blushed. I was at a loss for words and I feared Paul liked the idea of marriage and was waiting for the right moment to ask me. My stomach was in knots by the time we got to the theater. I caught the implication of his final word: *Yet.*

Silence enveloped me. I felt detached from the moment because I was thinking about Joe and Sara and going with Jennifer tomorrow to secure the venue for the upcoming party.

The changes in my appearance had given me greater hope of attaining my dream than I had thought possible when I started transition. I was torn between wanting to help other's like me and becoming an ordinary woman. It shames me to admit it now, but I did not want to be alone in a public place with the 'Un-passables'. Not even for one night.

It rattled me how much I longed to see Candy and I could hardly wait for the next weekend, the date she and I had made for me to meet her in the city. It wasn't that I was curious if the rumors about her were true —I was, but it was more than that. From that first meeting when she walked in carrying her boots in her hand and padded across that wet floor, I think I fell in love. Not in a romantic sort of way but like a crush you get on a teacher the first day of school. You feel safe and want to be around her all the time. But on some level, I feared that I wanted to develop that forbidden intimate relationship Traci had forewarned would be dangerous.

It's hard to stop living on the edge after years of having a death wish. I became addicted to the jive. That tickle in the blood that drives men to climb obdurate mountains, leap out of perfectly good planes or drive too fast on winding, unfamiliar country roads. I wanted Candy to come to the party but knew she most likely wouldn't be there.

At least with Candy, I would feel safer in the Magnum where two creepy guys might be lying in wait to do me harm. It wasn't rational to think she would be my replacement rescuer, but nothing in transition was solid. My dream was to become an ordinary woman but the temptation to fall into the arms of a wealthy admirer taunted my baser senses. Who ever heard of a male woman? At any given moment our dream might crack under the strain of our new persona and we would be swept away on the current of reality. Exposed and vulnerable. Fear and pain kept us in check.

"Evie?"

Paul's voice was raised, and Alison looked up apprehensively. We both knew that tone in her father's voice.

"What?"

"Can you take Alison to the bathroom before the movie starts and I'll get us some popcorn and a Sprite."

Paul usually got a large soda for the three of us to share.

"Sure," I said and took her by the hand.

Paul shook his head at me as we walked away. He did not look happy. Something was troubling him, too. I was sure it concerned me.

#

Chapter 33

The Committee

Sex is emotion in motion. – Mae West

I was mesmerized by the reflection of the girl I saw staring back at me in the stainless-steel wall of the elevator on the way up to the twenty-fifth floor of the same hotel Traci and I made our escape from a few months before.

The girl was not afraid. She looked cool and professional in her plaid wool skirt, white cotton blouse and smart blue blazer. The one her mother had bought for her last Christmas.

Dark mascara and black eyeliner set off her large green eyes, the eyebrows arched. Her lips were red and perfectly lined. I was fascinated with the reflection. I was getting to be a good actress. She had that bored expression on her face that read: *I don't want to be here.*

The elevator door opened, and we stepped into a modern office beset by sterile uncomfortable-looking furniture. A pimple-faced girl with short hair told us to sit anywhere we liked.

I sat in the faux-leather chair, hands folded neatly on my lap, head up and staring straight ahead at the attractive receptionist behind the big desk.

Jennifer sat with her legs crossed at the ankle on the brown leather sofa. She was wearing her long skirt and a matching earth-toned cardigan under her long wool coat. Her gray-blond hair was tied back with a thick brown ribbon and she was wearing a light foundation on her freckled face. She looked like a relic of a lost generation.

Julie had on her trade-mark noir. A black pencil skirt and black jacket. Her shoulder length hair was tied back severely with a plain black clip tucked in a knot behind her small round head. She stood idly at the magazine rack thumbing through the latest edition of *Cosmopolitan*. Every once in a while, her voice cracked the quiet of the room with a sharp rhetorical question and sometimes she directed a question or off-handed commentary at the young girl behind the desk.

"Did you know that the most popular lip color chosen by women in the U.S. is mauve but when men are asked, they say: red?"

A door opened and another woman walked in and took a seat next to Jennifer on the sofa. She smiled at her seat mate and picked up a magazine on the table beside her. She appeared oblivious that anything was amiss. Jennifer smiled back at her and nodded.

"Hey, according to the American Medical Association one out of six family members in the United States is gay? Did you know that?" Julie blurted out.

"No, I didn't know that," the young receptionist answered nervously. She did not look up from her typewriter. The incessant tapping slowed down for a moment.

"Do you know how much longer it will be before Mr. Kendrick will see us? We had an appointment at 1PM and it's nearly 2:30 now. I have to be back to New Haven by 5pm to start my shift. I intern at a hospital. I am studying to be a nurse—"

Julie's voice was flat, but I could tell she was nervous. She bit her lower lip after she spoke.

"He's aware you are here. He's in a telephone conference with corporate. It shouldn't be much longer."

The girl looked up and stopped typing. She reached for her liquid paper and tossed a sharp look in Julie's direction. She kept her voice pleasant.

As if on cue, the outer door opened and a tall distinguished gentleman in a gray pin-striped suit stepped out to wave us in. There was an eerie familiarity to his face. I retraced my memory to a time when Bernard was talking with a tall older man with silver hair in the hallway before coming back with that duffel bag full of toys. It could be him, but I was uncertain.

Jennifer and Julie exchanged pleasantries and sat down in the two chairs in front of the desk and I stood to the left of Jennifer where I could stare out a large window onto the spires and flat rooftops of the smaller buildings below. In the distance was Boston Harbor. Several large gray waves crested in the distance. I was easily distracted and staring off at some place I would rather be than where I would not.

"Here, miss, let me get you a chair."

Mr. Kendrick looked up and hesitated as if noticing me for the first time. His expression was a mix of bewilderment and formality as though momentarily distracted by a wayward thought.

The heat rushed to my cheeks.

"Oh, please don't bother. I can stand."

Kendrick's features were handsome and youthful for an older man. I guessed he was somewhere in his early sixties. His eyebrows and temples were light brown and trimmed. His long slender fingers moved gracefully over his chin.

"Oh, it's no trouble at all."

His brown eyes had flecks of a lighter color in them when they caught the light. I think they were almond-shaped. My favorite nut. His secretary came in pushing a chair in front of her.

"Ah, here we are. Thank you, Maddie."

He took it from her and pushed it on the end of his desk nearest him so I could be part of the conversation I presumed. He held the chair until I was settled and pushed it a little further like he was the Maître's. He sat down behind and folded his hands behind his head. He looked over at Jen and Julie.

Jennifer introduced herself as the president and Julie, vice president of the XX Club and she reminded him of their earlier conversation on the telephone.

"We would like to set a date for our party—if you agree of course."

"And you are?"

He looked over at me expectantly, catching me off guard. My face grew warm.

"She's the secretary of our club." Julie said.

Mr. Kendrick ignored her and continued to stare at me waiting for an answer.

"Um, Evelyn."

My voice embarrassed me. It scratched out breathless sounds that came out too lethargic and so deep in my throat they should have been carried into the room on a gurney.

His smile broadened. He tilted his head to one side, but he continued to wait as though I hadn't finished. He had an odd look in his eye. He was studying me. It made me more nervous.

"Stone. Evelyn Stone."

I didn't often get a chance to use a last name.

"Ms. Stone, I am so glad you came along. Can I get you a drink, a cola, coffee, water perhaps?

"No thank you."

He looked over at the others. Jennifer and Julie nodded in the negative.

"So, am I to understand that you are assisting these people—"

"She's one of us."

Julie's voice was brittle. Heat rushed into my face. I looked down at my lap. I'd been slapped.

"She's the secretary of our club."

"One of—?"

His brow pinched together. The wheels were turning rapidly in his brain. He sat back in his chair and shook his head slightly from side to side. It was more an involuntary gesture from the puzzled look on his face. I felt a wave of nausea wash over me. I'd been judged.

"Our club secretary."

Julie filled in.

"We are the transsexual support group that called you earlier. We have to live a year in our chosen gender and the party will be the first time some of our members venture out in their new identity and—"

"He doesn't need a lecture, Jennifer."

Julie snapped.

"It's a party. We want to come here and not have any trouble. We need to make sure we don't break any laws or rules but since we are dressed as women, we need to use the rest room obviously and—"

"Ah, you are one of them? Um—"

I nodded in the affirmative. His pupils widened.

"Oh, are you typical of your membership?"

"I-I guess."

I looked over at Jennifer for help.

"No," Julie snapped.

"There are no typical transsexuals any more than typical people in the general population. It depends on what you mean by typical." Jennifer attempted to explain.

Julie shot a nasty look at her.

"Some are new at it and will not look nearly as passable," Jennifer continued.

"What does that matter? We simply want to host a party here in your fine hotel. Can you do it or not."

"Julie, please. Let me handle this."

Jennifer's voice was firm.

Julie gave her another angry stare.

"We—" I began.

"Relax ladies."

He emphasized the last word as though driving home some point. Reminding himself we really weren't.

"We have hosted crossdresser groups here in our facilities before. We will reassign one bathroom on the next floor for your members to use to be more comfortable and give you 20% off our menu items and a flat rate of $120 per room if any of your members wish to continue to be our guest after your party."

Mr. Kendrick's irritation left his cheeks a bright pink or

maybe it was from something else. He no longer looked at me in that penetrating way men look at women sometimes when they are attracted. His attention was centered on the other two. I should have felt relief, but it bothered me more to be ignored so plaintively after having held his favorable attention moments ago.

"Of course, we will have to put on some additional security for your safety, so a $2,200 deposit would be appropriate for the room and—"

"That's a bit steep. You are trying to price us out," Julie snapped. Jennifer grabbed Julie's wrist.

"Don't touch—" Julie clenched her teeth.

"Mr. Kendrick, we are not wealthy. Unlike a crossdresser club, who are made up of men who lead dual lives, most of our members lose their jobs when they start transition and barely have enough—" Jennifer halted when she realized the futility of her argument. Trying to reserve an accommodation for a party in a luxury hotel for an impoverished class of individuals was a losing argument. So, I had said several times in our discussions, but neither she nor Julie listened. Her eyes dropped to her lap when he glanced at his watch.

The meeting was over. I detected a smile creeping over his face. When Kendrick sat back in his chair and folded his hands in his lap I spoke up.

"Is that the standard rate?" I asked.

He glanced at me.

"I believe it's fair under the circumstances."

"What circumstances is that?" Julie asked.

Jennifer pulled on her sleeve.

"Stop it." Julie snapped at her.

"Let, Evelyn talk."

Jennifer's voice was barely audible, but I took my cue.

"Mr. Kendrick. What my associates are trying to say is that our group represents one of the poorer segments of our society. Transvestites are generally heterosexual males with a fetish and maintain productive lives hiding their, um, unusual hobby if you will. They have jobs and lead seemingly normal lives, but our people are thrust into a situation where they are forced to alter their lifestyles. Most don't know how to wear makeup or dress appropriately. People may think there is something wrong with them or they are mentally unstable—"

"Shouldn't you be saying we—"

"Julie, please," Jennifer begged her partner to be silent.

"Mr. Kendrick, you are a businessman but also appear to be a humanitarian. I notice the plagues you have on the walls of your office and photographs with city officials and celebrities at various charitable functions."

One of the smiling men looked familiar. It caught me off guard and I hesitated.

"These are also held here in your fine hotel. You have even hosted, as you say, a transvestite group."

He began to gather paperwork on his desk.

"Can't you write off some of the expense on your taxes?" Jennifer added.

"Isn't your organization a legitimate 501(c)?"

Julie interjected and Kendrick reacted as if he'd been stabbed with a pen.

"Naturally, it's legitimate and no, it's not a non-profit organization. What are you suggesting?"

The look in his eyes told me that the party would likely be in the basement of the church again this year. Jennifer and Julie shifted in their chairs uncomfortably. I cleared my throat, gathering his full attention.

"What my colleagues are suggesting, Mr. Kendrick, is that you have a business to run. Anything that assists your bottom line can only enhance your responsibility to your owners or shareholders to manage it profitably. The clinic of which our club is a part is a charitable organization that provides documentation of any contribution including discounted services."

Mr. Kendrick leaned forward on his desk.

"These people—I mean we."

Julie shot me a cold hard look.

"We are different. Other people react in ways that sometimes may lead to violence. Security is important. We understand that better than most. No one wants to get hurt."

My throat was dry.

"If necessary, I can write a check out to you from my personal account, but it seems unreasonable to me to pay $2,200 as a security deposit for maybe 20 people and their spouses—"

"Is that all you have in your organization?"

Hendricks stopped me. His eyes lifted from mine to dart at paperwork on his desk as though looking for something.

"Well, the Tiffany Club will have more but, yes, around 26, but I think only about half will actually come and if they do, they may bring a guest and it shouldn't be over that number by much,"

Jennifer spoke up.

Kendrick picked up a paper that I assumed was our application and sat back in his chair studying it. His smirk became a smile as he looked over at me.

"Well, in that case, it is unreasonable."

He waited for my reaction then turned to look at Jennifer.

"So, you would only need one of the smaller conference rooms. Would $200 be more like it?"

Jennifer glanced in my direction and nodded.

"Thank you, Mr. Kendrick," I said, and Jennifer pulled out the clubs check book as Kendrick's hand extended across the desk towards hers. He gave it a quick shake then reached towards Julie.

"Are you married?"

Kendrick grabbed my hand. His palm felt warm and moist or maybe it was mine. I sensed a change in Kendrick's mood. He appeared genuinely curious about me, perhaps even interested—I shook off the thought.

Why would he ask me that question?

I wondered if he was aware of what went on after hours

in some of his rooms and what kind of people passed through the doors of his office representing organizations with a sinister purpose.

I shuddered. The hair on the back of my neck stood on end. Perhaps he was one of them. A club that catered to perverts that loved BDSM.

I saw an omen, and oddity, a shadow on a wall, a crow passing by the window, a leaf falling to the ground, something out of place that piqued my curiosity, and suddenly I am thinking about the macabre. I worried that I might run into an angry man with a tattoo around his finger—out for a little revenge, and this time Traci wouldn't be there to save me. The memory of our last tryst haunted me.

I looked down on his hand on mine.

That's when I noticed it. A little black mark around the ring finger caught my attention. I was unable to see it clearly before he pulled his hand away. It stirred a memory of the last time I was in a luxury hotel. Bernard had a similar tattoo and so did his friend Conrad.

#

Chapter 34

The Counselor

Credibility is a thin-shelled egg. – Anonymous

"I don't want to go."

Debbie stopped short of the door to the small office of the social worker and counselor that she had driven three hours to see. Canon Jones had indicated it was a mandatory meeting.

Our divorce wasn't final. I needed a social worker to sign off on my spouse's mental health before I receive my SRS letter.

Debbie pulled her hand from mine and looked down at her feet.

"You have to," I said.

Debbie stiffened.

"We are getting a divorce anyway, so why bother seeing a shrink?"

The D word caught in her throat. Her parents divorced when she was five. She swore that would not be her fate.

"We have to for your sake and for our children."

Before the operation, our divorce would be final. She was worried the counselor might ask her questions that may pique painful memories.

"It's for the continuation of my hormones. It has nothing to do with you personally."

"Then why am I here?"

"I told you. It's just a formality. They don't want you suing them if I am not able to perform my husbandly duties in the bedroom. They have to be assured that you won't contest my decision to undergo this—this change."

I didn't know how to describe it to her exactly.

"They want to be sure you are going to be okay—"

"I'm not."

Her eyes met mine momentarily then dropped back to

the floor.

Would you rather I be dead?

I wanted to say but thought it better not to. In many ways it was like a death to her. At the end of my transition, her husband would no longer exist.

"Deb, we spoke about this. You are not a lesbian. Look at me."

I waited until her eyes met mine.

"You can't stay with me after—It wouldn't be fair to you. You deserve to be with a real man. I can't take care of you and the kids when I don't even know what's going to happen to me or what I will be like. They aren't going to ask you anything personal."

I lied. I was not certain what they would ask, but the session was definitely about her. The clinic was concerned with liability.

What happened when the wife of one of their candidates for sexual reassignment surgery got angry and blamed them for taking her husband away and making him a eunuch? The heavy doses of hormone pills made males impotent over time not to mention sterile.

Debbie looked up. Her forehead pinched together in the middle as though struggling with some exam question. Her lips moved but no words came out.

"Please, Deb, it's a requirement, that's all. They meet you. Ask you how you are coping. What you plan to do after and— Either that or I'm all done." She knew what I meant by done. She had watched me put my 9mm away on more than one occasion. She knew that I would not ask for her help again.

"Okay, but I'm not saying anything. I want nothing to do with any of this."

The counselor's office was barely large enough to accommodate a table, a desk and three folding chairs. The woman behind the desk was startled when we entered. She stood awkwardly behind her desk and offered her hand.

She was in her late twenties, likely a graduate student

still in college and probably one of Doctor Higgin's pet assistants working under him to obtain her degree. After some small talk about the weather, traffic, and how we managed on the drive down, she introduced herself and sat back down. She looked down and began asking questions.

Was she really reading from a paper on her desk?

"So, are you planning to divorce or stay together?" she spoke directly to Debbie. Debbie's face collapsed at the question. She began to rock in her chair and stared out the window behind me.

"Divorce of course. I thought it was a requirement? But even if it wasn't, Deb is not a lesbian. We are in the process of divorce," I explained.

"Well, that simplifies things."

A small smile spread across her thin lips. At least I thought it was a smile. The girl looked down at some papers on her desk.

"Tell me a little about yourself, Mrs. Barcomb. How do you feel about your husband changing his sex?"

The question hung above us like some airy thing floating on the vapor that lifts from the moist earth after a hard rain on a hot summer morning.

"Whatever he wants. I just want him to be happy."

Debbie scratched the back of her hand. She didn't look up.

"Um, what about you. What do you plan to do?"

"I will get along, I guess, like anybody would when—their husband leaves—" Debbie rocked in her chair.

"Is this necessary?" I asked. "We are getting a divorce. The clinic won't have anything to worry about."

"We just want to be sure your wife is going to be okay. You have a weight lifted from you. No more inner turmoil. You feel elated because something is being done to alleviate the pain in your life but once a transsexual makes a decision to change their sex it leaves a void for those who love him. It's like a death. She needs to—"

"This isn't about me."

Debbie spoke up. Her voice strained to remain calm.

"I don't need your help."

"Mrs. Barcomb, the world as you know it has suddenly changed. It would be irresponsible of us to just sit back and pretend spouses and families—are unaffected. You will have to move on with your own life once he is gone. Your husband is being replaced with what will seem like a new person."

There was an uncomfortable silence where none of us looked at each other. Debbie sat back in her chair clutching her purse in her lap. She had already noted the change in my appearance. I no longer resembled the man she had married.

"Did you experience any sexual trauma as a child."

The question hung in the air. It materialized like some aberration in a serial horror movie. The counselor turned in my direction. I guessed the question was directed at me, but the counselor watched Debbie's reaction out of the corner of her eye. I nodded in the affirmative. I knew it was in the file on her desk. The counselor asked about my sexual trauma to garner Debbie's reaction.

"I've already said everything I'm going to say about it to the clinic psychiatrist."

I didn't think I ever told Debbie.

The counselor gave me an exasperated look. She made a notation in the file. Debbie stared down into her lap. She had stopped rocking in her chair, but her eyes moved side to side. She was looking for a quick way out.

"Our house is under contract. It is no ordinary home. Debbie will have plenty of money to survive for a couple of years if necessary and is planning to move in with my parents in Florida with our fifteen-year-old daughter in order to get a fresh start. Our middle daughter, Jackie, is going to FIT after graduation in a few months to become an aeronautical engineer in Melbourne, Florida. Our oldest daughter, Jen Rose, is at USMA at West Point."

"What are you planning to do?" she asked Debbie.

Frustration spattered across her face as though a balloon exploded.

"Get a job, I guess."

"What did you do prior to getting married?"

"I worked for Sprague Electric in a capacitor plant. I soldered electronic parts on an assembly line."

Outside of waitressing, there wasn't much opportunity for a girl without an education in Barre.

Debbie moved her sleeves up to show the small round white scars that peppered her forearms. I remembered each dot when she'd come home from work and showed them to me.

As soon as she walked into the kitchen, I saw the pain in her eyes and pulled her into me. I lifted her arms one at a time and I'd kiss the red welts as though it would somehow make the hurt go away. I'd carry her into the bedroom where I would place her gently down onto our bed. My lips moving over her arms and body like a feather. I peeled off her clothes then mine and we'd make love and lay there under the covers holding onto each other for hours sometimes until dark.

"Ouch, that looks like it smarted."

The counselor feigned concern. She was terrible at her job. She couldn't even fake empathy.

"Yes, but you get used to it and soon you know to wear long sleeves to work every day even in the summer months."

"Have you thought about getting remarried?"

"No," Debbie snapped. "I'll never get married again."

"Why not?"

Debbie stared into space. Her parents divorced when she was five. Her mother struggled to feed three kids and was pregnant, when she met Stanley Loving, an over-the-road truck driver.

When she was thirteen, her mother died of brain cancer. Debbie tended to her six- year-old brother, Gary, and her half-sister, Elaine, and new baby brother, Mark, who was still in diapers. Her stepfather was ill-equipped to handle anything without eighteen wheels. He expected Debbie to replace his wife. She had to change diapers as soon as she came home from school and get the kids bathed and off to bed before doing her homework. She dodged the misplaced affection of a lonely trucker whenever Stanley came home until an aunt finally stepped up to take her in.

"You are supposed to only get married once. I thought we would grow old together. I didn't know it would end—" her voice trailed off.

"It's okay," the counselor reached out and tried to touch Debbie's arm, but she pulled away.

"I thought we would grow old together," Debbie repeated and looked at me then covered up her eyes with the palms of her hands.

"It's okay, dear," the counselor stood up and reached out across her desk again.

Debbie stiffened. The counselor sat back down and turned a page in her notebook as though instructions on how to handle this situation were written in there.

"Have you enjoyed a good sex life? I mean do you enjoy sex, Mrs. Barcomb?"

Debbie looked at the counselor then at me.

"She has orgasms. I usually satisfy her before moving on to my own needs. If that's what you are looking for."

"I need for her to answer the questions to finish my assessment."

The counselor raised her hand in my direction. She looked at Debbie.

"Mrs. Barcomb, did you ever have a bad experience not necessarily with your husband but with someone else? Perhaps when you were a child?"

Debbie bit her lip until it bled.

The counselor didn't notice. She was looking down into her file. Perhaps studying some notes written by Doctor Higgins from my first visit. In my only session with the good doctor I mentioned there had been some incident with her stepfather, but Debbie would never tell me what happened.

Debbie got up from her chair and started for the door.

"I told you I'm not talking about me."

"Okay, calm down, we can move on—"

The counselor stood and held up her hand.

"We will talk about something else if you like?"

"No, I think we're done here. We are divorcing prior to the operation. That's all you really need to know." I was firm.

The divorce lawyer was an old school mate of mine. We were on the swim team together when we were thirteen.

"The lawyer says it will be finalized in July."

"I will pass that on to Dr. Higgins."

The counselor's face was red.

"Good," I said with a tone of finality.

I noted her leg was shaking under the desk when we left. I had a tentative date with Dr. Schrang in Neenah, Wisconsin for my operation, August 9th. The day before Deb and my anniversary. We would have been married twenty years.

We went for lunch to a Chinese restaurant and talked without staring at each other, mostly about the weather, April's new boyfriend, Jackie's upcoming graduation and about Parent's Day on the island in the Hudson River near West Point.

It's often not what is said between old lover's but what is left unsaid that haunts you in those empty days that follow a separation.

I wanted to reach out and put my arms around her like I did when we were young, kiss away the pain and tell her that everything would be alright again, but I knew it wouldn't. I no longer wished to lie to her, so I didn't say anything at all. I sat and stared at her face, memorizing every blemish, the sharp curve of her hips and the gentle rise and fall of her breasts as she breathed.

She must have thought me cruel.

#

Chapter 35

A False Friend

Betrayal is the only truth that sticks. – Arthur Miller

Excitement oozed from my veins like some invisible gas that pushed itself out of my pores and danced along the exposed skin of my arms and legs in tiny bumps as we pulled into the tunnel. Grand Central Station reminded me of a mausoleum, or a temple constructed as a tribute to the Gods who once lived above the clouds of Mount Olympus. It humbles anyone who dares to look up. We were ants crawling over one another trying to find a way out.

Joe and I threaded our way up the long marble steps through throngs of elbows, butt cheeks and wild-eyed stares like those first travelers to the city, who came by boat—a disenfranchised people in search of an uncertain destiny.

We passed through the revolving doors onto the sidewalk in front of mountains of mortar, concrete, and steel that reached up and blotted out the sky. It wrapped us up in an embryonic embrace that made it hard to breathe. The air smelled of fresh baked bread, popped corn, cheap perfume, sweat, gasoline, and vomit.

The city was aglow. 42nd Street bustled with activity all the way to Fifth Avenue. I shivered and pulled up my jacket's collar and clutched it tight at my throat. I shook, half from the cold, and the other in the anticipation of another experience.

I was trapped in that world between male and female, uncertain if I was perceived as a lesser man or a wannabe woman and never understanding what it was like to be either. I knew it would be short-lived.

Homeless men in tattered clothing and street vendors barking orders and waving papers, were huddled around battered garbage pails on bustling street corners. Their darkened faces and hungry eyes glowed like embers from the flames inside the dented cans as we hurried by. Watching a seasoned couple stand side by side to warm their hands stirred a quiescent longing inside me, and the desire for that warm comfortable feeling that other women feel in the arms of a good man beckoned me on.

Joe pulled me by the arm into a waiting cab. We were moving before I could sit down. I pulled on the ends of my short skirt trying to lengthen it against the cold seat. It provided little protection.

Joe wore a long wool skirt and boots. He dressed more practical for this trip. His face was painted up like some movie diva of the '50s, a time when his last fetishistic fantasy was ingrained in him as a rebellious youth. He looked more like the zombie version of the woman in the black and white photograph he kept folded in his wallet.

The taxi driver appeared to be in his mid-twenties. He wore an amused look on his face as a matter of course, but his eyes betrayed his curiosity when I stepped into his cab. He asked us where we were heading and Joe gave him the address of the club that we were to meet Candy. He barely spoke English. His accent was from somewhere in the Middle East. He wore a white rag on his head, and his beard was sparse. It didn't quite cover his pointed chin. His eyes bulged out at me in his rear-view mirror. He stared at me like the men we'd encountered on the train ride down from Connecticut. It made me nervous.

He wore the same, almost imperceptible grin as them— like he was looking at someone familiar. He continued to stare even when I caught him as if I'd invited him to look. He snarled at me in the mirror and clawed at the air. He was trying to mimic a lion to let me know that we reached our destination—the Lion's Den. Some of his upper teeth were missing. He looked pathetic.

The driver deposited Joe and I onto a sidewalk under the shadow of a building somewhere in the bowels of Manhattan, or maybe it was Brooklyn, where Fifth Avenue became something else.

The club was in a building sandwiched between two monolithic structures that rose up out of the concrete and disappeared into the night. It was made of rough-hewn brick stained with the soot of a malevolent part of the city. Moss clung to its sides and grew out of the cracks in its facade. The structures on both sides were polished gray, trying to blend in to the city so no one knew it existed.

The awning was torn in several places. Strips of red canvas fluttered in the wind. A string of bare bulbs hung along the underside of the torn canvas and lit the walk that led up to the large, black doors of the entrance.

In the luminescent glow Joe resembled an oversized manikin like the ones we passed on the way in the window of one of the many novelty stores or woman's boutiques. His skin radiated. It was white, smooth and sculpted. His hooded eyes, tucked under the shadows of a protruding brow, disappeared and reappeared at regular intervals each time he blinked like a no-vacancy sign in a cheap hotel.

The air was colder in this part of the city seldom visited by tourists. It was a place usually passed by natives on their way to somewhere else. The music poured out every time the door opened. It sent vibrations into my chest and a little panic. It was not a modern music but something of years past, timeless in its message about a circus, the sewers of a dark city and the people who live in its shadow.

I shivered. The nipples of my developing breasts tightened, anxious for the warmth that I imagined awaited me inside the club in the arms of some man waiting and wanting someone—if not like me yet—perhaps like I will be. I had mixed feelings. I was anxious and apprehensive. Hell, I was scared.

"Damn, it's cold," I said, hoping it would hurry him up.

Joe's head turned slowly in my direction. He held a compact in the palm of his large hand up near his face. His lips were puckered. The tip of his bulbous nose was redder than the color he applied.

"Well, if you'd have moved your tight little ass a little faster you would've generated more warmth."

He snapped the compact shut, put it into his red Gucci purse hanging from his shoulder, and pressed his lips together three times like he always did after applying color.

"Why on earth did you dress like that, or wear those fuck-me-pumps to a club? How do you intend to dance if you can't even walk in the damn things?"

"I can walk."

I stopped speaking when three young men about the age of one of my daughters walked by. They stared back in our direction. One of them murmured something and the others laughed. The doors opened and music spilled out. It blended with their male voices and made it sound melodious like an orchestra trying to harmonize before a concert. I hated my voice.

"If you wanted men to notice you, you sure succeeded," Joe said.

"You look like a prostitute. Where on earth did you get that outfit?"

I wore the outfit to the meeting earlier in the afternoon. He drove me there.

"Laura gave it to me. Why now, do you choose to say something?"

I was angry, and suddenly self-conscious of my appearance. I wondered if the skirt was sufficient to hide the maleness tucked up between my legs. It dawned on me why people kept looking at me instead of Joe. Then I remembered that I hadn't told Joe something important and I stopped.

"Joe, wait."

I grabbed his arm.

"You look fine, Evelyn. I was just teasing you."

"No—I need to tell you something."

He turned around. I wished I could see his eyes. My heart raced.

"I was the only one who was invited," I said.

Joe went silent. In the overhead light his dark eyes

blinked out again and again like stars in a cloudy sky.

"You can't sit with us. Candy doesn't even know you're coming."

"You bitch." He choked. His words were barely audible. He turned and started to walk back toward the street then he halted suddenly.

"You're a bitch, Evelyn. You've been becoming more like one every day."

"Joe, I'm sorry. I thought you'd like dressing up and going out. We don't have to stay long. Maybe I could--."

"Don't bother. You are not going to convince me to stay." Joe turned his head and looked back over his shoulder at me.

"Please don't go. Come in and get something to eat, drink, or whatever. I bet the guys will like your boots."

I stared down at his shiny boots.

"I'll just say hi to them and sit with you. Come on, Joe. It will be fun."

I spoke rapidly from the cold and panic. There was something pathetic in the sound of my voice and I felt ashamed. I did not want him to leave me alone in the city. Even though I could not see his expression, I knew he was hurt.

He was silent. My teeth chattered noisily while he pondered something—I was never quite certain whether it was to stay or whether to chastise me more for my callousness. I lost whatever composure I had and turned my head away.

I think my conscience had finally got the better of me— but perhaps too late. There was something that died in his eyes that day.

Even from that distance from which we stood in the cold, in the poor quality of the light at night under that torn awning, in the shadows of those monolithic structures all around us, I saw that glint in the center of his pupils, the one I noticed the first time he looked up at me from his chair in our imperfect circle in the basement of Christ's church, when he used to look at me with awe and admiration. It flickered like some flame grasping for oxygen trying not go completely out.

Friendship is a flower, someone said. It grows or withers depending on whether it is properly cared. I had doused ours with weed killer.

I don't know why I had always manipulated him. He didn't deserve it. I had never met anyone like him. I used to think that a man who dresses up in women's clothes to get his rocks off had something wrong with him. He couldn't be a real man but Joe had surprised me many times in the short time that I had lived with him. He fixed things around the apartment when they broke: the noisy garbage disposal, the plugged-up toilet, and circuit breakers when I had too many appliances plugged into the bathroom socket. Joe acted the part of the perfect husband. He bought me flowers, which admittedly had weirded me out, particularly in the beginning of our relationship. No wonder his wife had called him every night after he had left her.

Joe taught me more about makeup, hair and dresses and how to become a decent human being than I had ever thought possible. Caught up in the show, I somehow rejected his advice. I was still an infant when it came to being in my gender role. I was in a hurry to make up for lost time. I wanted to taste the life I had lost by living some other boy's life and waiting for my chance to live mine. There is nothing more selfish than a transsexual who first comes out into the light.

In the days ahead, I would try Joe's patience and good nature and push him to his limits—so much that I think in the end he hated me. But Joe would change my mind about transvestites, and those heterosexual men who liked to pretend that they were women. Perhaps they did have a twin spirit—a yin and a yang.

Joe walked away without saying a word. He headed back in the direction we had come. I knew from my limited experience that he would not be able to get a taxi.

He would walk two blocks cursing my name. He would ride the subway back to Grand Central Station alone, walk down those marble steps that we had ascended together and catch a north-bound train. The next day when I would call him, weary and drained, and ask him to drive down to the city to get me. He would come—without complaint—and we would drive back to our home in Stratford, Connecticut, in unremarkable silence.

Joe's assessment was correct. I was a bitch. But a bitch was female and for the moment, I could be content with that, or so I thought.

#

Chapter 36

The Lost Dream

No one ever told me that grief felt so like fear. – C.S. Lewis

Dressed all in black leather and looking like some doll in a 70's novelty shop, Candy was seated at a table near the end of the bar, surrounded by several men of varying ages, wearing tailored suits, loose smiles and gold bands wrapped securely around their ring fingers. She looked up and caught me staring in her direction and smiled.

Her eyes twinkled in that mischievous way unique to her, both inquisitive and seductive at the same time. It managed to enchant anyone who dared to stare back into that probing stare. Her slivered eyes broke apart at the corners when she smiled letting me and anyone who dared look know that all was good in the world, even if it wasn't.

I moved cautiously toward her, through the crowded bar, moving left then right and sometimes stepping aside for someone else making their way back through the sea of anxious faces. Eyes darted about me like minnows searching for something or someone to make their lives seem less desperate.

"Welcome to my city."

Candy's smile broadened and she slapped one of the many half-empty glasses into my hand that sat in front of her on the table that some suit had bought her hoping to get lucky before he went home to his wife.

I tossed it back and for at least that moment, when the heat coursed through me, all did seem right in the world.

# # #

It wasn't long after I gulped down a drink that tasted like a rum and coke with a lime twist. Sherlyn arrived and we left to find Candy's phantom boyfriend who had failed to meet her there earlier. "The shit," Sherlyn had called him, then she had put her fist through the wall outside the bathroom door. It folded up like paper.

"I think he loved me once, Candy explained.

"He had started seeing a shrink about his homosexuality. He'd always seen me as a woman with a dick. I know he loved me until that shrink told him it was still gay. He got violent when he got home. Like it was my fault, the way he felt about me when he'd look at me. If he'd just quit seeing that shrink."

Candy was looking at me when she said it. I think she opened up to me when Sherlyn had slipped and called her Rachel. I think she wanted to see my reaction but I was used to playing poker. Not that it would have bothered me. A lot of transsexuals kept secrets from each other. I was one of them. No one ever got that close to anyone to confide every detail. Not even to her therapist, if she had one.

It wouldn't have mattered to me if she had a different name for every outfit like Joe except, I didn't like being led on like I was some kind of narc or a stoolie. All those XX Club rumors aside, I think that, if anything bothered me most about their charade, it was being treated like an idiot. I liked Candy for who she appeared to be. The person she presented herself to be and that was all that mattered to me, nothing more.

Candy got quiet and looked over at the two men sitting at the bar. One of them had his back to us, while the other stared in our direction. I was pretty sure he was too far away to hear any part of our conversation. Again, I was confused by all this secrecy?

"We had a great life."

Candy shook her head. She closed her eyes and listened to the music playing in the background. It was soft, and low. The lyrics seemed a bit melancholy for my tastes.

"If I hadn't despised being male and taken more hormones, or tried to help so many others like me, maybe—."

Her voice drifted away.

She had an ugly red welt or rash on her neck that I assumed was chaffing from the scarves she always wore.

"I understand," I said, even though I didn't.

I thought I had to say something. At the time, I understood only what was in my province to understand. He dumped her for a natural born woman, moved away and tried to forget about her. But it didn't work.

Candy tried to commit suicide while he was on tour overseas and he had flown half way around the globe to be by her side. He was embarrassed by the press and kept their relationship secret. They had seen each other on and off. She moved into an apartment that he had bought her on the lower east side.

They loved each other but his obsession with homophobia, his public image, and her dysphoria became impossible to ignore. Even love couldn't save her, and in time, she made the decision to leave him and to change her sex. He went ballistic.

I kept my mouth shut and listened. Candy intrigued me. Anyone with secrets to uncover was interesting, a mystery to unravel or puzzle to solve.

Candy had many secrets, another name and a phantom boyfriend without one, a life in the shadows of a city I feared. I was afraid she would shut up and not talk anymore about things that I had always wanted to learn more about in my youth but was too afraid to inquire.

"He found out I had a date for my surgery. He got mad," Candy said. Her voice flat, matter-of-fact. It was a long time ago. The pain had dulled.

"How did he find out, girl?" Sherlyn asked.

She slid back down into her chair beside Candy and put her arm around her shoulders. I had surmised, perhaps presumptuously, that Sherlyn was their liaison—their Friar Tuck, the fateful monk in Romeo and Juliet.

"He's a fucking oracle. How the fuck do I know?"

Candy looked down into her glass.

"I asked him for money. He freaked."

"Life sucks."

Sherlyn removed her arm and got up to stand behind Candy.

"You got to start learning how to lie, girl. Didn't Sherlyn teach you nothin'?"

Candy forced a smile. Some person inside of me, someone I hadn't met yet, wanted to slide over and put her arm around her and tell her it would be alright, even if it wouldn't. Sherlyn bobbed her head with the beat of the music and began mouthing words that I did not understand.

Candy put her head down on the table allowing her hair to fall over her eyes. For the moment she was hiding from the world if not from herself. She was human after all. I felt guilty for thinking she was an addict, junkie or worse. I think back at all of our exchanges and discussion, and even the entire evening we just had and I could not think of any unkind thing she ever said or did.

I saw her give money away she likely needed. Wads of bills kept in her coat pocket handed without compunction to addicts and shadow people who came up to her on the street, blood-shot eyes pleading their cause. Her hand always found their outstretched palms—and she seemed ashamed to take their blessings and praise as she walked away.

Her criticism, often blunt, never seemed malicious. She thanked all of the men who bought her drinks and spoke to each one with kindness. I recalled the Puerto Rican lads we met on the tram. She dismissed their threats with a smile.

Candy, or the person who I knew as Candy, was not as young as I had first thought. The years had not been kind. The scars of an indelicate life were seeping to the surface. Fine lines etched her face. She was near my age, pushing forty, possibly older, but still beautiful in a nostalgic sort of way when you look at an old black and white photograph of your grandparents and see someone they used to be.

"What do you think they're talking about?"

Candy pointed her glass towards two women sitting at a table near the window. Both appeared to be in their mid-twenties. The blonde held a beer bottle by the neck with two fingers. She shook her head, pony tail flipping from side to side, a frozen smile pinned to her pretty face. The homely, darker haired one was talking. I shrugged. They were too far for me to hear their conversation. Only the trill of their laughter now and then.

"Do you think they talk about the things we do? Shoes, hair, makeup, sex?"

"I don't know. I guess," I lied. I could speculate.

I'd been doing it since I could remember. I'd seen girls in conversation, talking and laughing in their gay voices just like those two. Bright eyes darting about, while their delicate hands scrape at the air. I watched them from afar and dreamed I was in the mix, sharing some secret about a boy, or a missed period, or the latest gossip on a girl who wasn't there but I didn't want to encourage, Candy. I didn't like this conversation.

It reminded me how much I missed while being forced by some cruel trick of nature to live a boy's life. Candy was testing me. She knew real women didn't talk about the things Ts do, or if they did, it was not in the same context. I imagined when a woman told someone she liked her shoes, she meant it as a compliment. She was not thinking about how good they'd look on her.

"Do you think dreams can become real," Candy asked. Her voice broke like a saxophone when it misses a note.

"Yes," I said.

"What about us?"

Candy looked into my eyes. She was not herself. She was no longer perfect. She was old. Rough skin around the lids splintered into a thousand tiny smiles of dreams gone by.

"I don't know," I admitted. My honesty scared me.

"I hope so."

"What happens when we stop dreaming?"

Unthinkable for someone like us. Dreams were the only

216

things we had that helped us through the day.

"I don't know."

I lied. I assumed she meant the dream and not the dreamer. A dream isn't tangible. You can't touch it. It can't break. Or die. It isn't mortal.

Candy sighed and pulled on a loose strand of her graying hair with the long fingers of her left hand.

"I always thought maybe when I'm older? I just never knew when that would be. I kept putting it off. I thought it would always be there—"

Candy's voice trailed off. She looked down into her drink and touched her cheek with her fingertips gently.

"The young—they are stupid—they don't think they will ever get old. One day they wake up and look in the mirror and wham! Someone stole their face. What the fuck!" Sherlyn laughed at her own joke. She had no idea what Candy and I were talking about.

I stared across the table at Candy. She was still staring into her drink. She didn't look up. I didn't have an answer. I wished I had. She stayed silent for a while longer then she got up suddenly and went toward the bathroom.

"Rach—where are you going?"

Sherlyn seemed concerned. Candy nodded her off and kept walking.

When Candy or Rachel or whatever her name, came back to the table, she asked that question again, the one about the fate of dreamers.

"I guess they find another dream."

I breathed uneasily and waited for her reaction. Rachel cocked her head to one side as I finished the thought.

"Or it just fades away."

"Dreams don't just disappear."

She was angry.

"People might grow out of them, I guess. But I suppose they could go on forever."

I looked at my watch. It was nearly 11:30PM. I was more

217

an early bird than a night owl.

"Then what?"

"What do you mean?"

I hated it when she spoke nonsense. Forever means forever. It's like infinity.

"It never ends."

"What if you come to the end and there's nothing. Like God, you know, if you believe in something all your life thinking you will meet God and then you die and there's nothing?"

Now it was my turn to be silent. It was obvious where this was going.

"You mean, if a dream outlasts the dreamer?"

The question surprised me when it came out of my mouth. Candy looked straight at me. She nodded her head slowly. She wanted to know what happened to those whose dreams don't come true.

"Rachel—" Sherlyn started to say something, but Rachel raised her hand to stop her.

"Tell me. Please." She continued to stare at me, but I wasn't sure she saw me or something else. Her eyes had that far-away look. Like they were squinting into a sunset on a deserted beach at the end of some flick when one lover tells the other that she is dying and not to follow her—or to remember me—or what we had—or some such crap.

"You know what happens. You don't need me to tell you."

Heat rose up in my cheeks. I had never gotten angry with Rachel. In my bones I knew how she would react. It was part of my curse. Always knowing what was going to happen next.

"Please, Evie?"

She wiped the spittle hanging from her lower lip. Alcohol or some drug had a good grip on her. Or perhaps it was something else. Did I see an amber prescription bottle in her purse when she opened it up earlier? Saliva had dried onto the corners of her mouth. It looked brown in the dim light of the bar. Did she vomit in the bathroom? I shuddered. To think I wanted to kiss her earlier. Disgusting.

Some members of the club did not find Candy beautiful. They argued she was tall for a woman. Although she moved gracefully enough, she dressed kind of frumpy. She had big hands and her breasts were small. She bound them with tape to push them in to give the appearance of cleavage.

It surprised me how underdeveloped she was. As a newbie, I was fitting into a B cup after a few months on hormones. She had been living as a she-male for more than twenty years. She stopped taking them because it would have left her flaccid in bed she said. The first time I heard her voice I knew she was one of the shadow people. Joe was right, when she wasn't speaking softly, she spoke like a gay male, caressing her "Esses" and topping her "Tees" and dragging everything but the laundry out through her nostrils.

Despite her rough appearance there was something inexplicably sensuous about her. I could not put my finger on it. I was too new to the scene.

Men, and some women, cocked their heads in her direction when she walked by. It was not just her face. There was something seductive about her for lack of a better understanding, a chutzpah—she's got balls, literally—and a kind of compassion that oozed from her soul that only monks and missionaries seemed to have. She could light up a room with her presence, but the reverse was also true. Candy was the kind of person that when broken everyone could feel it.

A song started playing on the radio in the background. The singer talked more than sang his tune. Her eyes watered before turning back to ask—no, *begging* me—for an answer.

"Please, I need to hear it from someone real."

"I'm not real, Rachel. I'm just like you."

"No. You're not." Our eyes locked and in that split instant, I knew what she meant. As soon as you start living your dream – it is no long intangible but real. The dreamer stops dreaming—when it becomes a reality. She was asking what happens to the ones who don't.

In some past life we had this discussion before. She never

knew why she felt the way she did. We both attracted men and some women and were attracted to them. We felt feminine inside but only she was uncertain about her identity. It came over her slowly through the years as though she knit the skin that she was in herself. I have always known who I am.

"A dream unlike the dreamer, never ends."

Regret hangs by a thread. I knew she had been seeing Canon Jones and the staff at the Gender Identity Clinic and stopped. Suddenly I knew why. There were only a few reasons why a true transsexual would be denied her letter of recommendation for SRS—AIDs. The most misunderstood and dreaded disease of the decade.

Rachel bolted straight up in her chair. She rose in one fluid motion, pulled on her sweater, and walked away. She put her hand up almost subconsciously to touch the back of her neck, delicately as was her habit to smooth the scarf she wore even in summer as though it was made of paper. Was it to cover the rash, those ugly red welts that lay buried beneath her collar? Funny how I'd always seen them but I never noticed it before.

Perhaps I never wanted to.

She never turned or said a word as she left but as I look back over the years, I liked to think that somewhere in our discourse she found some consolation in my response to her question—if not closure—the kind people find when their dreams threaten to die before they do.

Sherlyn shot me an angry look before she grabbed her coat and ran out the door after her.

In the background I remembered that strange song playing on the jukebox in the corner, one of those censured songs you never heard on the radio, pounding out a bouncy little tune with a violin squealing in time and a man with a familiar voice speaking more than singing about: *some cunt that stopped breathing.*

#

Chapter 37

The Reluctant Hero

Sing your death song, and die like a hero going home. - Tecumseh

We raced out of the bar. The street was empty. The alcohol and fatigue had hit me hard. Everything appeared surreal. The cold night air did little to revive me.

I stood alone on the street trying to gather my wits about me. It was strange and silent. Ribbons of steam rose up from the vented sewer caps in a straight line every fifty yards. The city was quiet. I looked toward the subway station where we had last seen those Puerto Rican boys on the way down. Joe said not to look directly at them. They had been staring at us and saying nasty things in Spanish I did not understand. One of them grabbed his crotch and stuck out his tongue at me while the other's laughed. Every time I thought of them, my pulse quickened.

Sherlyn ran too fast. She had to wait for me. I was falling-down drunk. Or perhaps it was that I never learned to run in stiletto heels and a skin-tight leather skirt. I said "go," and waved her on. I would catch up. But I never did.

When she was out of sight, I was alone on the streets of the city of 8 million people. A place where death never sleeps and I was lost. I ran out of desperation, for some unknown reason, toward the subway—to the place I would have gone. I ran along dark streets with the hope that I would find Candy sitting on a bench in the subway station waiting for me and Sherlyn.

As I ran, I prayed that I would not step on anything sharp or that would slow me down. I didn't want to get hurt. Like every other T who finally made the decision to change, I wanted to stay intact. Preserve what was left of me for the transformation. The less scars the better. I was convinced that beauty would protect me in the days to come.

When I got to the subway station, I realized that I had given the last of my money to Sherlyn for drinks earlier and was lucky to find a few subway tokens. I searched for Candy along the platforms watching the people getting off and on trams that come and go in a rush. It seemed an impossible task. Like looking for a favorite rock you always carried for luck that fell out of your hand when you were climbing up a bank and it fell down into a pile of other rocks that looked exactly like it. For a moment, in my alcoholic haze, panic and fatigue, I thought I had seen her.

She was standing in the door way of a tram when the doors had closed. A man, the short one I thought I saw arguing with her earlier was there but maybe it wasn't him.

Perhaps it was one of those Puerto Rican boys that had taunted us. I wasn't certain if he had sideburns and the leather cap was missing. He didn't look young but menacing. I didn't really study his face long.

My eyes were drawn to Candy as they usually were. His hand was on Candy's shoulder. She seemed to let him. She appeared serene. There was no fear in her eyes. Just that far-away look she always gave me when she left without saying goodbye.

When I got to Grand Central Station, I made the call I dreaded. Joe answered in a fog. He said he would be there. He never failed to be my friend when I needed him.

\#

Chapter 38

The Omen

Wisdom consists of the anticipation of consequences. – Norman Cousins

It was late. I had not expected Joe to be waiting up for me. He had not said a word to me when he left that morning. Not that it was unusual. The days of sharing secrets and comforting each other ended when Paul came into my life.

I tried to be cordial. I really did but Joe's constant complaining grated on my nerves. It was harder to feign interest in Joe's many problems. His woe-is-me tales often ended with a hearty sob that shook his entire body until snot ran out of his nose and grossed me out.

Yesterday, a woman employee complained when she saw him go into the lady's room. He was supposed to use the one they made for him out of a broom closet. He said he had to do more than pee. They wrote him up. I sat and listened, but I no longer pretended to care about what happened to him. He was a man. He needed to suck it up.

Whenever he asked how my day went, I would say: Fine. I stayed to myself. My lack of candor dug into his self-esteem. He said I wouldn't let him be feminine. He wanted to be the mommy.

A familiar silhouette was leaning against the wall of the house with both feet up against the wood rail when I stepped up onto the porch. Joe's face emerged from the haze. He appeared one dimensional as if painted into the background. We were animated people, he and I. Dark shadows that run across the pages of someone else's life. Our lips curled into a smile when we saw each other but lately, it never reached our eyes.

Joe leaned forward to let me know that he was there.

"So, you found someone to take Traci's place already."

Joe's tongue got thick after three beers. He was barely understandable. He must have been drinking all afternoon.

"The committee was debating when you weren't there whether to have a party at all."

I moved toward the door to our apartment.

"You should have been there, Evelyn. Jennifer almost canceled it on us, but Kaitlyn stepped up. Everyone wants to move forward on the party. Even Sarah. So, don't worry, it didn't matter that you missed another meeting."

Another pause. He was trying to goad me into an argument. Talking with a drunk I have always found to be unproductive.

"She was looking for you after the meeting by the way, when you left with—"

"Who?"

"Sarah." Joe sat up straight. "She told me."

"No," I turned in his direction. "I was there, Joe, she knows it. I did not stay with the committee afterward. I went to lunch." Why would Sarah lie?

"With what's-her-name?"

"Candy," I sighed. No, Candy was not there. I went to lunch alone. I didn't owe Joe any explanation.

"Yeah, I knew it was something sticky sweet that will give you a cavity," Joe laughed. "Like, that's her real name."

I shrugged and turned toward the door. None of us use the name we were born with. I had no patience for his games. At times he acted like he owned me.

Who made him man of the house and arbiter of my life?

"The other little bitch. What's her name?"

Joe was drunk. His hands flailed when he was excited. He dropped his cup onto the floor of the porch.

"Shit. She never talks to me."

"Traci wasn't there at all, Joe. She's gone. Likely, none of us will see her again."

"Good riddance. Sweetness then. That fabulous famous fag no one cares or even knows about anymore. What the fuck does he want with you anyway?"

"Candy is a she. She likes to be referred to as a she but not to worry. I doubt she is ever coming back either. We have seen the last of her I'm afraid."

I felt a tug in my chest as I said it.

"Boo hoo. You sound broken up, like she is the only T who has a hard luck story."

He looked up at me and made a gesture as though rubbing tears from his eyes.

"She could have at least gone to Biscotti's' to say goodbye to everyone. Bet she's jealous of your new friend."

He switched subjects. Now he was talking about his old nemesis.

"Traci wouldn't have gone even if she was here. She didn't usually go to lunch with a group. You know that."

Joe knew how to get under my skin. Lately he was under there a lot picking and tugging at an old scab as though he hopped it would fall off and find some other person underneath. Someone he could bond with. Some old lover or spouse who gave a shit about his problems.

"Oh, yeah, the rule of three. She's full of pesky little clichés like that. One for the money. Two for the show. Three to get Read-as-a-T—Let's go! Is that why you ditched me at Biscotti's?"

I started to turn around but his voice rose.

"You are starting to act just like her." Joe's hand was shaking by his side. "Your other friend—is she going into stealth too?"

Okay I deserved that. He did me a favor after I dissed him, again. I let it slide.

"Candy is just being cautious, Joe. She is nothing like Traci. I am not certain whether she is even like me. She doesn't need rules. She is herself every day. In her world, she is the queen of the city. I think all she wanted was someone to talk to. It can get lonely where we are. She wanted to talk to me about something."

"Yeah, she's a fuck'n queen alright. Queer as a three-dollar bill. She's all that and a bag of chips. A tall tranny with big hairy tits."

I hated it when he tried to rhyme everything. It was annoying.

I shook my head and walked toward the door.

"She's too weird to be hiding behind all that attitude."

Joe forced a laugh and took another slug of his drink.

"You think you can do that. Walk away from your family, friends and all you loved like your old life never happened?"

"That's not what I meant. She—I don't know Candy well enough to say she's like me or you or even her friend, Sherlyn, but there has got to be something in between. Traci went deep stealth. I have family to consider."

They were Michael's reason for existence. They saved his life. Not mine. Stop it.

"I can't just forget them. They will keep my secret. I know they will."

"You're sure about that? You don't sound too confident. Do you think they can forget you were their father?"

Something in the way Joe said it made the hairs on my neck stand on end.

"And this new girlfriend—sweet thing—is she going with you on your journey, too? Are you going to let her in?"

He was jealous. He felt threatened by Paul, Traci, and now Candy—because it meant I would leave him.

I missed Traci almost as much as I missed Michael's old friends. I still saw Frank and Frenchy sitting at my kitchen table, their backs to me, sipping beer and chatting merrily on that last day. They never turned around. They talked to Debbie and the kids as though I was already gone.

The lights in the kitchen were on when I pushed open the door. Joe followed me into the house. There were dishes piled in the sink and a trail of grass on the floor leading into his bedroom. Joe must have cut the lawn when he got home from work early.

As part of our rent reduction, he did things for the

landlady. He patched the roof, organized the garage, caulked windows, and mowed the tiny lawn. He was a regular handyman, but inside our apartment he was Rip Van Winkle. He made a mess and spent most of his time in his bedroom—if not asleep—on the phone with Kathy, Big Kathy, or Kaitlyn, ironing or folding his laundry, polishing a new pair of pumps, or applying some new kind of makeup.

"Damn it, Joe. I just cleaned this floor before the meeting today." I didn't want to pick a fight. Lately he had been very short-tempered.

Joe looked down at the floor sheepishly. He put his empty cup on the table and stooped down to pick up the clumps of dirt and grass.

"Hold on, Mrs. Clean," he snapped, "I can't believe you get nervous over a single piece of grass."

"Single?"

I pointed to the hallway in front of the bathroom. He quickly ran over and brushed several clumps into his calloused hand with his thick fingers.

"Gee," he sighed, "you'd think you was a real woman the way you carry on."

He looked up at me nervously after he said it.

"Wow, you're full of compliments this evening."

I removed my coat and draped it over my arm. Looking at the remnants floating under the empty pot sitting in the sink basin, along with a bowl and some dirty silverware I doubted there was any of the New England Boiled Dinner I made yesterday left for me to enjoy. A few miscreant leaves of cabbage still floated over the plugged-up drain.

"Oh, shit."

Joe watched my eyes move from the sink towards him. His tone suddenly turned apologetic.

"I was going to clean it. Don't worry, Evelyn, I will get to it before I go to bed. I promise. Gee, you are worse than Kathy. At least she lets me put my dishes in the sink overnight."

I'm not your damn wife.

I turned and headed for my bedroom. Joe grinned. I think he reveled in taunting me. It made him feel at home. This must be how his relationship went with Kathy. The light bantering between spouses that made him feel comfortable. Debbie and I never argued, at least not ostentatiously. I would use my stern voice whenever she questioned my judgment and she always silently acquiesced. We lived in a patriarchal society. There was a time I took advantage of it when it suited me.

"You cook better than my Kathy does. Where did you learn how to cook? That was the best corned beef dinner I've ever tasted. Sorry about not leaving any for you but I couldn't help myself. It was sinfully delicious. You shouldn't have made it so good."

He was trying to ingratiate himself to me again. He knew I was mad at him.

No one ever taught me how to cook. I paid close attention to my mother when I was young and later to my wife, Debbie after I married. I would steal into the kitchen whenever I could without giving away an interest in some chore that was traditionally considered a woman's domain. Poor Debbie, I had not given her much thought not even a call in more than a week. It's like we were on two paths in a wood that ran along side of each other for a while then took a sharp turn away in different directions.

"Get your beauty rest, sweetie, you have a long day ahead of you tomorrow."

Joe had that look again. I hated the way he looked at me when he'd been drinking. I forced a smile and closed my bedroom door.

I'm not your damn mistress.

#

Chapter 39

Divorce Papers

Grief can be the garden of compassion. -Rumi

When I was young, I planned out my life as though it was scripted. The voice inside my head sounded like a narrator telling a story as it unfolded. I even knew the track of the tears shed by my wife on our final day together. Once transition started, I became a different person.

Planning became difficult. I was so distracted that I couldn't dwell on details. Some might call it spontaneity, others panic. I was in a hurry. I looked forward to the end result. I wanted it terribly and trusted that God would make it come through for me—in time.

As secretary of the club, it was my responsibility to coordinate the party. Julie gave me a number of someone at the Tiffany Club that she knew. I had no idea what this would entail. Once Joe got involved, he was the proverbial devil with the details. He called the other club's representative, organized some of his friends as an unofficial decoration committee, and started buying stuff. Party favors, hats, condiments in paper bags, rolls of ribbon, all kinds of decorative stuff cluttered every corner of our apartment. Worse yet, was when he held meetings with his make-shift volunteer staff in our living room.

Joe had been a construction foreman for over thirty years prior to walking off the job to work at Home Depot in drag. If he handled his personal life as well, he wouldn't be wailing loud enough to be heard in the street as Paul pulled up to drop me off. The wailing was louder when I opened my door to get out. Paul rolled his window down.

"Should I come in?"

I walked back, leaned into his open window, and gave Paul a wet kiss.

"You can if you want but it looks like a parade stopped by." I lifted my chin towards the driveway where several cars were lined up and one in the street. Paul gave me a queer look and glanced at his watch. "I am sure it's nothing, Joe gets loud when he's around his friends."

"Come home with me, Evie. It's not safe. I'll respect you. I've slept on the couch. It's comfy. You have nothing to worry about with me."

It's been almost a year and he has been a gentleman. He's stuck his tongue down my throat a few times, felt my tiny boobs through my clothes but for some reason he stayed away from my crotch. It made me wonder. Traci and even my mother warned me about admirers. But I am certain he was not because he was too homophobic. Perhaps he suspected but was afraid to find out. On several occasions he told me that I was the best thing that ever happened to his life in a long time. I laughed. If he only knew.

"It's fine. I have a lock on my door," I lied. "I'll sneak in. No one will even know I'm there."

I kissed him hard on the mouth and we both pulled away gasping.

"Get some rest. You have a long drive to the city in the morning."

Paul smiled and started to roll up the window then stopped. My heart pounded in my throat. If he walked me to the door and saw some of the committee, he would have questions or press me on moving out. I couldn't leave until my final operation. I needed Joe. I was not in the mood for a lecture on why women need men to watch out for them or how vulnerable I was to miscreants and why I shouldn't be living with a man who wears dresses.

"I made an appointment for you."

"What?"

"No girl of mine is going to live with some fagot. It's dangerous, Evie," he said. "You don't know when this guy will come unhinged. He could attack you in your sleep. I'd let you live with me but it's a studio. Only temporary until I get more money for a bigger place."

"But I am in a lease—" I protested. I wasn't ready to leave just then. I still needed Joe to help me. There was one more procedure. An important one. Someone would have to pick the new me up at LaGuardia Airport when I came back from Neenah.

"Fuck that. Break it. People do it all the time. You don't owe that fag anything. And judging from what I see now, it's better if you move sooner than later. I don't want to keep worrying about you."

There was no arguing the point further. In the year we had been dating, Paul had always been obstinate and dominant. He liked to control things and I was one of them.

"I called a number in an ad. Some guy has a house with a room available for rent in Milford. His name is Vince. He sounds like a nice older guy. A lawyer or something for Sikorsky. I bet it's a nice house. He'll meet you at La Cu china on the Old Stratford Road at 7pm tomorrow night."

I shrugged. I felt trapped. He'd gone too far.

"You know where that is, right?"

I didn't respond. I was still trying to think of something to say to change his mind when his face got instantly red—

"Evie!"

"Alright."

I jumped and audibly exhaled. I couldn't give him an excuse without piercing some invisible barrier between us.

"It's only $750 a month. You said you got that much, right? I don't have anything to lend you this month because the bitch wants her back support."

"Yeah, alright. How will I know him?"

I purposely kept my voice low and my eyes diverted outside my window. I thought I heard murmuring voices and peals of laughter coming from the house. They were distinctively in the male vocal register.

It may not be a bad time to leave. Joe was a mother hen and picked up strays from the club. Sarah moved into our living room seemingly overnight and never left and now a committee of gender misfits hung out belting out show tunes in C minor every weekend. Joe expected too much from our relationship. We were supposed to be trying to blend into our role not creating a new one in society.

When I first started, I was surprised to find others like me and even more shocked to learn that there were other kinds of gender people whose ideas of femininity and sense of self and sexuality conflicted with my own. It not only confused but frightened me.

Joe's constant complaining and inability to pass well made it uncomfortable to be around him for long periods or go out with him now that I passed. It wasn't fun anymore. In his own word's the "Pizzazz in our Jazz" was gone. Maybe he would still help me if I moved out. It seemed he clung to some chivalrous code that belonged to a gender he no longer had faith in.

"We don't know what each other looks like."

It felt hopeless. I tried to stretch my smile. Paul laughed.

"He will know you. He'll be looking for a white girl with big hair."

I punched him in the upper arm playfully.

"Alright."

A change may do me good. Another howl from the house rang out. *Maybe, I don't belong here.* Paul rolled the window down a little further and stuck his face out. We kissed quickly then he put his truck in gear and pulled away. I watched his tail lights disappear before going up the steps. When I walked into the apartment, Joe was wailing like a sow in labor.

"What's wrong," I asked Sarah.

"He got some mail and opened it during break then went into his bedroom and closed the door. He started crying. Big Kathy and Kaitlyn gotta leave. Evie, I am so glad you're home."

What could I do? The three of them looked at me expectantly. A quick glance in the living room revealed a mess for me to clean up later.

"Okay," I said. "Let me put my things away and hang up my jacket and I'll see what I can do."

When I came back out of my bedroom, Joe had quieted down. Big Kathy and Kaitlyn were shouting goodbye through his door. Sarah stood back watching me. There was something different about her but I was too preoccupied to dwell on it.

"Goodbye, Evie. Let us know how Joe is tomorrow. We tried to get him to talk to us, but he won't come out. Maybe you'll have better luck," Big Kathy explained. She leant down and gave me a quick hug with one hand, held onto some papers in her other.

"Have to work in the morning and I have an hour drive—" Kaitlyn looked apologetic.

"I know," I said. I remembered the drive to the hospital near Boston to visit a broken face after I first moved in with Joe. She seemed happier. I wondered what changed in her life.

When Big Kathy and Kaitlyn were gone, I knocked lightly on Joe's bedroom door.

"Joe, can I come in?"

Without waiting for an answer, I opened the door. Joe faced away from me as I went in. I looked for the light switch.

"What's wrong, Joe. Can I do anything?"

I raised my voice an octave.

"No, please leave me alone."

He sounded tired.

"Can't do that, big gal. We're roomies remember. Tell me what's wrong. Maybe we can help."

I tried to sound cheerful and sympathetic. Sarah leaned against the door frame looking around the room as though seeing inside for the first time. It did not evade me that her last domestic situation ended in violence. I flicked the switch on the wall. Light flooded the room.

Drool ran down Joe's chin as he sputtered unintelligible phrases: *Why me, why now, why this, and what am I going to do?*

His wig sat on the coffee table along with his beer mug and a bowl of popcorn and something else, a frame of a photograph, tangled in the phone cord. He ran his fingers through his thinning hair on top of his head. Fresh tears filled up his puffy eyes when he looked up.

"No one can help me. No one. It's too late."

Joe's voice dripped with contempt.

"Turn off that fuckin' light."

In the last few weeks we had barely spoken to one another. It seemed the party was the only thing in his life that gave him a purpose. The closer I got to my dream the further away he was from his own. Faint music was coming from somewhere above us, through the ceiling. Our landlord's daughter had forgotten to turn off her radio again. She had left for school two days ago. Joe's room was directly below. He hadn't complained about that or if he had, I hadn't noticed.

"We are not leaving until you tell us. We are concerned about you."

Before I finished speaking, he turned and flung some papers at me. They struck me in the shoulder and fell to the floor at my feet. I stooped to retrieve them. They were official court documents. I recognized the bold type: Dissolution of Marriage—divorce papers.

"It's no longer a discussion. She filed last week. My life sucks." He sobbed. His body wracked under his covers as though in pain.

Reality is a harsh matron. With the safety net gone, Joe was petrified that he would be alone, but it was more than fear that wracked his body. Thirty plus years of intimacy and friendship was about to be dissolved. I opened my arms instinctively and he leaned over and wrapped himself in my embrace. I was surprised he let me. I hadn't been kind to him lately. In fact, I don't recall many times in our short relationship that I had lent him my shoulder. When someone is starved for the touch of human kindness—I guess any port in a storm will do.

"What am I going to do? I love her. I never stopped loving her. In thirty years, I have never cheated. I didn't want this. I never really wanted to go through with the change. All I wanted was some hormones to get back my zest. I was happy with my life and being me."

Joe's revelation came as no surprise. He had mentioned this before on several occasions. It was another way we differed. Although I had a charmed life, it had never felt like mine. Even my children felt like they were temporary, on loan from God to give me comfort for as long as I survived.

"She will still be your friend, Joe, if you want her to. Kathy still loves you but needs to move on. You want her to be happy right?"

I patted him gently on the shoulder. I'd never seen Joe cry before. I was not particularly sensitive. I was guarded, hollow inside, but seeing Joe breakdown disturbed me at another level.

"Evelyn, what am I going to do?"

I didn't have an answer. No one does. I think all you can do is keep moving and see what happens next. Take it one day at a time.

"Joe, I'm sorry."

I turned the light off. Words seemed so inadequate. My own divorce was less painful. There was no emotion left in me at the end and the fight to keep her husband nearly killed Debbie. We had no choice. But for Joe, who already told me he wasn't going to have an operation, it was a tragedy.

"Goodnight, Veronica," I said backing out of his room.

Joe's sobs grew louder behind his door.

I put the papers on the kitchen table, turned to wish Sarah a goodnight, that's when it struck me. I should have thought about it before. Sarah was connected to Candy. Candy had come from the City she had said looking for someone, a friend. Sarah was the only one at the XX Club who seemed to know her.

Although I had never seen them speaking to each other when she was around, I caught that look. The one someone uses when they don't want to let others in on a secret. It was odd she showed up on our door step all beat up. Was that the night she disappeared—was that the time she went to the city to look for Candy?

#

Chapter 40

The Request

Never give a sword to a man who cannot dance. Confucius

She followed across the hall to the entrance of my bedroom. I looked up at her. Her eyes were like saucers. The kind my Nana used to have that lined the rack behind her gas stove in her small apartment. Small, round, silver discs. The colorless branches of some lifeless tree embossed around the outer ring and a tiny rose in the center. It appeared darker and contrasted with the other designs on the plate as though it had bled up through the seasoned metal. Your gaze is drawn to its dark stained center to see what secrets lie beneath the tarnish.

"Sarah?"

I wondered if she would mistake the want in my voice for fear. Ever since she revealed her shady past it worried me to be under the same roof but Candy was a friend.

Our kind were not supposed to get involved or even care about each other, particularly during transition but I would like to think she would have at least inquired about me. Sarah was my only chance to do the right thing, if that were possible. Something I had said, set Candy off on a course I was afraid would end badly.

There was a curt nod of her head. Somehow, there was a connection like we had an earlier conversation in my head. I imagined she knew what I was going to ask. "Do you think you might find out—about Candy. I am worried about her."

"Sure. No problem."

Sarah bowed her head and backed out of my room closing the door.

I breathed a sigh of relief. I crawled into bed and collapsed onto my pillow. I hadn't been this exhausted since I was on maneuvers as a Scout Platoon leader for an armor battalion. It was only last summer. My last summer camp at Fort Drum as a Guardsman. But it felt like a million years ago. I was so different now. Some layers of my former life had peeled from me faster than others. I hadn't even noticed.

Michael would never have left a friend behind. Evelyn, it seemed, would do almost anything to achieve her dream, even make a deal with the devil.

Since learning about her sordid past, I know longer saw Sarah as the innocent victim of a pedophile. Sure, she still looked at me with those wide eyes, like I was some kind of hero, but there was another fire smoldering beneath the surface. There was another side of Sarah that came out when she got excited about something. It scared me. What would Sarah expect of me in return for my request?

What if I had said: No?

#

Chapter 41

Return to Jacques

Everybody, soon or late, sits down to a banquet of consequences. –
Robert Louis Stevenson

It was a dangerous game we played in those days of transition.

We were anxious, wannabe women, gaining confidence by going into the places where straight men and natural born women would grade our appearance. It was pass or fail. If they perceived you as a man in a dress there would be consequences. There were consequences even if you were not read.

There was a dark side to being a T that seemed intertwined with our destiny. We were people who can only survive in the shadows. There was no place for a she-male in the world except in those dark places where men go to satisfy their primal urges. The kind that bring sex and violence to the surface, usually at the same time.

Men could do things to us that they would not dare do, to a real woman, one who was natural born, for fear of being arrested. We were used to living on the edge day to day, not really caring whether we lived or died.

We took risks that no one else would. We felt out of place like defective toys waiting for someone to fix us, but deep inside we knew that no one really could.

We clung to the hope that someday, when we were older, we would find a way to walk away from ourselves and achieve a normal life.

We were hopeless souls. Fools who didn't realize until it was too late that some things are broken that can never be mended.

Going into a club dressed as a woman while we still

possessed the tools of a man tucked up tight between our legs was expected of the femmes of the XX Club. It was simply a rite of passage. Unofficially, of course.

#

Chapter 42

The Changeling

There is nothing permanent except change. – Heraclitus

Boston is three hours from Central Vermont, nearly the same distance as the ride down to those XX Club meetings every other Saturday in the Hartford-Springfield area. A trip I had gotten quite used to in the past few years, since my journey to find myself began. The reason I had moved was primarily to be close to my daughter, Jen Rose, struggling to fit in at the USMA at West Point, a school that was less than 15% female in 1993. She needed my support. We had grown quite close over the years, as did her little sister Jacquelyn, who had grown a foot taller than her by the end of her Sophomore year at Spaulding High School. I was not just their father but their coach and both had become my super-star athletes, dominating at state championships in several sports. Ripping their father away from them was not an easy decision, but the alternative had been worse. At least this way, I felt I could support them from a distance, and be their guardian angel if needed.

There was another up-side to moving closer to the cities where the trans experience was beginning to emerge. Bean-Town is only a little more than 90 minutes from Hartford and NYC is about an hour or so by train. I could usually go out, practice wearing heels and a dress, test my voice, build confidence, and be back in bed a little after midnight, in order to be fresh enough to get up and go to work the next day.

I got all dolled up. Ran a brush over and pinned up my unruly hair, used a moisturizer and foundation and applied an earth-toned eyeshadow along those high arches I had been blessed with, besides the usual mascara and liner that I usually donned, to enhance what everyone said was my best feature, my big-sexy-eyes. I put on a slinky white silk blouse and the skin-tight leather skirt I had borrowed from Laura and forgot to give back. The transformation was nothing less than amazing. I didn't just pass, I was striking. I had to look my best. Traci was no longer there to correct my little indiscretions or run interference for me. It was a Friday night. Things would be hopping at the clubs. I intended to go out after the meeting Paul had arranged for me with some guy who had the name of a ship-wrecked-sailor I read in a book in third grade—Caruso. He would become my new landlord.

We met at La Cuchina as Paul had arranged and sat across from one another at a table negotiating the rent for the room. He was a short wiry man with a dark complexion. He wore his coal black hair slicked back over the top of his head like Sammy Davis, Jr. His brown eyes peered out from behind a pair of thick-framed black glasses. Every time I'd look up at him, he'd look away. He didn't look me in the eye. It made me nervous. He wasn't creepy or anything like that. My gut told me he was not offended by my appearance but crushing on me. Too shy to look directly at me, like the bashful dwarf in Snow White.

The meeting went well. Before we had finished the Jalapeno poppers he ordered, Vince agreed to rent a room in his home, waive the security deposit, and help me move in on Saturday. He was small-boned and kind of wimpy to do much heavy lifting but I didn't have much stuff to move. I didn't take much from my old life and hadn't accumulated a lot of baggage in my year of living dangerously. Actually, it was less than a year. Much too soon to be on my own.

I didn't know what prompted me to move out. I wasn't ready. There was still so much to do and learn. Maybe I was anxious to get on with my life or a little afraid Paul was finally catching on to my charade. It had been a stressful month. Traci was gone. Joe was crying almost every night. He was losing his house, his money and the life he had loved including his loving wife. My daughter, Jen Rose, almost dropped out of West Point and the sale of our house nearly fell through at the last minute.

Our out-of-town buyers were well off financially but heard about my upcoming unusual change and used a clause in the contract that made the sale contingent on financing at a reasonable interest rate to get a better bargain. We accepted half of the original deal, $240,000 lower. It hurt but life in Barre was getting difficult for Debbie and April. We had no choice. It was a chance to start again for all of us.

All I ever wanted was to feel comfortable in my body. I thought once I was female everything else would fall into place. I could settle down and marry a good man. I already raised a family. I didn't want another one, but I yearned to have an ordinary life that had been denied me because of my unusual birth. The ugly truth hit hard one day near the end of my transition.

One afternoon, Joe and I were sipping cheap wine out on our porch in those plastic flutes and he commented that Traci and I were male women and would never be anything less than *extra ordinary*. He separated the word to highlight his point. To dream otherwise was ridiculous. I started shaking. I needed to get out, to have some suit buy me drinks, whisper sweet things in my ear, try and put his hands on me. Have some guy, any guy, fall all over me to vindicate my existence. I had a taste of it and now I felt a fire in my belly that I couldn't quite understand. As soon as Joe suggested no straight male would ever accept us no matter how beautiful we were—I was in a panic.

I left several messages on Traci's answering machine. It was a few days before she was scheduled to leave but she never returned my calls. She was gone and if she kept her promise it meant no one, not even me, would ever see her again. I wanted to stop by her mother's house but decided against it. If she wanted to see me, she would have found a way. I guess I chose to drive to Boston because part of me was hoping to run into Traci by going to our old haunts. She couldn't accuse me of violating her trust. It would be inadvertent.

Maybe Joe didn't get to me. Perhaps I was lonely. Paul worked late on Fridays. He generally never came back in town until after midnight. He would usually call the next morning. I feared he was getting ready to propose. Perhaps even this weekend. It was close to his birthday and our one-year anniversary. I was trying to avoid confrontation. I intended to dump Paul after he helped me move into another man's home. I had lived in fear long enough. I simply outgrew him, like Joe and everyone else at the XX Club.

Someone, I forgot who, once told me that there is nothing more selfish than a transsexual who first finds herself. There were some things I still had to figure out. That feeling like happiness is something owed you for all those years of suffering. The years of teasing and taunting and the beatings. The same boys who dunked your head in the toilet, took your pants and ran you through the walk of shame in the school yard were the ones gawking or craning their necks to look as you walk by or falling over themselves to ask you out. We begin to get delusional. We mistake lust for love and sometimes as femmes we forget ourselves and our origins. We want it all. All those experiences we lost during those years we had to live some other boy's life and not our own.

That's how I ended up at Jacques, alone and trying to remember all of the things Traci taught me to get along in this world. My life in transition was like some wild dream, unreal, and so unconnected to the woman I had become. I had watched Traci smile and play coy, twist men around her little finger. They bought her drinks all night long. She danced and teased them, and sometimes she would leave with them and I would have to find my own way home. It left me wondering and wanting to be more like her. It took a while to learn those lessons but I was a fast learner. With all the attention I was getting from men without even trying lately I began to dream again and think the impossible might happen. Perhaps one day, someone, a real Prince Charming, may even fall in love with me and we would live happily ever after.

The writer knows well that tragedy begins and ends in the mind and not on the stage.

We began to think of love as a game, something we can win. We play along with the big girls—the ones born that way—and step up to those high-stake tables, albeit, a little late to the party, where men, the drop-dead-handsome-ones, with money and power, take what they want. We are like rag dolls hurriedly stitched together, hoping to last a few years, but sewn up so tight that if we didn't stay detached, we would eventually come apart at the seams later. We knew the ending before we began, but we played anyway.

Even a short life is better than no life at all.

#

Chapter 43

The Sadist

Never forget that only dead fish swim with the stream. Malcolm Muggeridge.

A long black Cadillac limousine pulled up in front of me and stopped on the icy street. It blocked my path. I had ridden in a similar one years ago, on my first visit to Boston, the night before I enlisted into the USAF in 1976.

A gay Italian designer met me and two other new recruits at a hotel bar. We were waiting to be taken to the Armed Forces Induction Center in the morning. Viet Nam was still going on, or so we thought. God had a sense of humor. We called him Mr. V. He paid us to drive to go to some party with him and to model some of his designs at a speak-easy in NYC. It was the first time I had dared dress in women's clothing since the sixth grade, when I wore a princess costume on Halloween. My father had put an end to it when he told my mother I looked like a squirrel.

An electric hum disturbed the night air. The passenger window came down. A black face under a driver's cap looked up and beckoned me to come closer. I hesitated. Traci's voice entered my head: *Let them buy you drinks, dance if you like, but whatever you do, never get into the car.*

"Mr. Black would like the pleasure of your company this evening. Have you eaten?"

The driver's voice was baritone, deep, and assertive. It vibrated in the cool air. I felt it in my chest, from four feet away. His neck was bigger around than my waist.

"Are you hungry?" the black driver asked. He presumed I didn't hear him the first time.

I wondered whether Mr. Black was a real name, or whether he was patently gay like Mr. V. had been many years ago, or if Mr. Black was black. Not that it would have mattered. I had fantasies about Nubian lovers. I stood there shivering, trying to make up my mind, when another voice spoke up from the void in the back of the car.

"I know a very nice place around the corner where they make the best lobster ravioli in town. We can have a quiet dinner. I'll return you to your car, if for any reason you are not satisfied with the meal or my company."

It was a pleasant voice, low, firm, and masculine. It belonged to a confident man, I thought. A powerful man.

"Okay," I said.

The door opened and I got in. I was alone with a strange man in the back of a limousine. Mr. Black stared from the void. The vanity lights went on suddenly at the base of the doors and I saw the outline of his face leaning back on the bench seat.

Never, never get in the car, a voice in my head that sounded a lot like Traci whispered, or had it sounded more like my father? I was nervous.

Mr. Black continued to stare at me long after I settled into the seat beside him. He did not turn his head, but I knew he was looking. If I could have read his mind, I would have guessed that he had been pleasantly surprised. Since I had ventured out without Traci, men have bought my drinks, picked up tabs at restaurants, whistled, and stared unashamedly. One man even vouched for me at a store when I attempted to use a starter-check. He told the clerk I was going to be his future bride. I had never met him before.

Despite my newfound confidence I shook like a leaf inside whenever someone looked at me. When I looked into a mirror, I sometimes saw the man I used to be hiding under thick mascara, pressed powder, and lace. On those rare occasions I shared my secret with someone, they were always surprised to learn that I was male and had been born that way.

I felt uncomfortable under Mr. Black's gaze when he first inspected me but when he smiled, I relaxed. He had a genuine smile. Part of being a bisexual is appreciating the beauty in both the male and female of our species in aesthetic and sensual ways. It was a time I did not know my sexual orientation and was still searching for my identity. I hadn't known what to expect when I entered the car. Whether he would like me or I would like him. I was pleasantly surprised that I was attracted to him as well.

I had never seen Mr. Black before. I was certain I would have remembered him. His features were remarkable. He had the trim athletic build of a man who spent a lot of time at the gym and was particular about the food he ate. His brown, wavy hair was cut short with a touch of gray at the sides. His dark brown eyes hid under a pensive brow that pinched together as he studied me. He had a handsome face, well-proportioned and kind. There were a few lines across his forehead from thinking too hard and smiling wrinkles at the corners of his eyes. I guessed he was around 45 years old and an important man.

We made a few stops on the way to wherever we were going. One was at a dingy little bar at the end of a dark street where a man with a nasty red scar across his forehead handed him an envelope. The other, a small clothing store where we met a sleepy woman who opened the door to let us in. He said I needed a change of attire for the evening before going to dinner.

"You don't like what I am wearing?" Laura would be mortified.

He smiled and handed the woman his credit card. She led me around like a new-found puppy pulling things off racks as we passed for me to try on. I dressed and undressed in silence until she appeared satisfied, I would meet his standard. I rethought about the man I was with. He was an important man. A very wealthy one.

A powerful man.

The restaurant was in the North End. A large converted building that had once been a warehouse during prohibition. The inside walls were made of a rough-hewn stone. A few scattered paintings of Boston Harbor at the turn of the eighteenth century adorned the walls. The room was dim, lit by large yellow bulbs that hung down on long cords from a black ceiling. As soon as we walked in, heads turned in our direction. People stopped what they were doing and stared. Whispers were all around us like flittering butterflies trying to alight without being noticed. I pulled on the ends of the little black dress he had bought for me, as though I could somehow lengthen the hem.

The waiter escorted us to a table in the corner and lit a candle. Mr. Black's eyes darted about like he was looking for owls that might come out of the night and snatch us away at any moment. Two guests, an older man and woman with blue-gray hair, were the first to get up from their table and walk over. Then two others approached us. They called him Stephen and spoke with him as though he was a long, lost friend, a celebrity, or politician.

Nobody we met in the restaurant or on the street walking back to the car had called him Mr. Black. I think he was surprised by his own notoriety or perhaps he did not expect to run into anyone he knew or, more importantly, who knew him in this part of town. Maybe he took risks with his reputation and future, like me.

He was tense when people started to come up to our table. He watched closely out of the corner of his eye waiting for me to say something stupid or embarrass him. I nodded politely, spoke sparingly but eloquently, held out my hand when appropriate and thanked each for their kind compliments. They liked my dress and my naturally curly hair, and one man was taken by my eyes.

Mr. Black smiled when I had compared my hair to a feather-duster. He was a perfect gentleman. He pulled out my chair, ordered my meal and spoke to me with kindness about various subjects that put me at ease. None of which had anything to do with my past, sex, or any anticipation of what was to come. I must have acted appropriately. He smiled and nodded his head to let me know that I met with his approval. I relaxed. It was easy to play the part of a lady because he treated me like one. He was handsome and charming, and I had begun to wonder if fairy tales came true. I felt that any moment I might be whisked away to some castle on a hill to live happily ever after.

After dinner, Mr. Black put his coat around my shoulders as we walked out to the car. It was made of real fur, warm, and smelled like him. It draped down to my bare legs that were raw from the cold. He was a considerate and cautious man.

We drove further into the city where the buildings rose like spires into a bronze sky. We stopped at one of them and parked under it. He ordered the driver to escort me up to the room while he made arrangements with a man at the front desk. The man stood erect as soon as Mr. Black walked up to him. Did he just smile at me? Had I met him before? He seemed familiar. He handed Mr. Black a small tote bag, the kind you bring to the gym. He held it with both hands and close to his chest as though it contained something precious. His misshapen head twisted around to stare as we got onto the elevator.

The room was large with a wall of glass that looked out over the silhouette of the city. We were alone for the first time all evening. Mr. Black put his arm around me. We sat on a leather sofa staring at a large screen television that was not on. The sounds of the city twenty-one floors below drifted in from a crack in the balcony door. I sensed a change in him. He was quiet. His fingers made small circles on my shoulder creeping closer to my right breast. Joe had helped me bind my small bosom with tape to create the illusion of cleavage. My boobs were small. I feared he would be angry when he found out— even though he knew what I was.

His fingers stroked the base of my throat probing that soft flesh between the collar bones. He moved his hand up and down along the front of my neck. Sometimes he stopped under my chin and lifted my head up. His touch was gentle as though he was afraid to break me. I think he found it remarkable I did not have a noticeable Adam's apple. My heart beat fast. In the muted light of the room I saw a smile creep across his face as he stroked my throat with his two fingers. I couldn't see his other hand.

"You amazed me tonight. Mrs. Kendrick was particularly taken with you."

"Thank—"

He squeezed my throat at its softest point. I gagged but didn't try to remove his hand.

"Don't speak unless I tell you." My body went rigid. "I like you. I don't want to hurt you. Do you trust me?"

I tried to nod. Panic was not an option. I sensed he was training me. Grooming me for something more ominous.

"Good girl."

He loosened his grip and put something in my lap. It was made of leather and looked like a collar with a hole in the center with three long cords attached. A black ball was threaded into the center cord. It slid up and down and looked as though it fit into the hole in the leather collar. His eyes followed my hands as I slid the ball up the cord and pressed it into the opening. It was a tight fit. He was waiting for me to ask him what it was. As I looked up, he handed me a pair of leather panties. His eyes were dark holes in the night.

"You are not like the others I've met. You're interesting."

He put something else in my hand. It felt like a wad of bills. I didn't know we got paid for this. It scared me.

"More champagne."

His voice was flat.

"No thank you," I said, uncertain if I should speak.

He laughed.

"No, I want you to get up and pour me more champagne."

"Oh," I said, and pulled myself up out of the cushions. Away from his warmth, the air was cold.

I found the bottle chilling in an ice bucket in the next room. When I came back, he was not on the couch but sitting on the bed. His jacket was off. His shirt unbuttoned, and his pants were unhitched. I handed him his glass of champagne and stared out the window over the balcony. We were high. A long, long way from the ground.

"Take it off," he said.

"What?"

"The dress. Take it off."

I was stunned and embarrassed. Traci had said these guys were sensitive about seeing male parts even though they know we have them. When I hesitated, he grabbed my wrists and pulled me into him. The scent of his cologne and sweat was overpowering when I'm pressed up against his hard stomach.

"Do you want me to do it?"

"What?" My voice scratched at the air.

"I won't bother with the buttons. You may not have much to wear tomorrow."

I was shocked both by the content, and the manner he said it. His voice was as calm as it was when he was ordering my dinner from the menu earlier in the evening. He let go of my wrists. I reached behind my back and began unhooking the hasp. I slid down the zipper. The dress slipped to the floor around my ankles. I consciously slowed my breathing. The champagne had made me lightheaded. I wondered if he slipped something earlier into my drink. I didn't think I drank enough to make me feel lightheaded.

Mr. Black stood up. He slid his pants off his hips. They fell to the floor like a whisper. He had on boxer shorts with tiny stars stitched in gold thread. He reached under my breasts and pulled on the duct tape pinching them together. He laughed. He pulled the tape up and with a snap of his wrist he jerked me into the air and again and again, until it came off in his hand.

My eyes teared up. It hurt. I wondered if I was bleeding but I didn't dare look. I didn't move. I didn't scream.

"Good girl." Mr. Black was impressed. He knew I was scared. He put his hands on my shoulders and rubbed gently until my breathing slowed. "Shh, it's okay. You're going to be fine."

He ran a hand across my flat stomach. Something tugged

between my legs. I felt betrayed by my own body. I was growing aroused.

"If you cooperate, no matter how rough it gets, you will walk out of here tomorrow with only a few bruises. If you struggle, you will hurt more."

The shaking became more violent, uncontrollable. I prayed my homemade gaff stayed in place. I was throbbing.

"I have to go pee," I said. My voice was barely audible. Mr. Black smiled and nodded his consent.

"Come right back when you are through. And put these on."

He handed me the leather accessories. My knees buckled as I walked. I staggered toward the bathroom. What did I get myself into? I was scared. I blamed it on the hormones. I have ridden over frozen rivers with openings that would swallow a sled and man and not spit him out until spring. I have ridden a snowmobile at speeds in excess of 100 mph inches above the snow-covered ground, flown combat missions where Russian fighter pilots had their weapons locked onto our fuselage but I had never been that afraid of anyone in my life like I was of that man.

I relieved myself and fixed my gaff, tucking my sex away for whatever was going to happen. I was already sore. I pulled on the leather panties he had given me and studied the rigid contraption around my neck in the full-length mirror. The cords hanging from the collar were different lengths. The knob was threaded into the center cord and was not made of plastic as I'd first thought but some other material that reminded me of a cue ball. It was hard, smooth, and heavy. The two sides were smaller and had hooks on each end. It looked like some kind of a leash.

I wondered if I could make it to the hallway without being detected before I bolted toward the elevators. I could yell for help, but Mr. Black would claim that I consented to his strange sexual proclivities or that he had thrown me out when he found out that I was a male prostitute. Either way, I would be arrested. It was a no-win situation.

"More champagne, sweetheart, and bring two fresh glasses from the wet bar." I heard his voice and wondered how it never raised an octave and managed to scare the living hell out of me. My knees began to shake again. I found the glasses and brought him the bottle of champagne. He was lying back on the bed. He took a sip, handed the glass back to me and nodded toward the nightstand. I put down the glasses. He spread his legs and pulled me down to him. A musky scent wafted up from his shorts under my knees. I marveled how warm they were as I pushed them away.

He pulled on one of the cords and the ball slid into place. It jerked my head straight-up and when he pulled down on the string, I couldn't breathe. I was his mannequin or some pet. He ran a hand through the thick curls on top of my head and said, "good girl."

"You're beautiful," he said. He stroked my hair with the back of one hand. He parted my lips and he pushed his fingers into my mouth. They tasted salty and a little like champagne. There was a soft click and I felt the prick of a blade in the soft flesh under my chin.

"If you want to keep your pretty face, act the part of the pretty girl I see, and nothing more."

Despite the fact that I had just gone pee, I wet myself.

Never, never get into the car, the voice in my head had said.

I should have listened.

# # #

Trauma has an effect on memory. Some victims repress it. Others simply relive the fear without thinking about the event. Anything may trigger the memory. An image, a smell, a sound. For me it was the smell of damp, dirty socks and odors that emanate from a musty room that has been closed up for a long time. It becomes Billy Houston's room. The teen-age boy who sexually assaulted me when I was a four-year-old boy, or trapped inside his body.

Victims may exhibit seemingly unexplainable and odd behavior days or even years after an event. In the days that followed my sexual assault, I used to climb out of my crib during the night. My mother would find me curled up on the floor of my closet, sucking my thumb with my blanket wrapped securely around me. Sometimes, I would hide in the backseat of my father or my uncle's car. They would find me after they got to work. No one understood my sudden odd behavior.

The XX Club's clinical psychiatrist, John Felber, invited me to his home in West Hartford one evening to accommodate my busy schedule. The meeting was part of the Harry S. Benjamin Standards of Care the clinic followed regarding its recommendation for sexual reassignment.

I presented his wife a check for $400 at the door and she showed me to his study. Dr. Felber was a robust man with a Vandyke beard that gave him an uncanny resemblance to Sigmund Freud. He was seated behind his big mahogany desk beside the active fireplace and I sat on the other side at his bequest. He asked me a series of four simple questions before asking me:

Have you ever been sexually assaulted?

Billy Houston's bedroom unfolded before my eyes as vividly as it did that first time, in 1959. It was the first time I had cried during my transition, if you could call wiping a few tears off my cheeks crying.

Rain tapped lightly against the windows. The snow had turned to rain in the early morning hours. The soft pattering of the water splashing on the balcony deck through the open window sent a wave of panic through me. Billy had a knife. He had lured me into his room with it. Mr. Black surprised me with his blade under my chin. I never intended to go back to Jacques, not ever. I never intended to run into Mr. Black again either. I repressed his memory. Oddly, I lost my love of champagne in the years that followed.

#

Chapter 44

The Big Day

Everything has beauty but not everyone sees it. – Confucius

Laughter scurried under the door into my bedroom. I threw off my covers and walked out of my bedroom to find a group of wannabe women sitting around our kitchen table and snickering into their coffee cups. I didn't have to be a savant to know they were discussing the party. A party that, if not the physical death of each of them, may be an end to whatever happiness they managed to eke out an otherwise pathetic existence.

Sarah's normally passive voice made me pay closer attention. She sounded excited. My eyes landed on a woman trying on a red satin party dress talking giddily to Joe. I didn't recognize her. Not at first glance. Not until she looked up and her dark slanted eyes alighted upon mine. She blushed as though caught in some embarrassing position.

"Well Sleeping Beauty is awake. You sure been sawing a lot of logs in there. Thought I was going to have to wake you to go to work." Joe's voice came from behind me. He sounded inordinately cheerful and kind.

I got up earlier and left a message on the answering machine at Dunhill. First sick day I had taken in over a year for the service.

"I am not working today."

I looked at them. Joe had on a long wool coat. Everyone was dressed to go out. Big Kathy, Sarah, and Kaitlyn, too.

"Wow, what are you all doing?"

"It's the big day, silly. Aren't you coming?" Big Kathy buttoned her collar. Her stare was one of concern.

"We got a room at the hotel. We will be decorating the party room all day and changing later." Joe explained.

"You should come along. We've got room in my car."
Kaitlyn rattled her keys up in front of her for effect.

"No, that's okay. I've got—"

"You're coming, right?"

Kaitlyn sounded worried.

"Of course, she's coming. She wouldn't miss it for the
world. Would you, Evie?" Joe blurted.

His tone was threatening. I owed him. It didn't matter
that I had done several favors for him in the beginning of our
relationship. Driving all the way to NYC in the middle of the
night to fetch me after I dissed him had reset my account. A
suitcase clutched in his large hand caught my eye. I shrugged
and forced a smile. Paul made plans for the weekend. We were
going to his favorite restaurant. The one near the harbor where
we first kissed. It looked like I would have to pull a sick card for
this party. Taking him as my date to this function never entered
my mind, but I nodded in the affirmative and kept a smile
pressed to my lips.

"Great. If you need a place to rest and get ready, Jorge and
I are in room 627." Kaitlyn said.

Jorge? Was that the name of her married boyfriend? The
one who beats on her? I thought it was Jose? Didn't she call him
Georgy or Gerry once, too? I looked over at Joe. His expression
soured. He wore his protective-father-face me, not his usual
mother hen puss.

"Oh, Evie, you haven't heard?"

Kaitlyn held out her hand. A ring with a large blue stone
sparkled under the overhead lamp of our kitchen. It didn't look
real but I guess to her mystery lover neither did she. I thought
Gerry, Georgy, Jose or whatever his name in Spanish, was
supposed to be married?

"He's getting a divorce?" Kaitlyn added. She must have
caught my bewilderment. Her voice shook. I couldn't tell if it was
from nerves or excitement. "He's a changed man. Since you and
Joe came to visit—" she doesn't finish her thought.

To dwell deep on any subject where the object of

affection is a tranny has an ultimate tragic conclusion. Love is reserved for the natural world. Perhaps it was the physical pain she was avoiding. The word hospital has its own negative connotations. Her bandaged and swollen purple face flashed before me. She healed well. For as often as he hit her, she had no permanent marks. Some memories are best left unmentioned.

"He said he is leaving his wife at the end of the month. We have been looking for apartments near Wilmington. We will be moving in together." Her voice became more nasal. She reached out and wrapped me up in her long stringy arms. It shocked me.

"He says he can't wait to see you again. You really impressed him."

What, in my ten second exchange when he knocked me over a chair fighting with Joe in her hospital room? She released me. She stared into my eyes looking for a reaction I hoped was well hidden under my frozen smile.

"He's looking forward to seeing you at the party. He wants to meet some of my friends. Isn't life grand?" Kaitlyn twirled around nearly knocking the copper tea pot off the stove with her loose lacy sleeves.

"I didn't know he liked—" I searched for the proper words— "our kind?" I muttered under my breath. Joe silenced me with a look. Kaitlyn caught our exchange again and frowned. For some odd reason she wanted my approval.

"He had a come-to-Jesus-moment." Joe held up his fist. Kaitlyn erupted into laughter.

"You two crack me up." Kaitlyn laughed like a little girl.

"It's a different world," Big Kathy added.

There was no conviction in her voice. She must have had some reservations. She had made more trips to the hospital than any of us and lately her drawings concerned a trans with blackened eyes and men with sinister faces staring over their shoulder at an innocent victim.

"Come on, we're going to be late. I have to pick up my wife at her work on the way." Big Kathy ordered.

"We are meeting some of the Tiffany Club members at the

hotel for lunch. They are helping with the decorations." Kaitlyn squealed and rushed by me out the door. "Try to get there early. It will be fun."

I wanted to tell Kaitlyn that this was not an official Tiffany Club function. A few members Jennifer had known had agreed to help us set up our first party, but I didn't want to dim her enthusiasm. She and other members had come alive in the last few months in ways I had only seen the femmes during their transition since I had been there.

There was no reason for me to share any of my fears with them about my suspicions of what I thought went on in that hotel or even in telling her to be careful. She was already with someone who could break her in half seven times over and likely would before their relationship ended, if ever. Besides, mother-hen would be there. Nothing got past HER!

"Sarah, get our dresses off the bed would you, dear," Joe instructed his new protege.

"Keep them on the hangers and don't tear the plastic. It took me a time to get them in there. Sarah, did you hear me? What are you staring at?"

Sarah was staring out the side window. I presumed she was watching Big Kathy and Kaitlyn find their way down the dark drive toward their cars. Is that Kaitlyn's red dress? How could she forget that one? Ah, we will have to bring it. Grab it, will you?

The phone rang. Joe answered then handed it to me.

"He asked for doll face."

He let the smile fall of his face after holding it there for two seconds. Now you see it, now you don't. Happy, not happy. He drove me crazy.

As soon as I heard the familiar baritone voice, a shiver ran over my skin and my heart beat faster. I wasn't certain if it was fear or excitement. At first blush, I jumped. Someone wanted me? Desire—that single heart thump just below lust—one of those little known, deadly little sins that Santa had left off the naughty list, pounded under my breast.

"Meet me at the Star Lighter Cafe," the voice said. It was Mr. Black.

"What makes you think I would ever want to see you again?" I suddenly understood the meaning of the word flabbergasted.

"Because you can't stop thinking about me."

I couldn't suppress the sound that escaped my lips. A cross between a laugh and a gasp. "Huh?"

"Would it help if I told you that I can't get you out of my head?"

"You put a knife at my throat and made me give you—"

"I am reluctant to discuss that on the phone, my dear, but if it makes you feel any better. I am sorry."

"So am I, Mr. Black, or whatever your name is—"

"I want to see you again—"

"I don't believe we are compatible."

It sounded like a business proposal. Instead of making a deal, I should have been making him apologize. I should be mad at him.

"If you give me the courtesy of—"

"I don't date admirers." I was not into S&M either. The collar he put on my neck almost choked the life out of me.

"Hear me out, please." I should have hung up. Did he really expect me to put myself in danger again? The audacity of the man. I stayed on the line. Putting myself at risk was part of transition, wasn't it?

"You were not harmed. It was just a game. I mistook you for—no, no I won't make excuses. Let's just start over again, shall we?"

I was speechless. There was panic in his voice that intrigued me. What was wrong with me? Maybe a real woman might have been flattered by a man who found her so interesting that he was compelled to beg for another chance.

"Evelyn, please, I am not perfect. I have my proclivities, for lack of a better word. Meet me this evening. Have one drink at the Star Lighter and hear my proposal. I promise if you do not want to ever see me again it will be the end of it. We will go our separate ways."

"Not on your life." I scoffed and told him I was busy, but he would not take no for an answer. Successful men seldom do. He begged me again to meet him and that scared me. Powerful men don't grovel. He was not the kind of man who was used to begging and certainly not rejection. Perhaps, he was luring me into some trap. Still, I wondered.

"I am busy tonight. It's not just a line."

My voice waivered. He was right. I was unharmed, at least physically, and he treated me well before he got rough. Despite my instincts telling me not to see him again, I wanted him to convince me otherwise.

"I know you have a party to attend at the Magnum. The Star Lighter is on the 18th Floor. I thought we could meet before your gathering." How did he know about the party? I looked over at Joe. He turned to stare in another direction. He purposely averted my gaze. It was unlike him not to be nosy. That's when I knew Mr. Black had called before. *Why didn't he tell me?*

Joe stopped in the door way.

"You better be there. People rely on you. For some reason Kaitlyn and others look up to you. Don't let them down." Joe pointed his finger in my face.

He left with Sarah following close behind him with an armful of colorful linen and lace. He lived in a world of colorful clothing and fantasy. I wondered if he realized what he was doing to me. How vulnerable it was to try to walk away from yourself and try to become someone else? How easy it would be for someone, a powerful man like Mr. Black, to come along and poke a hole in my world and watch all of my dreams come undone.

#

Chapter 45

The Party

Write something, even if it's a suicide note. Gore Vidal

An uneasy feeling crept over me as I got into my car.

I was going back to that place. The hotel where Conrad hurt Traci, where Bernard tried to hurt me, and some powerful man put a knife to my throat. They were related. They had to be. It was too coincidental. Some S & M club was operating out of the Magnum, the hotel where the XX Club was having its party.

Was I crazy? Did I have a death wish?

Sure, I took risks. I always lived on the edge. It was like a drug in my bloodstream but was I willing to throw it all away now that I was so close to attaining my dream?

I caught a glimpse of the frightened girl in the rear-view mirror. I barely recognized myself. Soon Michael and Evelyn and the XX Club would be a memory, and everyone I had ever known—gone.

"Stealth's a bitch."

Traci's voice popped into my head. Her words spill into my head from out of the darkness.

"Following a dream is never easy."

She was sitting next to me, patting the hollows of her cheeks as though she could make them swell. Jealous of my high cheek bones.

"There is pretty and there is beautiful. You are definitely the later," she said, then looked at me and added, "try not to let it get to your head, sweet cheeks."

I looked up at my reflection again. I didn't feel beautiful. There was fear in the dark eyes. Traci was not there. Fear was my companion now. I was utterly and completely alone.

Paul was an enigma. Even though I agreed to move out of Joe's apartment and into the house of another man, I wasn't sure I would stay with him. He wasn't much of a boyfriend. More a brief encounter, another experience to put behind me as quickly as possible. I had never seen our relationship blossoming. I didn't know what he saw in me and to be truthful, I was uncertain what I saw in him. I believed I was heterosexual.

I dreamt of girls growing up. I had wet dreams, got erect, masturbated, like most boys, and intercourse with girls was fun, at least in the beginning until the novelty wore off. I could not understand why I got aroused in locker rooms around other naked boys. I usually dressed in a corner where I didn't have to look at them and showered quickly or waited until I got home.

When Paul and I first kissed, I did not know what to expect. I thought I would be revulsed but when my sex strained against its restraint and almost betrayed me, I was shocked. I thought maybe it was the excitement of a near-death experience or something like being on an aircraft that almost crashes and your heart pounds so hard, you feel it everywhere, even in your crotch.

But then it happened again, when I danced with men at clubs, and again standing next to someone on a train and he was so close I could smell musk wafting up from his tea shirt under his jacket. I found myself leaning closer. At Jacques, on the dance floor, goose flesh, and then there was Mr. Black that set every hair on my body on end. It was frightening how much it affected me when a man took me in his arms. Men and women, but only certain ones, turned me on. It was confusing.

Despite uncertainty about my own sexuality, I was pretty certain that BDSM was not my thing. I didn't need to be tied up or have pain to get it on, but when I hung up, I had agreed to meet Mr. Black in the lobby of the hotel at eight.

It was a public place. I thought it would be safe. Still, I wondered. What was I thinking? If I changed my mind, he would be there lurking in the shadows watching me. That wicked smile. Those irresistible dimples. That knife. I was driving back to Boston, to a hotel where I lost my innocence.

Not the virtuousness natural-born women have, but the loss of that child-like illusion where we wannabes feel safe behind closed doors, locked behind a facade of masculinity. Those easy smiles that shield men from intense scrutiny do not work for women.

I was not much different than those new members of the XX club, the she-males who believed we could still fall back on that privilege we were born with to protect us.

A tall man, his face covered in shadows, stood alone by the elevator doors in the parking garage. I recognized the swell of the shoulders under the tailored jacket and the shock of thick black hair combed back over a high brow.

Bernard's crooked smile faded as I pulled into a nearby space and threw the gear shift into park. I should have been afraid but I was not. I felt a rush of excitement instead like when I boarded those flights in the military that took me to the edge of enemy territory and an uncertain destiny. He won't recognize the confident new me, I thought.

Bernard's eyes ran up and down my body as I boarded the elevator trying hard to remember where he may have seen me. I looked different. I hoped it was enough. A hand reached in. The doors halted. A signet ring clicked against the metal on the casing. There was that tattoo, the one with the crossed whips. I glanced up as the door slid back open.

Bernard stepped on. I held my breath. No hint of recognition or fear could escape my eye.

I knew from my numerous prechecks in the mirror on the way over that my makeup was impeccable, precise. I could still hear Joe breathing on the back of my neck every morning in those early days: practice makes perfect. Be perfect or be read.

The facade of a beautiful professional woman stood erect, unflinching under his gaze. She was so different than the slut he picked up at Jacques that frigid night. I gave him a casual glance and an inconvenient smile. Inside my chest a mustang thrashed against the stocks.

"Hello." He smiled at me.

It prompted a nasty kick at my ribs from the inside. I nodded and turned away politely. The door silently closed behind him. We stood alone, me staring at the closed doors, he staring at my stern profile. The enclosed space grew warmer with the doors closed.

What the fuck was wrong with the AC?

"Lobby please," he asked, then in the same breath, "have we met?"

I realized I was standing in front of the panel. The L button was unlit. Dare I stare back into those cold, steel eyes? I shook my head in the negative and stared straight ahead like I had seen many waitresses do when ignoring a pest.

"I'm sorry," he stammered and stepped around me. The door suddenly opened again. An old man and woman dressed in evening attire entered. The man pressed five and the older woman smiled politely at me.

"Forgive me for the intrusion but you look like someone I knew," Bernard fumbled. He appeared embarrassed. I wanted to take a deep breath, but I didn't dare shake the facade of the annoyed prey.

"Are you sure we haven't met?" he delivered the oldest line in the book with flair as he ran a quick hand through his thick black hair. I shook my head and tried to look annoyed.

The door opened and I stepped out into the crowded lobby past the old couple. Bernard bumped past them and stepped out before the door closed.

"Miss," he called after me.

I ignored him and pushed through a group of tall women in flowing gowns before realizing they were not real women. Their strong perfumes overwhelmed my senses. Their makeup was near perfect, perhaps too perfect. There was a faint line against the underside of the chin of the woman in the purple dress to my right. Her Adams Apple protruded noticeably like a knot in an old oak.

These were not XX Club members. I didn't recognize any

of them. They must have been from the Tiffany Club. Drag queens and crossdressers with lots of practice. One was asking a young clerk behind the counter for directions to the Marshall Room in a deep throaty voice that reminded me of my own only huskier and more confident. The clerk smiled and pointed a shaky finger toward a corridor behind her. A firm hand gripped my elbow.

"I would be most humbled if you would allow me to buy you a drink."

"Stop following me," I snapped. My voice was unnaturally high.

Bernard let go of my arm and raised his hands up in defense. In that moment of exchange, I thought I saw a glint of recognition that I had hoped to avoid.

"I don't mean to intrude. It is not like me to be so bold. I don't mean to follow you, but my future children would never forgive me if I let this opportunity pass without trying. It is only the fear that I may never see you again that makes me act the buffoon. I am completely under your spell. This is not my normal—"

"Oh, honey, he had me at hello! I mean if you are not with anyone, have a drink with him. He is gorgeous. I am so jealous."

One of the crossdressers said in a voice deep and nasal.

Bernard's head snapped around. A pile of blond tresses set up high on a blond head tied in with a gold tiara made her appear taller than him.

"Just one drink, please, I am harmless. I promise to be the gentleman."

He went down on one knee and extended his hands out with their palms up. The crossdressers and several people nearby laughed at his antics.

"Please," he insisted. "Just one drink. I adore you!"

He slipped into a familiar East European accent. That glint of recognition I had seen in his eyes earlier was missing. I was suspicious. He was sly. I wondered how I was going to get away from him.

"Ah," two of the crossdressers sighed almost in harmony. The one in the chiffon dress with a white faux fur bolero over her broad shoulders placed a hand over her heart. Her long nails were painted pink to match her dress.

"No. I can't."

I softened my voice trying not to appear the total bitch. "I am meeting someone."

"Eve?" a familiar voice rang out from behind me as if on cue.

Bernard's eyes sparkled in the light of the rhinestone chandeliers spinning overhead as he turned.

A tall slender woman in red moved toward me with her long, bare arms outstretched. The satin dress was tapered into a New York waist line giving Sarah's usually emaciated lanky frame a feminine appearance. Sarah looked like an eloquent and sophisticated debutant wearing one of Joe's human hair wigs. No longer that skinny effeminate man sitting, head down in the corner, listening to everyone else's woes at the XX Club. A new air of confidence surrounded Sarah. I folded myself into her embrace and stepped back to admire Joe's handiwork.

"You're beautiful. I almost didn't recognize you."

I hesitated to add: You look like a girl. Despite taking a femme name, Sarah had always presented as some overgrown adolescent male.

"You too, Eve, gorgeous as always. I'd know that big hair anywhere. You can't hide from the world with that mop."

She looked up as if noticing Bernard and the crossdressers for the first time. She blushed when she realized she was the center of their attention.

"You're friend? Takes my breath away."

Bernard bowed toward Sarah.

"Come, please, join me this evening ladies. Both of you. I promise you a grand time."

Sarah was stunned into silence. Bernard took her by the hand and kissed her wrist. The color in her made-up face deepened. She looked at me like a little girl who found a kitten.

"I am sorry. We must decline. We are late for a prior engagement."

I began, before being cut off by the crossdresser in blue.

"I'm available, sweetie."

Blue lady held out her hand. Bernard looked startled.

"Sorry, I have eyes only for—"

He nodded in my direction then tipped his head back at Blue lady.

"I am Sorry, too, Sweetie," Blue lady giggled.

"Joe saved a place for you at our table. He said you'd be coming. We're in—"

I took Sarah's hand and pulled her away from Bernard hoping she wouldn't say--,

"The Marshall Room."

Sarah finished her thought.

Bernard's gaze locked on mine. Fear slipped by my guard. That glint of mischief was back in the center of his pupil. He knew. I thought he recognized me.

The crossdressers realized there was some connection between us and began cooing like pigeons in a Notre Dame courtyard. Damn my voice. Pink Lady's eyebrows arched up.

"Oh, honey, you look great!"

"I never would have known," the one in the bronze gown exclaimed.

Blue Lady shrieked: "Baby, take me. I'm game. What's she got that I ain't?"

She jutted one hip toward Bernard.

He moved away instinctively. Bernard's ears turned bright red at the tips. The squeals and shrills that came with the added attention intimidated him. He looked around to see if anyone was staring. Anyone of the normal persuasion. Even though he wanted a sexual tryst with a twist, I don't think he wanted it public. He looked at the clerk sheepishly before turning away.

The crossdressers followed Sarah and I down the corridor toward the Marshall room.

"I'm Bonnie," Pink Lady introduced herself then the others.

"This is Gracie in gold and Margaret in blue."

She held out a hand with long, pointed red nails. I took it. Margaret and Gracie nodded hello.

"I'm Evelyn and this is—my friend—Sarah." Sarah nodded. It didn't go unnoticed when I called her my friend her eyes watered.

"XX Club?" Bonnie asked. I nodded.

"Wow, hormones do make a difference."

Her sapphire eyes danced in the light.

"Wish I could get my hands on some. Hint, hint."

Gracie's voice was thoroughly male. Like Joe, she didn't try to soften it. She held out her large, calloused hand, palm up, as if waiting for me to give her something.

"Those are real, huh?" Margaret eyed my boobs. I nodded again.

"Shit, must be nice."

She pulled down on one side of her bodice and exposed a silicon tit. The nipple painted in bright orange glared like a third eye.

"Behave, Margaret," Bonnie scolded her.

"Someone might see you. Besides, you are embarrassing our guests."

She looked over at Sarah.

"Your friend is quite shy."

"She is not used to dressing."

"She is beautiful. If she wasn't so tall, I would have figured her natural-born like you."

Bonnie pulled at a loose strand of her blond wig and tucked it behind her ear. I was flattered.

"At least at first, before you snapped at your suitor," Bonnie added.

"Your voice is good but not perfect. I've had too many lessons not to know the difference."

I looked at Bonnie.

"You're not wearing an evening gown. I mean who wears a pantsuit anymore, especially to a ball? It's so gay seventies. Besides, it looked like you needed help getting rid of him. The panic on your face, priceless."

Her lips curled as she looked me up and down.

"Am I that obvious?"

I thought I had done a great job masking my fear.

"You looked like a deer in the headlights when he grabbed your arm."

"I thought I was going to have to lift up my skirts."

Gracie erupted into laughter before she could finish.

"Don't laugh it works."

"I'd have blown him for you. He was cute."

Margaret added.

Bonnie and Gracie laughed, and Sarah smiled. The elevator doors opened as we passed, and several other people dressed to the max fell in behind us coming from the direction of the rooms.

At first glance there were more women than men in reams of satin and lace, a field of wild colorful orchids, the kind with those miniature faces peering back at you from a distance. Sarah took my hand, pulling me deeper into the room.

As I surveyed the happy faces, it occurred to me I had been wrong about the danger of men in dresses parading around in public. The reactions of the staff and guests were not hostile or even shocked but more amused.

Some appeared to revel in the show as though tall men in dresses were there to entertain them. Margaret, Gracie and Bonnie, the tall graceful shrews of the Tiffany Club, drew stares and praises as they paraded through the lobby like it was their own private runway. The trio of crossdressers were treated with dignity and they reacted in kind, like royal dignitaries from a foreign land, anxious to spread goodwill.

Joe may have been right all along. The world did not fear him. When everyone knows who you are, a gender bender is good clean fun. The world would laugh but welcome him. It was our kind, those capable of blending so well we could stay hidden among them for days, months, sometimes for years, without anyone ever knowing.

As remote as it may seem, no straight male wanted to wake up in bed one morning beside some boy they made fun of or spit upon in chemistry class ten years prior. A woman may feel violated if she opened up to a friend about her teenage abortion to later find her friend had been some guy that dated her sister in high school. It's that kind of deception that terrifies them. They feel deceived regardless of whether it's for an illicit purpose.

Light spun out from a crystal chandelier in the shape of a globe and spilled color over the room. Large decorative bodies in glaring gowns, shiny sequined shoes and some flamboyant bonnets sat at tables, filled the dance floor, or stood near the walls. Hotel employees in black skirts and white blouses stood behind a long rectangular table near the entrance collecting coats, hats, and gloves. Their male counterparts in dark pants and plain white shirt stood behind another table dispensing spirits. Their broad smiles appeared genuine. I was glad I was wrong.

For the first time since my transition began, I felt hope, not for myself so much, as I had always been one of the fortunate ones but for those who, no matter how hard they tried, would never blend in.

Joe sat tall in his chair at one of the tables in the corner of the room set aside for the XX Club members and their guests. Big Kathy leaned in to speak to a small woman in horn-rimmed glasses to her right that I presume was her wife. The timid smile barely reached eyes that darted fervently from side to side whenever someone bumped her chair.

"You made it."

Joe held up a goblet of champagne and greeted me as I pulled a chair out beside him. He was wearing a black wig pinned up on top of his head with a silver pin, his solid frame draped in a long gown the color of an eggplant.

"Someone said he thought you would dis us tonight. No one expected to see you once you got your letter," Laura said. A dark blue gown stretched over her large frame, her stomach protruding notably.

"Yup, she's going stealth, guys, take a last look. In a month she'll be gone, maybe sooner."

Joe talked louder than usual. He was putting on a show to cover up his disappointment.

I had not officially told him that I was moving out of our apartment next weekend. I made the mistake of confiding in Big Kathy at the last meeting. Joe sneaked into my room while I was at work and emptied out all of the change that I had been saving in an old traffic cone. That's when I knew Kathy had told him.

"I knew you would come," he whispered. I didn't come to gloat or fight. Why did he think I hated him? Didn't he understand it was about survival, not personal?

"Where's Jennifer and Julie?"

I avoided his gaze and picked up a flute of champagne that appeared untouched in front of my empty plate.

"Sitting at the head table with the Tiffany Club biggies. I didn't even know that club existed. I've been such a recluse. My kind of people. I may have found a source of new best friends."

He laughed at his private joke.

"So, which doctor did you decide on?" Big Kathy asked. "Oh, and this is Penny, my wife."

She jutted her chin toward the small woman beside her, who smiled.

"You look—stunning in that pantsuit," Penny complimented me.

"Thank you."

I nodded in Penny's direction, then turned towards her husband.

"Schrang."

"They say Wisconsin is beautiful in the fall. They get foliage similar to New England."

Big Kathy leaned in. The music was loud and my voice

was low.

"Why did you select him? Biber has been performing SRS for years. Didn't Schrang just start?"

"Biber is retiring. I think it's important to find someone who can do follow up if needed."

Schrang had come to one of our meetings. He showed a really grotesque film of one of the operations that he had performed. It chased all but the serious transsexuals out of the room. I met him afterward. He was a bit arrogant, but I liked him. It was as simple as that. It made me self-conscious to talk about trans issues outside of the club setting. Big Kathy's wife was staring at me.

"If Kathy hadn't told me I wouldn't have guessed—I thought you were one of the wives," Penny said.

"When are you leaving?" Big Kathy added.

I shrugged. She was trying to patch things up between us or provide a prompt for me to reveal my plans to move out on Joe. The meeting Paul had arranged at La Cu china with my future landlord, Vincent Caruso, went well. I had already confided in Kathy that I was leaving.

I looked over at the empty places at our table. Only about a dozen members had ventured out into the light. Some apparently paid for tickets but had second thoughts. It was not uncommon to spend hours dressing and preparing hair and makeup and get to the door before getting the shakes. We area an odd lot.

"Where's Kaitlyn? I thought she'd be here."

I changed the subject.

"She left with a guy she met downstairs. Nice looking. Some foreign dude. I think she introduced him as Jerry or something."

One of the newbies at the table spoke up.

"I thought I had seen her in the lobby with that married guy she was bonkers about." Someone else added.

The hair on the back of my neck was standing on end.

"She wouldn't leave like that." Big Kathy said.

"Not without saying goodbye and not alone with some strange guy she just met."

Joe sat upright in his chair.

"She's here with her boyfriend, right?"

I recalled seeing them. A man standing by the elevator doors holding her hand. There had been no recognition in his eyes when I passed him. "Gerry, Georgy, or some Spanish version of that—"

"Mr. Homophobia? Not on your life. No f'n way he would come near this place tonight. He thinks gayness is contagious."

Laura laughed as she came up from behind my chair.

How she knew him, I wasn't about to ask.

"Jorge, he's Puerto Rican."

Sarah jerked her head up to look at me.

"Relax, people. Kaitlyn calls him Georgy, sometimes. It's a private joke between them." Big Kathy added.

"Danielle doesn't know Kaitlyn or her boyfriend like we do. He used that name when they first met. Funny because he works with her. You think she would have known but she said he worked on another floor."

"Gee, I guess even admirers use false names. You can't trust anybody these days. Where is that tall chick-a-dee from the city you seem chummy with?"

A sharp shrill voice cut into our conversation.

Julie walked up behind us. Her acidic tone cut me to the bone. Sara tensed visibly and stared away. Julie placed her hands on the small of her back and stretched behind me in her long black evening gown making certain all eyes were on her before the final flex. A few inky plumes stuck up over the top of her head and several branched inward making what looked like a pointy hat rather than a feathery black tiara. She wasn't wearing her glasses and she resembled that wicked witch from Oz.

"I'm sorry, who are you?" Laura mocked her. "I think the yellow brick road is that way."

Julie put up her middle finger.

"Have you seen Kaitlyn?" Joe was anxious. He ignored the insult.

"I saw her with some foreign dude in the lobby bar downstairs. Dressed quite nicely I might add." Julie said. "Finally, she looks like someone who belongs in our club. Being on his arm though is the best part of her wardrobe. He's a hunk."

"That doesn't sound like, Jose." Big Kathy put in. She looked concerned.

Joe pushed back his chair.

"Oh, someone is going to get lucky tonight," Laura added.

"Can it, Laura. It's not always about sex," Sarah snapped.

The hair on the back of my neck had stood up. Bernard and his friend, Conrad, and Mr. Black popped into my head. Could it be possible that the S & M crowd were here in the hotel by coincidence and spotted an unwary victim. Someone like Kaitlyn. Even though she was nearly thirty, compared to my and Traci's life experience, she was just a kid. Were my instincts correct

"What foreign guy?" I reacted slowly. Joe was already standing.

What did Jennifer say about coincidences? Chutzpah? Hutzpah? Hitsuzen, about some preordained event? I grabbed Julie's arm.

"What did he look like?"

# # #

Chapter 46

The Search

Those who look only to the past ... are certain to miss the future.
John F. Kennedy

"Hey, where you heading so fast? The party's just getting started."

Bonnie raised her glass. Her broad smile dropped when she saw how somber I looked.

"What's wrong?"

"Our friend is missing. It's not like her to be gone more than an hour without telling someone. We think she may be in trouble."

I was surprised how breathless I became from the short jaunt across the room to the door. Stress will do that, suck the breath from you and sometimes, not give it back. Bonnie didn't hesitate. She placed her glass down on the corner of the table and waved for her friends to follow. One was an older man in a dark suit and Texas tie, with long gray shoulder-length hair neatly pulled back behind each ear. He looked like a character in a wild west show—Wild Bill Cody. The other, clearly a fresh transvestite in his early thirties with dark stubble already bubbling through the thick dry pan-cake makeup on his narrow face. She had a white carnation on her wrist. I explained we were looking for a wannabe in a long red evening gown.

"And silver shoes," Joe added. "You will know her when you see her. She has a freakish big schnoz."

"We fear she may be in the company of the guy that tried to pick me up in the lobby earlier or possibly his friend, or another admirer like him. Someone of East European decent."

"Admirer?" Bonnie looked puzzled.

"What, they want her autograph?" Her burly escort

asked. "Is she famous?"

"It's not funny," Joe pressed his thumb several times on the button to close the elevator doors. He glowered at Bonnie. They were nearly the same height.

"She's been beaten up several times and hospitalized. She has poor judgment when it comes to—"

"Relax, big fellow—" Bonnie bristled and the man we dubbed Wild Bill moved in beside her.

"Joe." I grabbed him by the upper arm. "We don't have time for this. They are here to help. Please."

"You should have told me. I can't believe Traci led you into this dump and now, Kaitlyn is—"

"We'll find her." I assured him with more confidence than I felt. It was a big hotel.

"She's not like you. We better."

He shrugged my grip from his arm. The threat hung in the air for a while before he finished his thought.

"If anything happens to her—"

"Some admirers are into S & M," Sarah's soft voice was calm. All eyes turned in her direction.

"Oh," Bonnie said. "Sounds like one of those treasure hunts where you get one clue at a time."

"Sounds like fun." A transvestite in blue suede shoes placed his hand on her shoulder. The smell of alcohol filled the compartment as soon as he opened his mouth.

Wild Bill grabbed him by the shoulders so he would not fall when the elevator stopped on the next floor. He straightened his wig. "Hold up there now, Brenda. I think you'd better sit this one out. Bonnie and the rest of us can handle this from here."

"There are 20 some odd floors in this place. Where do we begin? This was not going to be easy if she's not in the lobby, restaurant or bars." Bonnie sighed.

The doors swooshed open.

"Fuck." Joe exclaimed into the face of a short dark-haired woman dressed in a black cocktail dress that was coming onto the elevator. She halted abruptly. Her long lashes fluttered. She stepped quickly back into the hallway. The door closed on her wide-eyed expression and everyone erupted in inappropriate laughter including, Joe. It deflated some of the tension.

"So, you think this is some kind of S & M group?" Bonnie asked.

"I didn't say that."

I wanted to add that I got lucky but to what avail. From the way eyes diverted from her to me around the elevator the time for judgment had already passed. This wasn't the time to defend my honor. Brenda smiled weakly. She swayed on her feet even when the elevator wasn't moving, and Wild Bill nodded his head in some automatic social response that signaled his acknowledgment.

If this was a posse—hell—if I was the sheriff, Kaitlyn was in trouble. I did not want to be around men in dresses, much less leading a pack of them on a search for someone like me, who would risk everything for one moment to feel normal in her own skin. She could be anywhere, with anyone and doing anything. Our kind were unpredictable. I wanted to be as far away from this time of my life as possible, anywhere but here, but here I was and no one else in sight to take the yoke from my shoulders. There was that damn morality bred into me by parents of a Greater generation or threaded into my DNA, I was never quite sure how it got there, but I always did what I thought was right regardless of whether it was in my best interests.

Whether I liked it or not, I had to stay—not because it was the right thing to do but because it was time to become the woman I always wanted to be. In the year of living dangerously I had come to realize transition from male to female was more than mere physical. Joe was the first to point it out to me. I was becoming a bitch. That is not how I envisioned myself all those years I dreamed of my miracle. I don't think any woman sets out to be one. If there was a chance to alter my destiny, now was that time.

Canon Jones had said it best when he told me that the GICNE and the XX Club was not here to show us how to become women. We already were. The clinic and club merely facilitated the process so we didn't become frustrated and kill ourselves along the way. What really happens during the transition period is unraveling. We must unlearn all those masculinized habits, biases, and prejudices we adapted to over the years hiding and living as a woman in a male body.

Essentially, they help us walk away from ourselves and become the woman we were meant to be. I was so caught up in the rapid alteration of my physical appearance and successes that I almost missed the internal rebuilding that would make or break me in years to come. The process of becoming a woman in our society was as much mental as it was physical.

I mistakenly believed that to fight was strictly a male trait while flight was female. That steel thread of moral fiber stitching my inner being together bound me to a course, like it or not, to do the right thing no matter the cost. Lately, I found myself doing less and less of doing the right thing and more running away from my problems—and it haunted me. I didn't like who I was becoming any more than Joe. It was time to find out who I really was.

I jabbed a finger at Wild Bill.

"You, Joe and Laura search the bars. Bonnie, you and the rest of your group look through the lobby where we last saw Bernard. Sarah and I will make a quick pass through the lobby then go upstairs."

I was not sure if they would use the same rooms but it was worth a try before we went to management. They were an isolated cluster of rooms used at the end of a hall or given out randomly. I believed it had to be the former should anyone hear a scream.

"Bonnie knows what Bernard looks like. They rest of you should pair up with someone who knows Kaitlyn."

"She is blond, in her twenties and wearing a red evening gown but you will know her as soon as you spot her large hawk-like nose." Joe added.

"I think it's more like a burgundy," Sarah corrected him.

She was wearing the red one I had seen at the apartment earlier in the evening.

"So, we are looking for a big burgundy-nosed tranny in a red dress?" It was hard to tell whether Brenda was trying to be funny or boisterously drunk. Joe exhaled audibly and shook his head.

"Conrad is dirty-blond, shorter than Bernard but stocky and speaks in the same foreign accent. German, I think, if that's any help. They are both probably well-dressed in sports jackets and have tattoos on their hands and arms."

I hesitated to tell them more. They would likely be covered. I had no real recollection of the room number only that it was past floor twenty. Even if I had, what were they going to do? Knock on every door and say: Excuse me, we are looking for an admirer and our trans-sister. Please stick out your hand so we can see your tattoo?

The whole thing seemed futile and I could tell by the slow way Bonnie shook her big red-head that she knew it too. But we had to try. I thought about going to the manager but quickly shook off the idea. Mr. Kendrick would take the complaint and chuck it into the basket. He would be more interested in protecting his hotel and secretive patrons than alarming his clientele by searching for some missing tranny—who no one was certain was in any danger.

Shadow people should stay in the shadows. People would rather believe we did not exist. Sadly, in the 1990s, we tended to agree with them.

# # #

Chapter 47

The Proposal

Difficult choices, unlike red wine, rarely improve with age.
Richard N. Haass

The lobby was not nearly as crowded as it was earlier. The gourmet chocolate, jewelry store, and other boutique shops were closed. Only the bar at the far end of the great hall was brimming with activity.

Something cold and firm gripped my arm and I halted abruptly. Mr. Black's driver stared at me from the back of a line of people standing at the end of the open-air bar and I began to stiffen against the hold. It registered in my tired brain that Mr. Black may be nearby. I heard the smooth baritone voice whisper in my ear:

"You look real—beautiful tonight. Emmy, is it?"

I heard the emphasis of the word real and that slight hesitation before beautiful that made me cringe. No one wants to be reminded they are a freak in drag even if someone thinks they are attractive. I expected to find Mr. Black's smile when I turned. Instead, Bernard's face beamed down at me.

"I was wondering when you would come down to find me."

Bernard gripped the inside of my bicep more firmly. He squeezed to let me know it would be futile to try to break free. I gave a quick look toward Sarah. She read the fear in my eyes and quietly moved away but I hoped she would follow close behind.

"Let go of my arm or I'll scream."

Bernard laughed out loud.

"I don't think so."

He shook his head from side to side. He knew I would do no such thing. Our kind doesn't scream, at least not the ones who spent more than three decades trying to hide their feminine side. Bernard tightened his grip. He wanted it to hurt. He directed me back toward the elevators.

"Let go before I hurt you."

I tried to sound assertive but I knew he could feel me shaking. We halted abruptly. Bernard bumped into a taller man in a long navy coat draped over his arm. Mr. Black's driver was larger than I remembered. His dark eyes bored down on Bernard, his mouth was drawn into a fine line. His brow humped and furrowed like an Irish field.

"Will your friend be joining us this evening, miss?" the voice was deeper than I recalled.

"What the hell—" Bernard let go of his grip on my arm.

"No, James," I forgot his name but it seemed appropriate, "he has another pressing engagement. Don't you, Bernard?"

I smiled and narrowed my gaze at the smaller of the two men. He sheepishly nodded and moved away. Seeing Bernard made me breathe a sigh of relief. At least Kaitlyn wasn't with him. Then who had her, Conrad?

Mr. Black came up from behind us. Without complaint, I allowed him to sling his arm inside mine and walk me towards the bar. I nodded to Sarah to quell any reaction. She maintained her pace behind us. Her eyes darted from side to side presumably still scanning for Kaitlyn or other trouble.

"Nice outfit. Great taste as usual. I approve." He said, I had hoped he had not noticed Sarah but as we walk past the concierge desk he asked,

"Who's your friend?"

"None of your business."

I said through my teeth and nodded toward the concierge who I had hoped remembered me. He did and smiled as he looked up.

"Ouch. I guess we did kind of scared each other last time." He sighed.

"You were the one with the knife as I recall."

I rolled my eyes at him. Mr. Black laughed quietly. He is damn handsome and I felt turmoil stirring inside of me. I was turned on despite my fear. He was freshly shaved and smelled of a rich cologne that reminded me of the sea. His coat was open and his tie loosened and pulled away from his sinewy throat.

"And what's with that contraption with the straps and that ball? You nearly choked the life out of me."

"I'm sorry if it startled you."

His smile broadened.

"It was—"

"Wholly unnecessary. I was yours for the taking. All you had to do was ask."

"I didn't know it was your first time."

Some young men shouting at one another at of the tables drew our attention.

"It's not funny."

I tried to elbow Mr. Black, but he flexed his bicep trapping my arm to his side as soon as he felt me move.

"I thought—that was why you gave me your roommate's telephone number. After he calmed down, he was quite helpful. I don't think he likes you very much."

"We share an apartment together. It is our phone and no; I think he likes me just fine."

Mr. Black escorted me to a table by a window overlooking the dark street. It was snowing. Large white flakes drifted slowly down and caught the light from the overhead lanterns that jutted out from under the awning. They sparkled like miniature diamonds appearing suddenly out of the darkness and melted quickly when they touched the wet street below. A life extinguished before it lost its glow.

"The phone is in his name only and he gave up way too much information about you without prompting but if you say so."

He shrugged and pulled out a chair for me. He waited until I sat down before pulling another one out for Sarah. Mr. Black smiled at her. It made me worry when Sarah smiled. She was not used to such attention. I was worried for her.

"He said you are from Vermont but don't worry, I don't

think he knew much more about you than I do at this point."

The news that he knew that much alarmed me. Why would he do that? Then, as if he had read my thoughts:

"If we are to have more than a cursory contact, it is imperative I learn who I am associating with. I have a proposal for you."

"Desperate, are we?"

He ignored the dig.

"Hear me out, please—"

"I am not interested."

I watched the driver take up a position at the end of the bar. I turned to Sarah.

"Please keep looking for Kaitlyn. Don't worry. I'll be alright."

Sarah started to get up then sat back down. She leaned forward and put a crumpled piece of paper in my hand under the table as she leaned in to hug me and whispered something I thought sounded like: "She made it. No more pain."

What did she mean? Was she was talking about Candy?

When she sat back up in her chair, I searched her eyes for an answer but she turned her head away from me. I stuck the paper in my purse for safekeeping. Mr. Black's attention was still focused on Sarah.

"Oh, what's the hurry. Surely, she can join us for one drink. What would you like, dear?"

"No. I have to go."

Sarah's voice was barely audible. She grabbed at her wrist. Drawing his attention to those ugly red scars on the backs of her hands. It seemed to excite him. His gaze washed over her—scrutinizing every inch of her boyish frame.

"Let me know when you find her, please."

My voice cracked. The intense way he stared at her made me nervous. Sarah nodded and pushed away from the table and left without looking back. I watched her leave the bar and hurry into the great hall of the lobby before turning my attention back to Mr. Black.

"I really should go with her. Our friend is missing. We must find her."

Mr. Black's eyes narrowed. He didn't believe me.

"So, what do you want with me? I am sure you have girls standing in line to go out with you, including your wife."

He stiffened.

"I have my own sources,"

I noted the ring line on his left hand.

His smile fell off his face.

"Let's not go there."

I shrugged and hoped it looked nonchalant.

"There is no time for bitterness. Life is too short."

His voice was flat. I shut my mouth before I could utter the next retort. The last statement sounded like a threat.

"You made quite an impression on Mrs. Stratham."

"Who?"

"The woman who came up to us at Corelli's—"

"That restaurant in the North End?" He nodded.

I remembered her well. The blue-gray hair swept up on top of her head like a crown. Her warm smile, The strong scent of Channel No. 5. Cold, bony hands clasping mine as she rambled on about how I reminded her of herself at my age. The impromptu meeting at the little Italian restaurant turned out to be the only pleasant part of the evening.

"So?"

I tried to act indifferent. If I seemed disinterested, maybe he would let me go.

"She gave us an invitation."

"Good for you. Another contribution to your campaign from a wealthy benefactress. A glowing tribute to your charm, Councilman."

I remembered seeing the flyer on the floor of the limousine that night we first met. I couldn't read the name or don't remember if I did. It appeared to be Greek or Slavonic but his face was unmistakable. I emphasized the last word to impress upon him that even if I did not know him, I knew how to find him. Knowledge was my protection, or so I thought. He sat staring at me for a moment before speaking again as though in deep contemplation. I had piqued some other thought deep within his brain.

"I said she gave *us* an invitation."

He emphasized us. The muscles in his lower jaw visibly tightened.

"I didn't know we were a couple?"

His brow pinched together. I was getting to him.

"Is that how you treat all of your mistresses?"

I pressed on. I needed to get away and find Kaitlyn. Time was of the essence.

"Please. Let's not trade barbs. Can't we start over. People do it all the time."

"You scared the shit out of me, literally."

He smiled and looked away.

"I said I was sorry."

"I don't get that warm and fuzzy feeling deep in my tummy when you say it."

I lied. It bothered me how much I believed him. How much I wanted to believe him.

"I won't say it again."

An implication hung in the air.

Was that another threat?

"Eve, you really need to calm down. You'll get frown lines."

He reached up and brushed a curl off my forehead.

What did Joe tell him about me?

Worry bubbled up from my belly. He looked genuinely remorseful. It was hard to understand.

"I can see why she liked you—"

He stopped speaking and caught himself. Mr. Black turned his head toward the window but not before I saw—some expression of what: pain?

Damn, was he pretending to be hurt? He was a politician.

"Why me?"

The sudden return of those steel-gray eyes staring into mine made me shudder and I hesitated.

"I mean you could take—anyone." I softened my tone. "Isn't it a bit risky? I mean—to have someone like me go as your mistress?"

He caught the inference. A real girl would be less damaging to his reputation. He let out a sigh and looked over his shoulder toward the crowded bar where his driver stood guard. What was he afraid of?

"I thought politicians were conservative."

He arched his eyebrows at the mention of his career.

"Politics is full of risks but it has limitations. It's the variables we can't control. By limiting the number and type of variables into the arena we contain the risk."

I had no idea what he had just said. If Traci was here, she would tell me that he was a man aroused by the thrill of exposure. Admirers love the thrill of getting caught but you never know what a desperate man would do once backed into a corner. A man and a woman pass by our table and Mr. Black stopped talking. When they passed our table, he said,

"She was quite explicit. I take you or don't bother coming."

"I guess she is adding to the number of variables to spice things up?"

He smiled. We both knew she was unaware of my type. I glanced up into his somber face then down at my hands. Silence is a slippery serpent at times. It slithers through our clothes dampening our skin, tightening around our throats before we realize its true form is fear. It is cold and clammy.

This was all new to me. Everything in my transition had moved at the speed of light. I felt locked into some kind of dream where the outcome is unknown. I was not in control of my own dreams anymore. I looked up at him and he shivered but not from fear.

"Damn you—"

Mr. Black snapped. He stopped short of spilling his last

thought.

My throat tightened. Is he playing a game with me? He angered me, too. *I am real, damn you, even if the world doesn't know it yet.*

Maybe it was my paranoia, psychic nature, or psychotic disposition as some social scientist might say but I thought, if only for a moment, he was fighting the urge to like me.

"My wife and I have an agreement. Everyone knows we remain together only for appearance. She had a stroke a few years back. She doesn't usually mind my indiscretions so long as they are quiet. Mrs. Stratham has put up with my other ruminations but for some reason she insists on seeing you again. It looks like she is forcing me to oblige her."

He let go of my hand. I felt relieved. I had not been aware of when he began holding it and he settled back in his chair and stared at me. He was that little boy who just asked his mother if he could play outside—in the rain. Something in his confession disgusted me. If only he hadn't reminded me that he was married. Technically, so was I.

My father broke off his lucrative business partnership with a man who left his wife and twelve children for another woman. He was a man of principle. He believed in doing the right thing. I had always admired that trait and strove to emulate him in ways that I could not understand. Some unwritten code that set him apart—as a good man. Mr. Black was waiting for my reply. It was a lucrative opportunity for someone like me. A golden parachute for a tranny—to be a rich man's mistress someday but—something felt wrong about it.

There was no question what my father's son would have done. Michael would have said, No.

I knew I could always lie. Say yes, I will go with you. Tell him that I would meet him at some station or coffee shop then just not show. It tore at me. I did not want to—lie. Not this time and didn't know why. So, it surprised me when I said:

"Okay, but you have to promise not to hurt me again. I'm not into that kind of kinky stuff."

He stiffened and looked at me sharply. The waitress was approaching our table. A muscle in his jaw twitched.

"I will think about it, but only if you ask me nicely. I'm not one of your ruminations."

"Unbelievable." He said under his breath.

His angry eyes were drawn up at the waitress.

She halted. Her otherwise cheerful expression mixed with bewilderment. Her eyes darted from mine to his like a bee debating which flower to alight on first.

I tensed and put my hands on the edge of the table ready to push off if necessary. Mr. Black looked in good shape from spending hours at the gym but I felt fairly confident could outrun him. It was only a few months ago I had coached a Division I boys' high school soccer team and out-sprinted all but two of the best runners. It was the tall black driver watching us from the bar I wondered about.

Mr. Black shook his handsome head and grinned up at the waitress. He ordered another gin and tonic. She babbled a lame apology and scurried away.

"What the fuck are you doing to me?" His smile waned. He shook his head. A lock of hair fell across his right eye. He brushed it away. I stared back at him wondering what he meant.

"Alright, alright. You win. Evelyn. Will you please spend the weekend with me at Mrs. Stratham's Rhode Island estate?"

"Weekend?" Holy shit! He wanted me to commit to more than an afternoon tea." I thought it was just a party?"

"Ah, I am such a dunce. You need a wardrobe?" It was more a statement than a question.

"Do you have any clothes at all? No, of course not. Come down on Thursday? I will put you up at a hotel closer to downtown and send someone to take you shopping. I don't want to take a chance on what you might wear."

I was stunned. Did he just ask me to be his mistress? My suspicions had been correct. Will I have the willpower to do the right thing as my father had all of the years instilled in me?

"Don't worry," he added, "She'll have my credit card."

"I'm not sure I can take a Saturday off. Some of us work for a living."

I realized my error as soon as I had spoken. I forgot that I sold my business. I am only a temp, but before I can recant his eyebrows rolled up like a broken shade.

"If you think I am going to pay for—"

"Relax, I'm pushing your buttons. What girl could pass up a new wardrobe?"

I felt like I had made a deal with the devil. His lips parted into a grin.

"I'll call you tomorrow with the details," he said as I pushed away from the table and stood up. It bothered me that he had my number.

"What is your hurry? Have a drink with me. I just ordered—what's wrong?"

"I have to get back. It has nothing to do with you or—" I was worried about Kaitlyn. No one had come to tell me they found her.

Maybe worry was the wrong term. Guilty perhaps. I kept telling myself that I didn't care, not really, I didn't even know her. She was just another bump in the road on my journey. We all take risks on the way to become someone else, but it bothered me. That magnetic pull toward true north was tugging at my moral compass.

"What's wrong?" he repeated. I moved away from the table but when he stood up from his chair, he blocked my path. He knew full well what was wrong. It occurred to me this whole scenario was acted out to keep me distracted until— "Is it that man you were with earlier?"

"I've got to go." He did not grab at me when I passed.

"Evelyn, please let me help." I halted and looked back over my shoulder. "What are you afraid of? Why don't you tell me what the hell is going on? I want to help."

"Don't patronize me. You know damn well what goes on in this hotel."

The words spewed out. I was livid. He raised his eyes in

surprise.

"Don't act like you don't know."

Whether the hormones or the year of living dangerously had finally grabbed hold of me, the numbness I had been living with for years was beginning to lift. It wasn't full blown but I was tingling along the edges. Emotions, I had not felt in years were rising to the surface. I was starting to care again—about someone other than myself.

"What? I've never been to this hotel." He threw out his hands palms up.

"You, you and your cronies in that sick club that hurts people. You think because we are shadow people that we don't matter. We do. We are just as real as any woman, only broken and trying to find a way to fix ourselves. You take advantage of us because we can't complain."

"Club? What the hell are you talking about? Are you insane?" He looked frustrated.

"Don't pretend you don't know."

I reached up and touched my throat with both hands in a choking motion and his eyes registered awareness. I didn't care whether other people stared at us when I did it.

"Evelyn," he snapped. His voice broke and I felt my temper crumble and catch in my throat. I wounded him. Somehow it touched me. Why? Why did I care what he felt?

"You hurt people for some sick reason I can't understand. We don't do anything to you. All we want—"

I twisted and pushed to get by his big bodyguard-driver who suddenly appeared beside me. The room was spinning.

"Stop it. You don't know what you are talking about. This is not the time—" his voice became a harsh whisper.

"Are you alright?"

"Your friends better not hurt her the way they hurt her, or Traci, and who knows what you did to Candy. Poor Candy. Poor Kaitlyn. She's more fragile. Just a kid."

I rambled. I felt light-headed. He stepped toward me with his arms extended.

"Don't come near me."

The room was spinning faster. My legs buckled. He reached out and pulled me into his arms. He and his driver each had an arm as they escorted me from the room. I didn't try to fight them. I didn't understand why my head felt funny. Did he put something in my drink?

We moved quickly through the lobby. It was late. Only a scattering of faces jumped up here and there and shoes, high heels, low-riders, a pair of bright white sneakers, and taupe sandals, scooted by. They were not lingering in one place but moved haphazardly across my vision with a purpose. They were heading for revolving doors on their way out into the night air or down a long, carpeted hallway, perhaps to some party room or up to the bank of elevators, everyone going to their respective destinies.

The elevator doors closed behind us and Mr. Black shakes me, not unlike shaking a blanket before going home from some sandy beach. I felt listless but alert, trapped in some dream.

"Get your hands off from me or I will hurt you."

The definitiveness in my voice surprised me. He let go of my shoulders. I waited for him to chastise me for making a scene, but he only stared at me with that pained expression on his face as though I had slapped him.

"You're acting crazy. I had nothing to do with the disappearance of your friend. I don't belong to any club."

I picked up his right hand and moved the signet ring up his finger. There is a tan line beneath but no tattoo. I had expected to find one similar to the one I had seen on Bernard and Conrad.

"What are you doing?"

"Even if you don't have the tattoo. You still hurt people."

"What?"

"The whips and chains thing. Do you think I'm stupid? The other guys had a tattoo."

"I don't have any tattoos."

Mr. Black looked sheepishly up at his driver then back at me. Bewilderment etched upon his usually stern face. Is this an act? I used to think I knew all men's secrets. How naive I must have been.

"It had a whip in a circle. One had it beneath his ring."

I made a circle around my own finger to illustrate.

"Sounds like a gang mark."

The driver's deep baritone voice penetrated the stillness. We both looked up at him. He shrugged.

"They tied up my friend. Did awful things to her."

I shuddered. I wasn't there. I did not know for certain but my imagination ran rampant. I have made and art of assimilating facts and drawing conclusions I'd hoped were correct.

"An S & M thing. Like you did to me with the—"

I struggled to find the words and reached up and touched my throat. I had no idea what to call that contraption that nearly choked the life from me. His eyes darted up toward the driver who moved to the back of the elevator. The corners of Mr. Black's mouth curled up making his pained expression look comical. I've embarrassed him, again.

"I assure you Evelyn, I am not part of some conspiracy or some sick club that has your friend."

"Then why—"

"I thought you were or are a—" he hesitated.

I tilted my head waiting for him to finish his thought. I gasped aloud and shook my head trying to make sense of what he did not say—did he really think I was some street walker—a prostitute? Is that why he bought me a dress before we went out and gave me money? I thought he was an admirer. Isn't that what admirers do?

"You were dressed a bit light for the weather. Don't you think?"

"You took me to a restaurant?"

I was confused. My head ached. I remembered wearing his jacket afterward and shivering on our way back to his car.

His thick brows pinched together into a straight line. I smiled despite my fear of him. He seemed genuinely confused.

"Is it that hard to believe I was attracted to you?"

"But it was outside of Jacques?"

I assumed he knew it was a gay bar. He blinked rapidly.

"You—were a whole new experience for me."

"Did you know I was—"

"Not at first," he cut me off.

Careful, Traci's voice echoed in my head.

An admirer hides his sexuality even from himself.

"You saw me come out of Jacques, didn't you?"

I was intrigued. *Do I look that good?*

"Can we save this conversation for later."

It was an order not a question. He looked uncomfortable. The driver's face was buried in the corner pretending to read a placard that had a photo of an elephant on it. I nodded. The driver knew, but some secrets are best not discussed, even if obvious.

"I am not going to your room."

My voice sounded hoarse and syrupy. He shook his head. The couple beside him were amused. I couldn't quite tell if that look in his eyes was surprise or embarrassment?

"Do you really think that's why I am here? I would not stay one night in this dump. You seem a bit tipsy. I just want to be sure you are okay."

I laughed out loud. For some reason I thought it was funny. I also thought this was the same hotel that Bernard and Conrad chased Traci and I through the halls. They must have Kaitlyn locked behind one of those doors up above the twentieth floor—lost in the den of inequity.

"Where are we going then?"

He didn't answer. Perhaps I was wrong about Mr. Black. He was not at all what I had thought. The girl staring back at me in the reflection in the elevator door had fear sketched over her pretty face, or was it confusion? I tried to recall the color of the carpet in the hallways.

I had run barefoot carrying my shoes and looking down, afraid to step on the scatter of trays stacked by closed doors with the remains of some other woman's enchanted evening, hiding under purple-stained napkins waiting for room service to take them away. The carpet had verdant fields and rows of Flor-de-lis etched in gold run in a straight line along the sides. Memory is a fickle thing. I pictured Traci pulling me fast away from those men and the danger of their association when in fact it was me pulling her. Our bare feet sounded hollow in the empty halls.

I stumbled and nearly fell. I looked down. I've had too much to drink. I remembered the oil paintings on the walls. Landscapes of English country sides and Continental villages. Men on horseback carrying muskets through a dark green wood. In one hand a hunter held a bugle or French horn, curved and golden, in the other, the reins of his mount. Round ruddy cheeks and plump red lips pursed, ready to blow. A dog twisted beneath curved hooves, mouth agape—like Traci's—in some frozen yelp as though she was about to be stomped. It had to be the same hotel, but I am uncertain.

I looked down again and a dark orange and tan contemporary carpet moved beneath our feet and shattered my confidence. It clashed with the one in my memory. The halls seemed narrower. Patches of tan papered walls were adorned by a host of square black-framed paintings with a spatial pattern of an ethereal and spatial design. The other hotel's decor was not contemporary but continental—something you might see in Europe in a fine old establishment.

An awareness that I have been drugged weaved its way through the threads of the carpet up into my feet and reached into my stomach.

I felt nauseous. I lilted forward lifted up gently by some invisible hand. It felt like I was floating then we stopped abruptly. Darkness, like a warm gray blanket drifted down and folded around me.

When I opened my eyes, Mr. Black was carrying me. The

elevator doors whispered open and we stepped out into a hall, wider and larger and brighter than I remembered.

Where are we? How did we get here?

I sounded tired. He looked down at me. My eyes closed involuntarily. I tried to keep them open but darkness fell like a heavy curtain.

I am trapped at the end of some macabre play. It kept playing again and again, and I am its only audience.

#

Chapter 48

The Menagerie

In memory, everything seems to happen to music. - Tennessee Williams

Candy's aging face popped into my head. She stares up glassy-eyed from behind dirty glass doors of a subway car. A short thick arm with a tattoo is draped over one of her shoulders. I can't see his face. His flat leather cap is dipped low casting a shadow over his dark eyes. His jaw is square, set firm against some invisible force pushing against him but he is determined to have his will. I blink. A hospital emergency room buzzes with activity around me. People waiting, huddled together against the wall crying. A single black eye peeks out at me from behind a dirty bandage. Sarah's voice was in my head whispering those words again:

She's made it. No more pain.

What does that mean? And that crumpled note stuffed into my purse. I haven't had time to look at yet. Panic rushed through my veins upsetting my peace. Bernard's wry smile is set firmly on the shadow-man's face. He has someone. Candy, I think. That deep cold ache in the center of my chest began throbbing. Suddenly, my vision blurred and they were gone. It was only a dream.

I looked up. Time stopped. It stood drop-dead still. Big white flakes appeared suspended in mid-air like a surreal painting closed behind the glass outer-wall. The billboard outside blends in. It's a poster—advertising some ski resort in Colorado.

I blinked again. I am that woman floating across the final pages in a scene from some romance novel. The image of some lover's face buried behind strands of wispy-hair briefly cuts in.

It's imprinted in my brain by some trick of fate. A handsome man leans in. An unintelligible whisper spilled into my ear as I am lifted up into his sinewy arms. It's funny how you remember things when you are under the influence of some drug or alcohol. I was locked in a bizarre dream. Truth and reality intertwined. Strange bedfellows, indeed!

My eyes are green. Hers are blue.

You can try to separate dream from reality later when you awaken? I think I can. I know it's not me. I watch from a distance as *she* leaves, floating across the dark screen. She overcame the odds and made it to the other side. Her dream came true. She survived.

Mr. Black held me in his arms. We moved steadily back toward the door to the elevator. I remembered something.

Did I chug that drink he placed in front of me, earlier? What was I thinking?

This can't be happening. I knew better. I don't do things like that. My eye-lids have grown heavy. Hard to keep them open. I shuddered. People were staring at us, at me. Their smiles melted into a collage of faceless putty as we moved steadily toward the door.

Another flash of light before the darkness falls.

Was that a camera?

#

Chapter 49

The White Knight

Forgiveness is a virtue of the brave. - Indira Gandhi

Some tall, broad-shouldered womanesque-person in an auburn wig was moving towards me with a purpose. My vision blurred. An aura glowed around the fringe. I was swimming towards the surface from the deep. Weighted down. My limbs were heavy. The harder I stroked the further away I got from the light. I tried to concentrate. Everything jumbled in my mind. I pictured Joe, or someone like him, reaching for me. I felt strange. I should have been afraid but I didn't feel anything. I floated, detached from my body and flailing up near the ceiling looking down at some scene unfolding from a dream. Suddenly, I was looking up at man's distorted face.

God, his nose is big.

"What the fuck do you think you are doing?"

Joe screamed in my face.

"While you are playing debutante, we are going out of our minds looking for Kaitlyn and then you go missing and everyone starts looking for you and not her. When Sarah told us, you are with some guy—"

He stopped and looked at the black driver and then over at Mr. Black, his arms wrapped around me tight. He was keeping me upright. Joe's face crinkled.

"You're drunk. Fuck, Evelyn. You, selfish bitch."

I tried to respond but my incoherent sounds spilled out of my mouth in slow motion and bounced in different directions. It was a struggle to hold my head up off Mr. Black's shoulder. When Joe reached for me the driver stepped forward.

"Sir, kindly restrain yourself."

The driver's voice was low but stern. A line was drawn.

"Who the fuck you calling, sir?"

Joe straightened up. Another couple on the elevator to my right moved away. Their amused smiles fell off their ruddy faces. A young man with a thin mustache and a chunky girl in a halter top and cut-off jeans. Traveler's perhaps, but no. Two teens out for a night of frolic in a fancy hotel. That's it. Or maybe—she was a prostitute. Her cheap perfume offended the senses and she had on a bright red lipstick, the color of a freshly painted fire hydrant. The boy was a member of a ball club staying in the hotel the night before a big tournament. He was dressed in sweats. A narrow yellow stripe ran down his leg. My bladder throbbed. I needed to pee.

"Back down. You don't want to go there."

A threat. Joe moved towards the driver. Mr. Black's hand appeared suddenly on Joe's protruding bosom.

"You must be, Evelyn's roommate. I believe we spoke on the phone earlier today."

Mr. Black's smooth voice vibrated in my ear. It dripped, thick as honey over me and I felt a tickle in my core. He becomes that strawberry sundae sitting on the counter at the Green Mountain Diner floating to the surface of my memory. A scoop of vanilla and strawberry ice cream with thin swirls of hot fudge drizzled over each. A child draws faces on the sticky counter with a finger. It's mine. I wanted to lick Mr. Black's hand. His wrist tastes salty. He pulls his hand away. Laughter flooded the small space.

Why am I acting so inappropriate?

"She's not feeling well. I am just taking her somewhere to rest before letting her drive home. No worries."

Mr. Black fumbled for an excuse.

Did he say we are going somewhere where I can lie down?

I felt tired. He said he didn't have a room.

Joe, don't believe him.

My lips move but no sound comes out.

Why can't I talk?

Heat rose up inside of me. I felt hot. My heart struggled to keep up. One thump, a pause, then two more. I wondered if it was panic, trapped beneath those waters with me trying to reach the surface. It was weaving its way out of my stomach and up into my veins. I felt strange. A distorted face looked down at me.

"Your nose got hairs in it."

Did I say that?

It sounded like me only much weirder.

Joe slapped my hand away from his face.

"No, need. I can get her from here."

Joe gripped my forearm. Mr. Black's arms tightened around me. I felt his heat envelope me. Joe tugged harder. They were ripping me apart, like some rag doll.

"You guys gonna fight over me? Ouch, Joe, don't break me."

Laughter filled the compartment but faded out when the lift slowed to a stop. The door opened. A collage of color rushed in, along with the cackle of cheerful laughter and strained voices.

"Oh, there you are, sweetie. We've been looking' high and wide for you. We can't find your friend. But someone said they saw her crying in the lobby and think she went home with her boyfriend because she—or he had a headache—something like that. One of them anyway. Oh—you got company. Nice—"

It was Bonnie? No, another crossdresser's voice penetrated the compartment. I forgot her name. Bonnie and two other wannabes from the Tiffany Club pushed into the confines of the elevator. Joe pulled my arm again more firmly.

Mr. Black released his hold on my shoulder but not before he whispered: "Later," in my ear. I should have been scared but I was numb.

Kaitlyn was crying, someone said. Who? Why?

We have to find her. It's all my fault.

Pain or guilt pounded between my ears. A dull ache, like some small creature trying to claw out of the dirt. I should have warned them, warned her. I shook my head vigorously, hoping it would loosen the memory or help sober me up. Awaken me from the stupor. I must have shaken it too hard. I lost my balance.

The first pin prick struck deep into the pallet of soft tissue behind my left eye. A sharp pain materialized inside my head. The lights went out before my forehead struck the floor.

Chapter 50

The Dumpster

Death is not the greatest loss in life, the greatest loss is what dies inside us while we live. - Norman Cousins

A slip of light winked at me as it twisted and bent through a maze of stone and steel and glass. It was morning. The sun was peeking around the corner and bouncing off the shiny hood ornament of a rusty red Ford pickup that someone had nosed up into the alley.

Indistinguishable shapes crept from the shadows. The large square box on rollers across from me was heaped with debris. Something odd yet familiar caught the light and held my attention. I stood up to get a better look.

A silver shoe fitted onto a foot dangling beneath a bony ankle and attached to a long slender leg stuck out from the debris. It was obscured under a pile of something yellowish and wiry that looked like dried spaghetti and an ugly brown-stained cardboard flap. The other foot was bare. Toes stubby and misshapen. The baby piggy missing, torn off when it struck something on the way down. On the way down—from where?

My head ached. I looked up at the magenta sky trying to remember. Was there a scream first or was I just imagining it?

No, no that was me. I was screaming obscenities at something—someone. Mr. Black, Joe, his driver, or Bernard perhaps.

The tattoo of a whip encircling a fat finger popped into my head. A gold ring with a tan line beneath. It has writing on it—Latin letters perhaps, or numbers—flashed before a sharp pain hit behind my eyes. It nearly struck me blind. I reopened them when it subsided.

The truth is, I don't know what happened. No matter how hard I try, I can't remember. Not everything. I've blocked it out.

Memory comes back like shrouds of broken glass, fragments much too shredded to be pieced together again, and too sharp to try.

Beside the dumpster were dark piles, some large and some smaller ones, scattered along the floor of the alley. Their soft edges came into focus slowly. The largest shadow resembled a man sitting on the ground with his back propped up against the cement platform beneath a closed overhead door. At first, I thought it was a remnant from some oversized container too large to put into the overflowing dumpster, then I heard a deep guttural sound coming from its direction. A familiar sob. A man crying.

"Joe?"

I leaned back against the door to the stairwell until I felt stable enough to walk without falling. I stumbled down four steel steps and crossed the alley.

"Joe, are you alright."

I noticed that shoe again and the foot and slim leg it was attached to dangling out of the dumpster and turned to get a better look. I remembered a woman in red—

"No, Evelyn, don't—don't look."

The shadow moved. Out of the corner of my eye I saw Joe struggling to stand then lean against the wall like I had earlier to keep balance. He wobbled as though he might fall. I pulled up on the broken cover to get a better look. A blinding light struck me behind my eyes. It was like the hand of God had taken a hot poker and drove it deep into my brain to burn out the memory of what I had seen. The next thing I knew, Joe was pulling me into his arms.

The image of a feminine body in a red satin dress unnaturally twisted at the waist flashed momentarily and was gone again under a wave of pain. The top half of the body was facing down and the head tilted on its side. There was a wad of matted hair over some purple flesh and bone and something brown and spongy where the face should have been. It didn't look human.

"What happened? What—who is that?"

I forgot what Kaitlyn was wearing. The color of her gown, shoes, size of her feet, whether her toe nails were painted red or black. Details are fleeting in the minds of wandering souls. Shadows stealing across the floor of some dank alley.

Joe wailed. He pulled me deeper into his chest. He held onto me like an overgrown child clutching a broken doll hoping he could squeeze me hard enough to put that image out of my mind. Something caught in my throat and choked whatever emotion I had left inside me. The numbness that had stolen my former life began to wrap its familiar steel tentacles around my heart.

I remembered men fighting. Joe, and some man with wide shoulders. His back was to me and there were some big women standing nearby. No, not women. Men in dresses. Some were familiar. They were arguing and yelling at someone out of my view, and then each other. Crying. Shouting. Hysteria. Banging—at a door. The faceless bodies, a blur of color as more people scampered in and out of the room. A rush of cold air. More banging. The trill of glass shattering and the screaming in my head melting into strange laughter that seemed to be escaping from my lips and then—the fall. I fell. Hit my head on a table.

Was that when I heard the glass? Or was it before the scream. I don't remember. I can't remember because that damn blinding pain glows hot behind my eyes every time I try.

"What happened?"

My voice was a hoarse whisper. I really don't want to know. I just said anything to see if he was alive. He wasn't moving.

Joe didn't answer. There was blood on my hands. It wasn't mine. I wasn't cut. I wiped them on my silky pants until my skin and nails shined.

Kaitlyn would be there at the next meeting. Sarah, too, with news of Candy. No one really died in our world. The chair beside me, where Traci once sat, would be filled with another wannabe the very next meeting.

And when I did not return, another like me would take my place in that imperfect circle of chairs. Someone trying to walk away from herself, learn all she could about the feminine things, and if lucky, she will survive to become that woman she always wanted to be. This was merely another experience on my way to becoming someone else. Another memory to block out.

Joe draped an arm around my shoulder. We walked down the alley in silence like wounded warriors after a battle. This time allies, the next time maybe less than friends but never enemies. Joe always forgave me for whatever insult I made to his pride. He often called me a plague on his life. Damning him to worry.

We were going home to an apartment we shared on a street with the same name as his soon to be ex-wife, Katherine. Away from the shadows and those destined to inhabit them. Away from that body in the dumpster, never certain if it was a man or a woman nor whether it was Kaitlyn or someone else from the XX Club. It could have been Candy or Rachel or someone unrelated to anything or anyone I had ever known. Someone tired of her own existence, who jumped from a balcony, or got pushed. It didn't matter. If it was a transsexual, or someone not yet defined on the gender-spectrometer it didn't matter because to the rest of the world, it was a non-person. *She* wasn't real.

We didn't call the police. Once determined it was not a woman, they would perform a cursory investigation to identify the body. If learned, they may call someone to come in to pick it up to save the city the costs of cremation. If no one came in, they would write "John Doe" and suicide in their report and close the books.

In the 1990s, there were thousands of homeless people who died on the streets every day across this great country and were swept up with the garbage. Big cities like New York, Los Angeles, and Boston were rumored to have mass graves to dispose of their unwanted dead. Cold, unwanted corpses wrapped in plastic thrown into a hole some place at the end of the world where no one would ever find them. A blight on civilization to be kept out of sight. Someone that everyone in the world, including the person herself, would like to forget ever existed.

We are the shadow people.

# # #

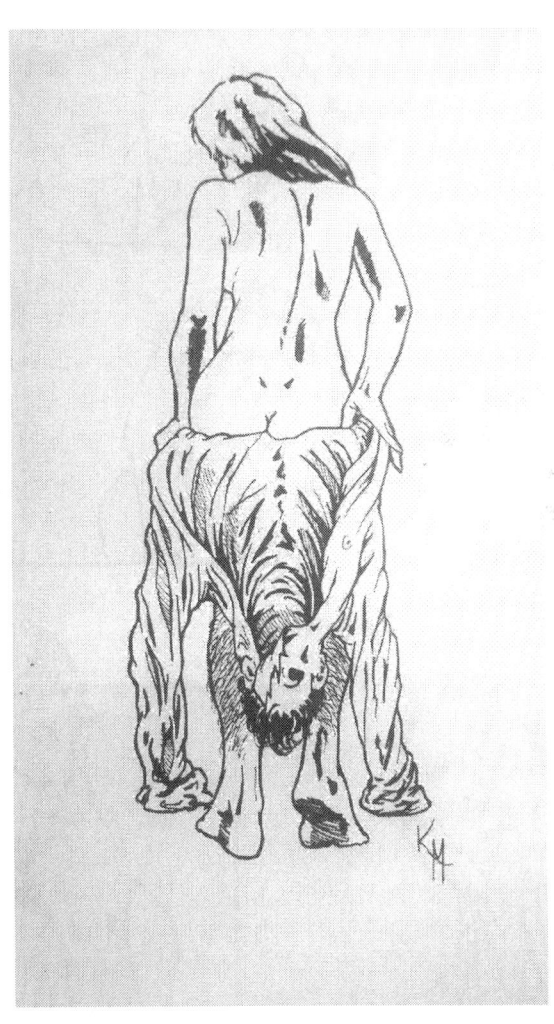

Chapter 51

The Move

Anatomy is Destiny. – Sigmund Freud

Joe stood on the front porch leaning back against the railing to our apartment. He was still wearing his short brown Elaine wig, pink housecoat and fuzzy white slippers from the day before. His strong arms folded securely across his heaving bosom. A look of defiance etched on his seasoned face. He had stopped screaming obscenities but watched us like a shrew as we huddled under the safety of Paul's truck. It was parked in its usual place across the street near Joe's garden. That patch of poison sumac and wild thistle that he loved so much.

Paul and I sat and stared out of the windshield, afraid to make eye-contact with one another. We watched the mist rise up in knots from the puddles of last night's rain showers and intertwine in some primal dance like poltergeists from our pasts' desires. Neither one dared to speak. We sat in silence. Joe's words, as he chased us out of the house, still vibrated in our ears.

After nearly a year of a tacit truce, Paul had entered our apartment without an invitation. He knew he was not invited. Joe would have never allowed it. He had always waited on the porch or in his truck for me to come out but on this final occasion, the last day I would be living with an aging transvestite, he decided to inspect our living arrangement.

It was moving day. Joe was seated at the kitchen table when Paul walked in. I was finishing up in the bathroom when I heard the commotion. Paul was not expected for another half hour. Plenty of time to tell Joe that I was leaving, breaking our agreement, and sticking him with the rent, if any remained. Joe had already broken into my room and rifled my drawers for the balance.

"Evelyn got sacked", became the joke circulating around the XX Club. People snickered when I inquired. Big Kathy had already told them.

Joe alluded to our relationship status in the past tense when talking to the Tiffany Club contingent at the party. "We used to be roomies," he told them. He looked right at me when he said it and when I asked him what happened to my money, he simply gave me that grin, like the proverbial cat that swallowed the canary.

He knew I was leaving but he didn't know when. In all fairness neither did I—not really—I mean, I did speak with my new landlord and gave him a deposit on the room he had available in his home, but I was hoping I could slow things down. There was one major operation left, my SRS. I would need Joe to help me during recovery. It was not my idea to move. Paul pushed me into it and no matter how hard I tried to think of what a woman would do? I couldn't find an answer. I honestly didn't know. Not many natural born women desperately needed a vagina.

As I came out of the bathroom, my heart was beating out some show tune from the Phantom of the Opera. It had been pounding in my head since I awoke that morning. The sinister music. The demented laugh. It mesmerized me. I was looking down at the buttons hitching up my pants, when I heard Joe tell Paul,

"She's just like me."

I looked up into Paul's red face when he said:

"She's got a dick."

I was aghast. I put my hand up to my throat in an attempt to keep myself from overreacting. I had to preserve the illusion that I was real, and somehow convince Paul that Joe was merely trying to embarrass me—a mature woman accused of being a man—how ridiculous!

He was simply trying to get him mad enough to hurt me.

Paul looked right at my crotch then back at Joe—and burst out laughing.

When he laughed, I released my breath and ran out the back door with Paul following close behind me. I didn't stop until I reached his truck.

The muscles in my legs ached. I struggled to keep them closed tight, while waiting patiently between Paul and his daughter and trying not to let them feel me shake. No excuse existed. It wasn't cold and I the tight black blouse with a low neck line to show off my newly formed cleavage revealed moisture. I sweat when warm or nervous.

"You look beautiful, today, Evie. Better than ever."

Alison beamed up at me from the passenger seat closest to the door. Her father insisted she sit where she had a seat belt. I got the hump in the middle, my bony-ass in a pair of too-tight-jeans, that had belonged to my daughter, squeezed in between the both of them. No seat belt, just a firm hairy hand once in a while on my knobby knee to keep me in my place.

"Why, thank you, Alison. That's sweet of you to say."

I felt bone-weary. It had been another long month.

My best friend and mentor, Traci had gone into deep stealth. I likely would never see her again. Candy was missing. I was alone. No one to confide in now that Joe turned against me. All I had was some cryptic note that turned out to be a telephone number to a mental hospital in Upstate New York scrawled hurriedly on a crumpled piece of paper that Sarah had thrust into my hand the night of the party and some odd assembly of words mumbled in my ear saying: she made it.

Whatever did that mean? She was finally at peace or something to that effect? And who was *she*? I assumed she had meant Candy. Now, Sarah and Kaitlyn were missing. Neither one had been heard from since the party. I didn't intend to go back to another XX club meeting. Like Traci, I intended to go stealth and shut off contact with the whole lot of them. So, I may never know.

Maybe, *she* was the woman in red without a face in that dumpster. If Joe knew otherwise, he would not tell me. I severed that tie when Paul walked in unannounced to help me move out.

It didn't matter, I told myself. He was just some other memory to block out, like those of Bernard and Mr. Black, powerful men who wanted to possess me like some exotic toy. I would forget everything, the good and the bad. Everything that had ever happened to Evelyn during transition, and all those years before, in Michael's life, except for Debbie and the kids. I would block it all out. Not that it was all bad, but it was taxing. I knew on some level that it would eventually hurt when my emotions came back. When the broken parts of me reconnected, but for the moment I could move forward unencumbered by memory or emotion—like some kind of machine—waiting for something to make it human again.

On the positive side, the house and business in Vermont had sold. Debbie and April were settled with my parents in Port Charlotte, Florida. Jackie had graduated and was to attend the Florida Institute of Technology in Melbourne, only two hours from them across the state. Jen Rose had decided to stay at the United States Military Academy at West Point after the worst Beast Camp in the school's history. It lost more than thirty percent of its Freshman class. At my last meeting of the XX Club, Canon Clinton Jones had handed me my SRS letter. I had a new identity with a license and social security card, not only my new name, Michelle, but it designated my sex/gender as female. I caught a glimpse of my face in the rear-view mirror. After several months of hormones and some facial surgery, I looked "better than ever" as Alison had said.

"She's right, Evie, you look great."

Paul surveyed me in a way that made me shiver. I stared back and tried to keep from shaking.

"When the police arrive—"

"What?"

"I called them. I've been through this domestic shit before. I am not going to jail again and don't want you to get into trouble either. So, we just sit and wait until—"

"Joe is not like that. I mean Elaine. I don't know why he—she was saying those awful things, earlier."

"You'd be surprised what people do in normal situations. I'm not taking any chances with a freaked-out freak."

At some point while we were talking, a black and white cruiser had pulled up in front of the house across the street from us and Vince Caruso, my new landlord had parked behind Paul's truck. Paul told Alison and I to stay in the truck. He got out to speak to a young police officer and Vince. When he came back to the truck, he didn't look happy.

"Evie, I'm sorry but he won't let me or Vince into the house—"

"But all my stuff is in there—"

"Relax, he said you can go in with him when he comes back out but only you will have to move your stuff from the house to us outside."

That didn't really bother me. I felt strong enough to handle the few things I had to pack but the shaky relationship Joe and I enjoyed thus far was over the moment a police officer walked up to him.

"Okay, Miss," the policeman called to me.

"Let's get this over with."

Joe was standing in the kitchen in his housecoat and slippers and the short brown wig he wore to work. He glowered as soon as he saw me.

"You look scared. You should be. Paul's about to find out you are really a man—"

"Get back fifty feet. I told you, no talking to each other."

The policeman stepped between us and pointed toward the living room. Joe retreated towards his bedroom instead. That's when he said:

"You know officer, she is just like me. She's got a dick."

"Joe." I shook my head sadly and tried to look at him pityingly. The officer looked down at my crotch. My jeans were tight. I choked every time I spoke.

"I know you are hurting but—

"I said no talking. Trying to taunt each other will end in an unpleasant experience, I assure you."

He said this to Joe, but I noticed he looked right at me. The policeman was suspicious but not convinced. I'm certain he had seen a lot of strange things in his line of work. I was thankful Paul called me his girlfriend and briefed him on the situation from his biased perspective prior to entering the house. None of it would have worked if God hadn't been good to me. The reflection in the mirror by the door showed me that I had exceeded the dream. The woman staring back was far from ordinary.

"I have to make a call. I am going to be right outside. If I hear any fighting someone is going to jail."

The policeman gave me a stern look. I nodded and swallowed hard. He left through the living room and out the front door where Paul and Vince were waiting on the porch. I packed up my things as quickly as possible. I didn't have many boxes. I threw my clothes in two garbage bags and dragged them out onto the front porch where Paul and Vince hauled them off to their respective vehicles. I put my pots, pans and dishes in a box but left my crock pot for Joe. I knew he would appreciate it later when he calmed down.

The move was inevitable. I was certain in time Joe would come to realize it. Perhaps a bit premature, thanks to Paul. In a few months I would be leaving for Wisconsin. Soon, like Michael, everything in Evelyn's world would be gone. No more Traci, Candy, Sarah, or Kaitlyn. No time to grieve. The XX Club and everything about the transition would be someone else's memory. Evelyn will no longer exist. I already had a new identity. A license and a social security card in another name, and female designated as my sex. I didn't have to do anything except show up and ask to have it changed. Like Joe's wife, Kathy had said: I looked like any other woman, like I was born this way. Nobody questioned me.

"You've won, Evelyn."

Joe came up behind me. His voice did not sound angry but unnervingly calm. I turned to face him.

"I've shouted your secret to the world, but no one

believes me. They think you are real. Congratulations. You've made it."

"Joe, I didn't want it to end this way."

"Oh, it's not over, Evie, not yet. I promised I would be there to pick you up after your operation. I always keep my promises. I don't expect you to do the same. I know you are going stealth."

I felt some relief, but his accusations hung over me like a noxious cloud. The threat of exposure haunted me. I wondered if Vince heard Joe shouting obscenities from the porch and accusations about my 'dick' being bigger than his before the officer ordered him back inside the house. I had never fed him the stories I gave to Paul. I wondered if he believed Joe and regretted inviting me to stay in his home.

"Besides," he added, "your rent is paid up in advance. You can recover from the operation here if you want."

His face broke into a grin. Joe smiled despite his sentient mood. He was an honorable man. He wanted to make certain I knew it. For some reason it was important to him. That male ego I never understood.

"What are you going to do?"

I asked him with as much concern as I could exhume from the blackness within me. I assumed he would crawl back to his wife and ask her forgiveness.

"Not your concern," he said.

"You have enough to worry about. I wouldn't trade places with you for all the money in the world."

I didn't ask him what he meant but as I started out the back door, he grabbed my upper arm, leaned in and whispered into my ear.

"How does it feel, Evie, to be looking over your shoulder for the rest of your life?"

It's funny, as a male you spend your whole life building an impenetrable wall around your emotions but to become a woman, one must learn to be vulnerable. I never realized how much courage it took to lower your shield and let someone penetrate you. Some members of the XX Club never let go of the shield. Some never stopped dreaming. But some had learned to peel back those layers of masculinity they spent a lifetime hiding behind. After a year of living dangerously, I hoped that I was up to the task.

It never occurred to me then that it might take another twenty years to peel off the remaining layers before I could truly walk away from myself and become that ordinary woman I always wanted to be, if at all.

#

Glossary of Terms:

Trassexual: a male or female who identify the opposite of their birth sex. They feel trapped in the wrong body and desire to change their body in order to feel comfortable in his or her own skin. The term is often confused with Transgender which is a category for all persons who challenge a binary gender paradigm.

Transgender: Trans is an umbrella term that describes a wide range of people whose gender identity and/or gender expression differ from their assigned sex and/or the societal and cultural expectations of their assigned sex; includes people who identify as androgyne, agender, bigender, butch, crossdresser, drag king, drag queen, femme, FTM, gender creative, gender fluid, gender nonconforming, genderqueer, gender variant, MTF, pangender, questioning, trans, trans man, trans woman, transfeminine, transgender, transmasculine, transsexual, and two-spirit.

Transvestite: generally, a male who dresses in the clothing of a female primarily for sexual gratification. It is an outdated term that was historically used to label people who cross dressed as having a mental illness; replaced by the more inclusive and respectful term, 'cross dresser', which is not considered a mental illness.

Stealth: the practice of living one's life entirely as one's self-determined gender without disclosing past experiences.

Transition: Refers to the process during which trans people may change their gender expression and/or bodies to reflect their gender identity, including changes in physical appearance (hairstyle, clothing), behavior (mannerisms, voice, gender roles), identification (name, pronoun, legal details), and/or medical interventions (hormone therapy, gender-affirming surgery).

Sex: biological attributes and legal categories used to classify humans as male, female, intersex or other categories, primarily associated with physical and physiological features including chromosomes, genetic expression, hormone levels and function, and reproductive/sexual anatomy.

Sex Assignment: legal designation of sex, usually made at birth

Sexual Reassignment Surgery: SRS: the surgery performed to alter the genitalia of individuals with gender dysphoria to resemble the sex of their chosen gender. It has been replaced with Gender Reassignment Surgery (GRS) to conform to present standards of understanding for treating the condition known as Transsexualism and in some cases other psychological disorders under the broader category of Transgender.

Sexual Orientation: patterns of emotional, romantic, and/or sexual attractions to groups of people (e.g. men, women, trans* people), a person's sense of identity based on those attractions, related behaviors, and membership in a community of others who share those attractions; re: pansexual, bisexual, LGB, heterosexual.

Privilege: Refers to the social, economic and political advantages and power held by people from dominant groups on the basis of attributes such as gender, race, sexual orientation, and social class

Outing someone: accidentally or intentionally revealing another person's gender identity or sexual orientation without their permission.

Passing: Pass: the ability to pass or blend into society as the sex or gender opposite one's birth sex.

LGBT: acronym for Lesbian, Gay, Bisexual, and Trans people; GLBT.

LGBT2Q+: an evolving acronym for Lesbian, Gay, Bisexual, Trans*, Two-Spirit, Queer, and additional identities.

Male: a sex, usually assigned at birth, and based on chromosomes (e.g. XY), gene expression, hormone levels and function, and reproductive/sexual anatomy (e.g. penis, testicles).

Male-to-Female (MTF): may refer to a person assigned male at birth who identifies as female all or part of the time; transitioning-to-female; female-to-male spectrum. (QMUNITY)

Man: a human being who self-identifies as a man, based on elements of importance to the individual, such as gender roles, behavior, expression, identity, and/or physiology.

Normal – when used in this novel/memoir refers to anything more commonly associated with persons who conform to present standards, including appearance, emotions, feelings, identity and other internal and outward expressions universally accepted by the masses. Generally, it is a perception or state of mind that one fits in or is common to the group or society in which he or she is a part.

Intersex: a reproductive or sexual anatomy that does not closely resemble typical male or female reproductive or sexual anatomy, which may be related to genitalia, secondary sex characteristics, and/or chromosomal make-up; DSD replaced the outdated terms 'hermaphrodite'; see also 'disorders of sex development; DSD is different from trans.

Heterosexual: Of, relating to, or characterized by a primary sexual orientation towards members of the other sex or gender. Heterosexual people are often referred to as straight.

Hermaphrodite: an outdated term that was historically used to label people who have a reproductive or sexual anatomy that does not closely resemble typical male or female reproductive or sexual anatomy, which may be related to genitalia, secondary sex characteristics, and/or chromosomal make-up; replaced by the more respectful term, 'disorders of sex development' or 'DSD'.

Homosexual: An outdated term that was historically used to describe people who were attracted to other people of the same gender; replaced by the more inclusive and respectful term, 'gay' or 'lesbian', which are not considered offensive by many.

Hormones: chemical substances that control and regulate the activity of certain cells or organs; see also: sex hormones.

Hormone Therapy (HT): administration of sex hormones for the purpose of bringing one's secondary sex characteristics more in line with one's gender identity; hormone replacement therapy; HRT; transhormonal therapy.

Gender Identity: internal and psychological sense of oneself as a woman, a man, both, in between, or neither.

Gender identity disorder: Formal diagnosis set forth by the Diagnostic Statistical Manual of Mental Disorders, 4th Edition, Text Rev (DSM IV-TR) (American Psychiatric Association, 2000). Gender identity disorder is characterized by a strong and persistent cross-gender identification and a persistent discomfort with one's sex or sense of inappropriateness in the gender role of that sex, causing clinically significant distress or impairment in social, occupational, or other important areas of functioning.

Gender Dysphoria: distress resulting from a difference between a person's gender identity and the person's assigned sex, associated gender role, and/or primary and secondary sex characteristics. (WPATH)

Gaff: a garment that flattens the lower part of your body, concealing the penis* and the testes.

Femme: describes gender expressions and/or social and relationship roles that are perceived as being feminine, or refers to a person who embodies these qualities. Might identify as trans, but not necessarily. In this novel/memoir, fem or femme refers to someone overly blessed with qualities that are feminine or more commonly associated with the female sex.

Facial feminization surgery: Surgeries that feminize the face, which include Adam's apple reduction, nose feminization, facial bone reduction, face lift, eyelid rejuvenation, and hair reconstruction.

Female: a sex, usually assigned at birth, and based on chromosomes (e.g. XX), gene expression, hormone levels and function, and reproductive/sexual anatomy (e.g. vagina, uterus). Female-to-Male (FTM): may refer to a person assigned female at birth who identifies as male all or part of the time; transitioning-to-male; female-to-male spectrum.

Feminine: describes socially and culturally constructed aspects of gender (e.g. roles, behavior, expression, identity) typically associated with girls and women.

Feminizing Surgeries: gender-affirming surgical procedures that create physical characteristics reflective of one's gender identity and/or gender expression, including breast augmentation, vaginoplasty, facial feminization surgery, voice surgery, thyroid cartilage reduction, buttock augmentation/lipofilling, and hair reconstruction.

Female-to-Male (FtM): Adjective to describe individuals assigned female at birth who are changing or who have changed their body and/or gender role from birth-assigned female to a more masculine body or role.

Drag Queen: drag queens are performance artists who dress and act in a feminine manner and personify female gender stereotypes as part of their routine. Might identify as trans*, but not necessarily

CIS: cis Cisgender (also cissexual): having a gender identity that matches one's assigned sex; non-trans.

Cross Dresser: people who wear clothing traditionally associated with a different gender than the gender they identify with; cross-dressers may or may not identify as transgender or transsexual; 'cross-dresser' has generally replaced the term 'transvestite', as 'transvestite' is considered offensive by many.

Androgynous: a blend of other genders; a person who identifies a person with an androgynous identity might refer to themselves as an androgyne

---

*Many of these definitions are adapted from other organizations and resources. QMUNITY, Gender (Free) for All, the World Professional Association for Transgender Health, American Psychological Association, Institute of Gender and Health at the Canadian Institutes of Health Research, and Gender Creative Kids, influenced the creation of the glossary.

Evelyn Stone - August 1994 – at Vince's home – 116 Judith Drive, Milford, Connecticut.

ABOUT THE AUTHOR

Michelle Berthiaume is one of several names and identities she has had over the years. She was born and educated in the Northeastern United States. She served in the United States Air Force during the Cold War. She earned an air medal while flying special-operations missions for the NSA and worked as an intelligence analyst. She has degrees in computer science, law and creative writing (non-fiction) and a certificate in Russian Studies and is a retired civil rights attorney who currently spends her time between Colorado and Florida and is currently working on her second book: Fyrecurl.

Made in the USA
Columbia, SC
05 April 2022

58477520R00176